P

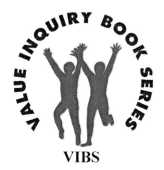

VIBS

Volume 217

Robert Ginsberg
Founding Editor

Leonidas Donskis
Executive Editor

Associate Editors

a volume in
Philosophy of Peace
POP
William C. Gay, Editor

POSITIVE PEACE

Reflections on Peace Education,
Nonviolence, and Social Change

Edited by
Andrew Fitz-Gibbon

With a Guest Foreword by
Arun Gandhi

Amsterdam - New York, NY 2010

Cover photo: Berlin Wall, ©Morguefile.com

Cover Design: Studio Pollmann

The paper on which this book is printed meets the requirements of "ISO
9706:1994, Information and documentation - Paper for documents -
Requirements for permanence".

ISBN: 978-90-420-2991-0
E-Book ISBN: 978-90-420-2992-7
© Editions Rodopi B.V., Amsterdam - New York, NY 2010
Printed in the Netherlands

Philosophy of Peace (POP)

William C. Gay
Editor

Other Titles in POP

Laurence F. Bove and Laura Duhan Kaplan, eds. *From the Eye of the Storm: Regional Conflicts and the Philosophy of Peace.* 1995. VIBS 29

Laura Duhan Kaplan and Laurence F. Bove, eds. *Philosophical Perspectives on Power and Domination: Theories and Practices.* 1997. VIBS 49

HPP (Hennie) Lötter. *Injustice, Violence, and Peace: The Case of South Africa.* 1997. VIBS 56

Deane Curtin and Robert Litke, eds. *Institutional Violence.* 1999. VIBS 88

Judith Presler and Sally J. Scholz, eds. *Peacemaking: Lessons from the Past, Visions for the Future.* 2000. VIBS 105

Alison Bailey and Paula J. Smithka, eds. *Community, Diversity, and Difference: Implications for Peace.* 2002. VIBS 127

Nancy Nyquist Potter, ed. *Putting Peace into Practice: Evaluating Policy on Local and Global Levels.* 2004. VIBS 164

John Kultgen and Mary Lenzi, eds. *Problems for Democracy.* 2006. VIBS 181

David Boersema and Katy Gray Brown, eds. *Spiritual and Political Dimensions of Nonviolence and Peace.* 2006. VIBS 182

Gail Presbey, ed., *Philosophical Perspectives on the "War on Terrorism.* 2007. VIBS 188

Danielle Poe and Eddy Souffrant, eds., *Parceling the Globe: Explorations in Globalization, Global Behavior, and Peace.* 2008. VIBS 194

Carmen R. Lugo-Lugo and Mary K. Bloodsworth-Lugo, eds. *A New Kind of Containment: "The War on Terror," Race, and Sexuality.* 2009. VIBS 201

Assistant Editor of POP
Danielle Poe

For Hilda Fitz-Gibbon
Thanks for everything Mum!

CONTENTS

Preface   xi
  ANDREW FITZ-GIBBON

Editorial Foreword   xv
  WILLIAM C. GAY

Guest Foreword   xvii
  ARUN GANDHI

ONE   Hope and the Ethics of Belief   1
           RICHARD WERNER

TWO   The Vulnerability Thesis and the Peacemaking Virtues   13
           ROBERT L. MUHLNICKEL

THREE   Gandhian Nonviolence as Not Presupposing Human Goodness   23
           SANJAY LAL

FOUR   Nonviolent Rhetoric in Geopolitics   31
           WILLIAM C. GAY

FIVE   Will Kymlicka as Peacemaker   39
           JOSEPH BETZ

SIX   Systemic Constellations and Their Potential in Peace Work   49
           ANNA LÜBBE

SEVEN   Peace Education: A Systemic Framework   59
           JOSEPH RAYLE

EIGHT   Building Bridges to Peace: Teaching Tolerance
         through the History of Art   67
           PAUL J. PARKS

NINE   Anti-War War Films   75
           DENNIS ROTHERMEL

TEN   The Power of Song for Nonviolent Transformative Action   107
           COLLEEN KATTAU

ELEVEN   Woman, Mother, and Nonviolent Activism   119
             DANIELLE POE

TWELVE   The Blue Guitar, Blue Frog, and the Blues   133
             KATINA SAYERS-WALKER

Works Cited   151

About the Authors   165

Index   169

PREFACE

This book arose from the Twenty-First Annual Conference of Concerned Philosophers for Peace, held at the State University of New York, College at Cortland, in October–November 2008. The theme of the conference was *Resisting War, Educating for Peace.* Around forty philosophers and educators gathered to read papers, engage in stimulating conversation, and debate about possible responses in education to contemporary unrest and war.

Presenters submitted papers for critical peer review and this book is the result. We examine peace education from a variety of theoretical and practical perspectives. The contributors all work in higher education and share a common desire for a more critical and reflective approach to teaching peace.

Arun Gandhi, grandson of Mahatma Gandhi and keynote speaker at the conference, sets the scene in his Foreword with a challenge toward positive peace. Positive peace, he suggests, is a resisting of the physical violence of war as well as the passive violence of the psychological structures present in all people that lead to conflict. Peace education has a large part to play in creating positive peace.

Richard Werner, in "Hope and the Ethics of Belief" argues for something like William James' "sentiment of rationality" that amounts to intelligent social action based on enlightened egoism. Nations should work cooperatively rather than destructively because cooperation serves their best interests. Peace is pragmatic and hopeful.

Robert L. Muhlnickel continues the theme of hope by examining the "vulnerability thesis." He suggests that vulnerability to failure is constitutive of being human. Nonetheless, humans develop dispositions to protect against failure. These dispositions are the virtues. Traditionally, philosophers have concentrated on courage as the primary virtue necessary to prevent failure. Muhlnickel argues that the virtue of care is more important and applies this thesis to resolving violent conflict.

It is conventional wisdom that when an opponent is "evil" the only recourse to a solution is violence. Nonviolence is seen only to work when one's opponent is a person of conscience. For these reasons, Gandhian *satyagraha* ("truth force") is said to be unworkable given human nature. In chapter three, Sanjay Lal argues, on the contrary, that Gandhian nonviolence does not presuppose human goodness. He suggests a more nuanced and complex view of human nature and human institutions—as neither wholly good, nor "evil." He argues that self-sacrificial nonviolence is as pragmatically valid as conventional violence and is a more adequate response to evil actions and institutions.

William C. Gay, relying as Muhlnickel does on the ethics of care, argues for a change in the rhetoric of geopolitics from "Wolf" language, the rhetoric of war, to "Giraffe" language, the rhetoric of peace. Gay uses the work of Marshall Rosenberg, Carol Gilligan, and Ellen Gorsevski to suggest that a new rhetoric of empathy, compassion and care is essential for the development of positive peace.

Will Kymlicka is a Canadian political philosopher who has written extensively on international justice issues. Joseph Betz, in his chapter on "Kymlicka as Peacemaker," analyzes Kymlicka's brand of liberal multiculturalism as a basis for peace not just between nations, but also within the four kinds of nation state that he identifies. Betz applies this most importantly to nation/minority conflicts.

Anna Lübbe, in Chapter Six, identifies a new approach to ethnopolitical conflicts. She borrows the concept of "Systemic Constellations" from systemic family therapy and applies it to violent ethnic conflicts. Systemic constellation therapy is a form of psychodrama in which participants, in a group setting with trained facilitator, assume the various roles of those involved in a conflict. Lübbe sees Systemic Constellations as an instrument in development cooperation projects when parties reach a deadlock.

Joseph Rayle also takes a systemic approach in arguing for a peace education policy. Peace education, he suggests, is more than a disconnected set of skills or ideas taught in isolation from the rest of the curriculum. An ecological framework would enable students to draw interdisciplinary connections to understand the interdependent nature of the problems of war and violence.

Just such an approach is the take by Paul J. Parks in his chapter on teaching tolerance through the history of art as a bridge toward peace. By studying the history of art in many different contexts, students learn to relish variety while at the same time recognizing aspects of themselves in artifacts from other cultures.

In Chapter Nine, Dennis Rothermel analyzes the potential for teaching peace through anti-war war films. He outlines thirteen anti-war film strategies that can be used helpfully in peace education. He argues that the direct portrayal of the experience of the horrors of war undermines the warrior-cult.

Continuing the theme of the arts in peace education, Colleen Kattau looks at the power of song in nonviolent transformative action. She analyses the use of songs in the civil rights movement, in the United States labor movement, in the vigils and protest over the School of the Americas, and in the *Nueva Canción* of Latin America. She concludes that song is essential to create communities that challenge and resist the forces of violence and repression.

In a chapter on mothering and nonviolent activism, Danielle Poe uses the work of Luce Irigary as a lens through which to view the nonviolent activism of Michele Naar-Obed. Poe looks carefully at the importance of "intersubjective mothering" and the place of extended community in peace activism.

In the final chapter, Katina Sayers-Walker reports on and analyzes a teaching project—again using film media—to raise student consciousness of social justice issues. She argues that film study has the potential to assist students to cross the "mental space" to imaginative empathy with the Other and the

Other's suffering. This "as-if" feeling enables students to take the further steps of care for the suffering of the Other and toward transformative social action.

This book, then, provides theoretical and pragmatic approaches to peace education and substantive clues for educators to follow in the search for a nonviolent future.

Thanks are due to the authors for their diligence in meeting deadlines, writing revisions, and their creative insights. A multi-author, peer-reviewed book relies on the kindness and dedication of a host of behind the scenes contributors: colleagues from many universities who carefully peer reviewed all the submissions form the conference, SUNY Cortland professional writing student intern David VanHamlin for copy-editing tasks in the initial round of edits, Elizabeth D. Boepple who works tirelessly and skillfully in making us all read better than we would without her, and special series editor William C. Gay for support and encouragement along the way. Funding was provided by the SUNY Cortland Offices of President Erick Bitterbaum, Provost Mark Prus, Dean Bruce Mattingly, and the Research and Sponsored Programs Office, directed by Amy Henderson-Harr; thanks are due to them all. Finally, I am privileged to work in highly motivated and supportive Philosophy Department at Cortland, chaired by Professor Kathy Russell. I am grateful to all my colleagues for such a delightful community.

Andrew Fitz-Gibbon, Associate Professor of Philosophy
Director of the Center for Ethics, Peace, and Social Justice
State University of New York College at Cortland

EDITORIAL FOREWORD

Within the field of Peace Studies the distinction between "positive peace" and "negative peace" is made very frequently. In brief, negative peace is defined as the mere absence of war, while positive peace is defined as also entailing the presence of justice. Often, when a war is occurring, the central goal of those concerned with peace is to find some way to stop the fighting. In this regard, a negative peace is judged to be preferable to a "hot war." The "body count" of hot war is reduced significantly with the "cease fire" of a negative peace. Of course, few are under the delusion that simply stopping the fighting is sufficient. The ultimate goal is to achieve social justice.

Much has been written about war and how to stop it, and much has been written about situations of negative peace and how to advance social justice under these circumstances. While the ideal of and need for positive peace is cited in many works, the literature on positive peace is not as robust.

The present volume is a welcome and needed contribution to the literature addressing positive peace. *Positive Peace: Reflections on Peace Education, Nonviolence and Social Change*, edited by Andrew Fitz-Gibbon (Associate Professor of Philosophy at the State University of New York, College at Cortland), includes the editor's Introduction, a Guest Forward, and a collection of twelve further essays by philosophers and educators. These authors explore issues of peace education, nonviolence, and social change. In so doing, each advances our understanding of positive peace.

A distinctive element of this volume is the Guest Forward written by Arun Gandhi, grandson of Mahatma Gandhi and founder of the M. K. Gandhi Institute for Nonviolence (now located at the University of Rochester). He was the Keynote Speaker at the 2008 meeting of Concerned Philosophers for Peace at the State University of New York, College at Cortland. At this conference, earlier versions of most of the essays in this volume were also delivered. Arun Gandhi eloquently addresses the question of why peace is so elusive. In addressing this question, he often draws on points that he learned directly from Mahatma Gandhi.

The essays in this collection address four major themes or approaches to the pursuit of positive peace. The themes of hope and care are central to three of the essays. Richard Werner, Robert Muhlnickel, and William C. Gay focus on the importance of hope as opposed to resignation, and of care and the web of relations in which we find ourselves. These authors eschew the formal and abstract principles of procedural justice precisely because they are less likely to achieve positive peace.

A continued focus on nonviolent approaches is central to two other essays. Arun Gandhi stresses support for nonviolence as a principled or deontological, a priori position. Sanjay Lal stresses pragmatic or consequentialist a posteriori grounds for pursuing nonviolence. These essays provide useful additions to the literature on the relevance of nonviolence.

Attention to new strategies is found in four of the essays. Joseph Betz applies the approach to multiculturalism developed by Canadian philosopher Will Kymlicka to the aim of peacemaking. Anna Lübbe draws on insights from family therapy. Joseph Rayle develops analogies with ecology. Danielle Poe stresses the relevance of practices found in mothering. These essays offer fresh, promising strategies for advancing positive peace.

Finally, four other essays consider issues in the arts. Dennis Rothermel and Sayers-Walker both analyze film, while Paul Parks looks at the history of art and Colleen Kattau stresses the importance of songs within social movements for forging community. While works in the arts have frequently served to show the horrors of war, these authors point out explicitly how the arts can help forge an orientation toward peace activism.

The essays in this volume provide a cohesive, original, and useful addition to the literature on positive peace. This volume fits very well with the themes of this Special Series on the Philosophy of Peace and helps to advance research and writing in an area that very much needs to receive the attention given to it by these authors.

William C. Gay, Professor of Philosophy
University of North Carolina at Charlotte
Philosophy of Peace Special Series Editor

Guest Foreword

WHY IS PEACE ELUSIVE?

For generations human beings have strived to attain peace, but with little or no success. When peace appears to be won, it is often temporary. Why is peace so illusive? Is it unattainable? Are human beings incapable of living in peace? I think the answer lies in the question, "what do we mean by Peace?"

For most of us, peace is the absence of war. Yes, we have ended wars and attained some semblance of peace at various times in history. Lest we forget, World War I was to be the war to end all wars, yet we have fought nearly 300 wars since World War I and continue to fight on several fronts even today.

If there is no peace in the world, we do not have much peace within nations either. Every day we see evidence of increasing crime in spite of harsh laws enacted to combat it. People live in constant fear of being robbed, mugged, or killed. There is no peace at home, either, with more than 60 percent of marriages breaking up, and children rebelling and loosing respect for their parents. Ironically, the more civilized we human beings become, the more violent we are.

I am sure my Grandfather, Mohandas K. Gandhi, would say, "If True Peace is to be attained, then nonviolence is the only way." However, to attain this peace, we must understand the depth and breadth of the nonviolence Gandhi talked about and practiced. He said nonviolence is not the opposite of violence or the absence of violence. Nor is violence simply the act of physical fighting or killing. Some aspects of violence we do not know, have never explored, and, therefore, cannot combat. It is difficult to cure a malady we know nothing about.

Since we have not been able to achieve peace in so many centuries of human existence, we have come to believe that true peace is a Utopian dream; that violence is inevitable and, therefore, the best security is to envelope ourselves in a culture of violence—a culture that has now completely dominated all aspects of human life. If we live, breathe, think, act, speak, and behave violently, and our relationships with one another are based on self-interest, how can we build peace?

When I lived with Grandfather in Sewagram Ashram, Wardha, in Central India, as a twelve-year-old boy in 1946, he once made me go out and search for a little three-inch butt of a pencil that I had discarded on my way home from school. At the time, I was surprised and annoyed that he would make me search in the dark for something so useless. Why would he not believe that a three-inch pencil is too small for anyone to use? However, when I found the pencil and showed it to him, he said it could still be used and demonstrated this by using it himself for the next two weeks. He did not do this to demonstrate his miserliness, but to demonstrate the need for frugality in our use of natural and man-made resources.

The lesson he taught me through this incident was that if we waste our resources, as we do every day when we throw away perfectly good and useful things, we are committing violence against nature. Since wasting leads to over-consumption of resources, then when we waste, somewhere, someone lacking the means to buy scarce resources is forced to live in poverty. That is violence against humanity.

This lesson was followed by an introspective exercise of building a genealogical tree of violence with two offshoots, "Physical" and "Passive." Every day before I went to bed, I was required to analyze the day's events and experiences and put them down in the appropriate column. Physical violence, obviously, is the kind of violence where physical force is used— fighting, killing, murder, and rape for example. However, passive violence is more insidious and extensive because often we do not even think of such action as being violent to anyone. Typical of these is the over-consumption and waste of natural and man-made resources.

A predictable materialistic justification of over-consumption is that because we consume more, someone has to produce more, and that provides jobs to people. This is one way of looking at the problem. However, the flip-side of this argument is that only those who have the means consume more, and those who have the wherewithal produce the goods. A large segment of humanity is still consigned to poverty and destitution. India and China are prime examples with booming economies producing for the wealthy nations of the world. Yet only half of their enormous populations benefit from this economic boom. The other half is so deeply entrenched in poverty and ignorance that they have little hope of survival.

The result of this exercise was that, in a few months, I filled a wall in my room with examples of "passive" violence. Later, my parent's explained to me the connection between "Passive" violence and "Physical" violence. Since we commit passive violence consciously and unconsciously all the time, victims of passive violence become angry and resort to physical violence to get justice, which takes the form of crime in society and wars between nations. Clearly, passive violence is the fuel that feeds the fire of physical violence. Therefore, in order to put out the fire of physical violence we have to cut off the fuel supply. In other words, *we have to become the change we wish to see in society.*

Grandfather found that anger was the spark that caused violence, and anger management became the foundation of his practice of nonviolence. Anger is natural to human beings, just as a circuit breaker is important to an electric circuit to avoid a catastrophe. However, if we ignore or abuse the circuit breaker and cause a calamity, the fault is not with the circuit breaker but our ignorance and carelessness. Grandfather taught me that anger can be used intelligently, just as we use electric power intelligently for the good of humanity, but that it could also be abused and the consequence of abuse is always a crisis. He taught me the importance of "thinking" nonviolently so that we can come up with nonviolent solutions to problems when we face them.

Reacting to an incident in anger, when not in control of our mind, leads to violence, either physical or non-physical. Taking time to regain control of the mind helps in finding a nonviolent solution. Whenever I became angry, I was taught to write the incident in an anger diary, not with the intention of pouring my anger into the book, but with the intention of finding a nonviolent solution, and then make genuine efforts to achieve the goal. Consequently, the diary, over the years, became a valuable resource for nonviolent solutions instead of a constant reminder of the incident that caused anger.

To practice anger management and retain control of the mind it is important to do mental exercises. Just as we neglect teaching anger management, we also neglect teaching mental exercises in the erroneous belief that education is adequate mental exercise.

In reality, education is not mental exercise. Education is the process of filling the mind with information and knowledge, just as we feed our hunger with food. Neither of these acts by themselves can be regarded as enough. To be able to digest the food and strengthen the body we need physical exercise. In the same way, to be able to digest the knowledge and build a healthy mind we need mental exercise.

The exercise I was taught is simple. I had to sit in a quiet room with no distractions of any kind. I placed a flower on the table in front of me and concentrated all my attention on that object for a minute. I then closed my eyes and tried to keep the image of the flower in my mind. Just as in physical exercises, in the beginning I found that this was difficult to do. The moment I closed my eyes the image vanished. But persistence is the key in physical and mental exercises alike. As the weeks went by, I found I was able to keep the image for longer and longer and that I was gaining control of my mind. Within a few months, I was able to keep out unnecessary thoughts and distractions from my mind at will. It helped me considerably in keeping my cool in moments of crisis.

In times of crisis, we tend to lose control over our mind and behave rashly in what we colloquially call "a moment of madness." By doing the mental exercise, we are able to control our mind from flying off the handle in a moment of crisis and to think rationally for a solution that will not deepen the crisis.

The third lesson that Grandfather taught me was about relationships, also an integral part of his philosophy of nonviolence. If we have poor relationships at any level, interpersonal or international, it is bound to lead to conflict and even violence. In materialistic societies around the world relationships are necessarily built on self-interest. Materialism thrives on exploitation and exploitation leads to all kinds of conflicts. To deal with these conflicts, we have developed "conflict management" courses. The question that arises is, should we create conflicts and then learn to manage them peacefully, or learn to avoid conflicts altogether?

In creating and managing conflicts, the danger is that we reach a stage where these conflicts become unmanageable and erupt into violence. In learning to avoid conflict, we are required to build relationships based on respect, compassion, understanding, acceptance, and appreciation where conflicts may be substantially minimized. Is this a pipedream? I don't think so. There is substantial evidence that human beings are capable of relationships based on mutual respect and understanding. Such relationships have flourished over many years without conflict.

The problem is that materialism has made us selfish, and this attitude is projected on our children when we exhort them to become successful in life by any means possible. The same attitude is also projected onto countries when we emphasize the need for nationalism and patriotism. In the prevailing culture of violence—in which these beliefs are rooted—this attitude leads people to believe that we can isolate ourselves in a cocoon to protect our nation and national interests and not be concerned about the rest of the world. We believe that we can preserve the sanctity of our nation with weapons of mass destruction and not be concerned about the consequences for the world.

In the Culture of Nonviolence, it is believed that all human beings and, by extension, all nations are interlinked, interconnected, and interrelated. The security and welfare of any country, however strong and powerful it may be, is inexorably linked to the security and welfare of the rest of the world. Just as no nation can preserve its security by ignoring the world, no family can ensure its security by ignoring the neighborhood in which they live. There is a limit to how far we can run in search of a safe nest. Thus, in the practice of nonviolence it is imperative that we broaden our vision of society and nation, and learn to build mutually respecting societies with a greater degree of compassionate sharing.

I must explain what Gandhi meant by "compassionate sharing." The kind of concern we show to the needy and the poor is motivated more out of pity than compassion. When we act out of pity, we give the poor what they need on a platter. For instance, organizations and societies have run soup kitchens to feed the hungry for generations. In the same way, individuals dole out charity periodically. Such actions are motivated by a desire to do good; they are easy and require no commitment—just write out a check and mail it. The result is that the poor become dependent on charity, whether from the government or individuals. Consequently, a population already oppressed by circumstances is further oppressed by the charity we give. When people are forced to live in any form of oppression the two things they sacrifice are self-respect and self-confidence. The poor buy into the stereotypes that society creates—that they are lazy, that they are incapable of doing anything, and they will forever remain dependent on society.

Gandhi's concept, rooted in the Culture of Nonviolence, speaks of people acting out of compassion, which means getting involved in trying to rebuild the self-respect and self-confidence of the poor, and launching "constructive programs" designed to help the poor stand on their own feet and do things for themselves. Gandhi called this, "Trusteeship." What this means is that we must consider ourselves trustees of the talent that we possess instead of owners of the talent, and, as such, we should be willing to use the talent to help the poor realize their potential. This, of course, needs a great deal more commitment than doling out a few dollars in charity. It means getting involved and spending more time and talent to bridge the gap between the rich and the poor, between the ignorant and the educated.

The Peace Corp was conceived as an organization of "constructive work," but it got mired in arrogance. Their approach was, "we know your problem and if you listen to us we will solve it for you." On the contrary, when working for the poor, we need a great deal of humility so that even if we know what their problem is, we are willing to listen to them, guide them, and try to lead them to a solution. The poor must become a part of the solution if they are the central part of the problem.

We need to change many more aspects of the Culture of Violence if we really want to build lasting peace. Briefly, these include our concept of Justice and our parenting of children. Our justice system is based on revenge and punishment. It is quick to catch criminals, give them a trial, and punish them by sending them to prison. This attitude has its roots in the belief that the world is made up of "Good" people and "Bad" people. In reality, all of us have the good and the bad in our psyches. That is why good people do bad things and bad people do good things. It all depends on the circumstances and the compulsions we face. Being punished for this does not always make a person better, especially if they have to come out of prison and face the same circumstances and compulsions again. Besides the emphasis on punishment, prison only makes people hardened criminals instead of enlightened citizens. If prisons were places of reformation rather than punishment the results would be startlingly different. People would come out better citizens rather than stronger criminals.

The same concept of justice is carried out at home. We punish our children for misbehavior, and for the most part, like criminals, they quietly suffer the punishment and make sure that the next time they don't get caught. In a Culture of Nonviolence, Gandhi said punishment must be replaced by penance, wherein parents accept responsibility for their children's behavior. As good parents, they ought to have taught the child not to behave in such a way and therefore, instead of punishing the child, the parent does penance such as fasting. They explain to the child why they were fasting, feed the children, and talk to them with respect. Since the relationship between parents and children is based on mutual love and respect, the children will feel bad for having misbehaved and learn not to to do so again.

Some may argue that this creates a "guilt complex" in the children. Without making a child feel guilty for the wrong it has done, the child will not realize the mistake it has made and will not learn the lesson that change is necessary. Of course, the effect of penance on the child is contingent upon the relationship between the parent and the child. If the parent-child relationship is not based on mutual respect and love, a parent's penance will have no effect on the child. We also instill in our children the need to be selfish when we urge them to reach for the top by any means possible. Usually this injunction is followed with the remark, "don't think about the others, just think about your own goals and reach for them."

You will notice that I offer no citations and I have no proof that my grandfather said all of the things I have explained. In all humility I say that Gandhi's philosophy, or any philosophy for that matter, can be approached in one of two ways—the scholarly way or the intelligent way. This is not to belittle the motives of scholars. However, when we seek proof for everything we reduce the philosophy to a dogma, and, in the process, we get trapped in what Dr. Martin Luther King Jr. once called, "the paralysis of analysis." In plain English, we "work the philosophy to death." The intelligent way is to learn of the essence of the philosophy, and to use one's deductive logic to work out what the philosophy meant and how it can be understood today. A philosophy needs to be kept vibrant and saved from becoming a dogma.

This paralysis of analysis has caused some scholars to view the philosophy of nonviolence as a "strategy" to be used when convenient. Gandhi said that nonviolence is not a jacket that you can put on today and discard tomorrow. Using nonviolence only as a strategy is the reason it has had limited success, and when it has been successful it has not been lasting.

India is a prime example of this. For Gandhi's compatriots, nonviolence was a strategy of convenience. Once independence was achieved, the leaders walked out on Gandhi and virtually said India would no longer follow the philosophy of nonviolence. Consequently, India has become one of the most violent nations of the world and spends enormous resources on weapons of mass destruction. India today is not the country that Gandhi envisioned.

If one does not live the philosophy of nonviolence, one cannot practice it effectively.

Arun Gandhi

One

HOPE AND THE ETHICS OF BELIEF

Richard Werner

These are dark times for humanity. We face serious problems such as global warming, AIDS, genocide, famine, and overpopulation. We foresee the grave possibility of diminishing nonrenewable natural resources and the dangerous consequences of their unequal distribution. We understand that the world faces acute economic problems of a structural nature caused by the general decline of the United States and the rapid assent of second world nations such as China, India, Russia, and Brazil. We sense that the spread of weapons of mass destruction across the nations of the world is an inevitable deadly game of Russian roulette. We realize that globalization leaves us with no one in charge—a dangerous situation should an extreme emergency occur as it did recently with the global economic crisis. Let's call this series of interconnected issues "the concatenation of problems."

Albert Camus, the great French novelist and existentialist, held that where there is no hope, one must invent it. He too lived in dark times. Perhaps we always live in dark times. But Camus taught that we must rebel against hopelessness and cynicism. *The Rebel* represents Camus' moral ideal (1992). Hope may require invention through a creative act of will and the refusal to accept defeat and despair even in the light of strong evidence that defeat is seemingly inevitable. Such a creative act of hope is an act that affirms life. It finds life in the fallibility of our knowledge and our times. It lies at the heart of what Herbert Marcuse, Camus' contemporary, called the great refusal, which is the refusal to sell our human capacity for hope short even when comforted by consumerism and its accompaniments (1991). While living in the lap of luxury and privilege, people fear the end of that luxury and privilege even if justice recommends it.

Moving on from two European thinkers to an American thinker, William James held that most practical issues run beyond the reach of reason and our present problems are no exception. Uncertainty is always a consequence of practical issues. David Hume postulated that uncertainty surpasses reason in the practical world because reason and certainty are both surpassed by our inability to predict the future. If someone decides, for example, that the issue of global warming is fully settled, it is, William James would say, rational sentiment functioning instead of reason and evidence alone. Emotion and imagination, in addition to reason and evidence, are playing what may be a deciding and a legitimate role in the judgment whether we can ameliorate the concatenation of problems.

However, I do not think, and James did not think, that this insight condemns us to either radical relativism or hopelessness and despair. Instead, the sentiment of rationality, as James called it, when confronted with a demanding practical problem entails a creative activism consistent with the view that some beliefs are better than others—an activism that sits between the two extremes of radical relativism's paralysis by analysis and a mindless dogmatism with the inaction it all too often commands. It is an activism that is consistent with the realization that our beliefs are fallible and that we must act creatively under conditions of uncertainty if we are to resolve problematic situations like the concatenation of problems. It is an activism recognized as a self-fulfilling prophecy, the marriage of theory and practice in the self-fulfilling nature of praxis.

Now there are many who will tell us that James' view is irrational because it relies on holding beliefs that trump the strongest evidence to the contrary. William Kingdon Clifford, in his famous 1877 essay "The Ethics of Belief," gave perhaps the boldest argument for what is now called "evidentialism," the view that "it is wrong always, everywhere, and for anyone, to believe anything upon insufficient evidence" (1999, p. 77). Clifford's view is the denial of James' sentiment of rationality. James responded to Clifford in his equally famous "The Will to Believe" (McDermott, 1977, pp. 717–734), where the debate turned theological and James made the important claim that I will defend:

> Our passional nature not only lawfully may, but must, decide an option between propositions, whenever it is a genuine option that cannot by its nature be decided on intellectual grounds. (Ibid., p. 723)

Lest you think the debate antiquated, recently, Richard Feldman (2000), Jonathan Adler (2002), and Simon Blackburn (2005) have taken James' argument to task in defense of Clifford.

My interest is not in the theological argument of the "The Will to Believe," but in James' lesser known, but equally important and earlier piece, "The Sentiment of Rationality" (McDermott, 1977, pp. 317–345), as it applies to practical, worldly problems.

Consider the following situation: You have a diagnosis of serious disease. However, the diagnosis is ambiguous. If you have disease A, no treatment is available and you will soon die. Disease B does have a treatment and a possibility of survival. Let us assume further that the evidence suggests that the probability that you have disease A is 99 percent, and the probability that you have disease B is only 1 percent. Assuming all other things are equal, despite strong evidence that you have disease A, it would appear to be obvious that you should assume that you might have disease B and seek treatment as long as the probability is not zero. In situations like this, choosing against the best evidence— to choose hope, to adopt the great refusal and become the rebel—is rational. In situations like this, choosing against the best evidence—to choose hope, to adopt the great refusal and become the rebel—is rational.

Just as you cannot win the lottery unless you buy a card, neither can you survive the illness unless you seek treatment for B. Someone wins the lottery, therefore to buy the ticket is not irrational. Likewise, to treat for B is not irrational if that were the only hope for survival.

You may object that this analogy is not quite right. We should believe that you have illness A as the strongest evidence suggests, and believe that, since your life could depend on it, we should treat you for B nonetheless. No contradiction is inherent in believing one thing while acting on another. I might believe that it is not going to rain yet take an umbrella as a measure of protection.

As Socrates said long ago, and as the classical pragmatists held in common, if persons do not act on their beliefs, then they do not believe. If I take the umbrella then I believe that it may rain. I believe that the chance of rain has a non-zero probability. Therefore, taking the umbrella against the risk of rain is prudent. By taking the umbrella I reveal that I am a pragmatic fallibilist about belief; that I believe that all beliefs are fallible and that none are certain.

Yet illness is different from rain. Whether I take the umbrella and my belief about the probability of rain does not affect the likelihood that it will rain. But in the case of illness, Jerome Groopman has cited strong *empirical evidence* that suggests that someone actually believing in the possibility of cure changes brain and body chemistry in such a way as to improve the immune system, which actually improves the likelihood of survival (2003). So while simply seeking treatment for B as a precaution may not help, *if one actually believes B, one actually improves one's chance of survival.*

To embrace despair by believing that surviving an illness is impossible obviously can have a profound effect on an individual. Our biology is systemic. It is not surprising that depression and stress change our chemistry in such a way as to impair our immune system and cognitive abilities, in much the same way as hope enhances our immune system and cognitive abilities and, thereby, improves our health and chances.

What is true of illness is generally true of belief. Empirical evidence reveals that positive thinking improves our ability to think clearly and act accordingly while negative thinking and stress impede thought and action (Groopman, 2003). So, we should expect that our chances of surviving a dangerous future are better, generally speaking, if we act from hope rather than surrendering to despair and hopelessness.

Therefore, it is not as rational to believe that we have disease A while acting as if we have disease B as it is to both believe and act as though we have disease B. The second belief enhances chances of survival better than the first. Similarly, it is not as rational to believe that humanity's future is hopeless while acting as though we have hope, as it is to believe and act out of hope. In both cases, we lose the important self-fulfilling prophecy contained in our positive attitude if we choose the first option yet retain it if we choose the second option.

Our brain and body chemistry improve in ways beyond our immune system when we have hope, ways that improve our ability to think clearly and creatively. Understanding the biology of hope begins best with understanding the placebo effect. Hope is a combination of belief and expectation: belief about the way things are and an expectation or desire about what they will become. The two behave synergistically. Our emotions influence our perceptions and reason as our reason and perceptions influence our emotions. We mistakenly believe that our decisions can be solely rational. Without emotion, rational choices are not possible (Domasio, 1994). Hope has a cognitive (belief) and an affective (desire) component that work together as one (Groopman, 2003, pp. 167, 191–203).

True hope takes into account the real threats that exist and seeks to navigate the best path around them. False hope does not recognize the risks and dangers that true hope does. False hope often leads to bad choices and flawed decision making (ibid., pp. 29–57). When I write of the positive effects of hope, I mean the effects of true hope and not those of false hope that are too often negative. The placebo effect while often thought a bad thing in medicine when it interferes with scientific outcomes of experiments are increasingly considered worthy of study in itself since it can improve health and well-being. The placebo effect is compatible with true hope.

Scientific studies show that the placebo effect can be produced in the laboratory so that the subject does not feel pain in response to an otherwise painful stimulus. The placebo effect can be explained in terms of the body's neurochemistry: More endorphins and enkephalins and less cholecystokinin (CCK) are produced. Hope, the belief and desire (expectation) to avoid pain in this case, can help activate the neurochemistry that does so (ibid., pp. 167–174). Hope can create a self-filling prophecy.

A scientific study shows that sham surgery that mimics arthroscopy for osteoarthritis of the knee provides equal benefit in terms of pain reduction and restored motion as the actual surgery. Positive results were observed with improvement in lower-back pain, the treatment of asthma, and the treatment of Parkinson's disease through the placebo effect. The latter illustrates that the placebo effect can go beyond pain to affect the capacity of voluntary muscles and motor skills (ibid., pp. 175–190).

When we feel pain from our physical debility, that pain amplifies our sense of hopelessness; the less hopeful we feel, the fewer endorphins and enkephalins and the more CCK we release. The more pain we experience due to these neurochemicals, the less able we are to feel hope. To break that cycle is key. It can be broken by the first spark of hope: Hope sets off a chain reaction. Hope tempers pain, and as we sense less pain, that feeling of hope expands, which further reduces pain. As pain subsides, a significant ob-stacle to enduring a harsh but necessary therapy is removed. (Ibid., p. 179)

What is true of physical pain is equally true of psychological pain: Stress wheth-er it is manifest by depression, anxiety, or fear can affect neurochemistry in-creasing the psychological pain of the stress. Hope can break the vicious circle by affecting our neurochemistry and, thereby, help us both to make better choic-es and to enact them. Resilience or the maintenance of high levels of positive feelings and well-being in the face of significant adversity is simply the habit of true hope in the face of stress and adversity. Like any good habit, it is self-reinforcing. We maintain it because it works; it can be self-fulfilling.

Simply consider that hope and resilience are a part of our neurochemistry and not a mystical phenomenal cloud or aura surrounding our physical head. It is not surprising then that hope and resilience can play a causal role in our ability to make better decisions and to live better lives. They are as physical as our head. There is nothing spooky here, nothing mystical, just old fashion pragmatic naturalism at work: What John Dewey long ago called the "the reflex arc con-cept in psychology" (1896, pp. 357–370).

But how, you might ask, does this information about individuals affect the social and political level? The answer is obvious: the social and political are composed of individuals. Insofar as hope and resilience can be created and main-tained among the population the positive effects can be expected to spread through the population. An excellent example is the tipping point phenomena experienced in American culture during the recent presidential candidacy of Ba-rack H. Obama and, in particular, how his "audacity of hope" against tremend-ous odds catapulted him first to the Democrat nomination and then to the presidency (Crown, 2006). Ronald Reagan and George W. Bush also initially ran on similar platforms of hope that spread like contagion among a discouraged populace. Politicians and political movements have relied on the contagious na-ture of hope throughout the ages: Mohandas K. Gandhi, Franklin Delano Roose-velt, Martin Luther King, Jr., and Nelson Mandela to mention a few. I suggest that hope can be contagious among a population when that population has reason to believe and desires better expectations. Sometimes that hope can create a self-fulfilling prophecy, especially when it is based on true rather than false hope.

I am reminded here of a famous story retold by Johannes Silentio (2006) from Søren Kierkegaard's *Fear and Trembling* of two dancers about to perform a difficult jump in their dance routine. The first dancer is unsure whether she can land the jump successfully. Her lack of confidence is apparent—by the stress evinced in her face and in her movements—as she approaches the jump. Sure enough, she fails. The second dancer is confident that she can land the jump. Everything about her dance routine before the leap reveals her confidence. Sure enough, her jump is successful.

I suspect that each of us has seen this sort of difference and even experienced it ourselves, if not in dance, then in other areas of life. Sports teams, advertising agencies, and political campaigns attempt to capture this positive attitude because it increases the probability of success. The self-fulfilling prophecy will occur.

You say this is still not right. When we consider all of the evidence including the chance of survival with disease B compared to that of surviving A, the strongest evidence supports B not A. Therefore, James is mistaken.

While the whole context of belief is surely important, if we make the move suggested we render the claim that we should hold true the belief with the strongest evidence an empty, non-verifiable claim. For we are claiming that whatever belief is best to hold true in a context is, by definition, the one with the strongest evidence. Therefore, "we should always hold true the belief with the strongest evidence for it is best" becomes an empty tautology. It is so by stipulated definition, by fiat. So, in our example, using this logic, diagnosing for B has the best evidence even though there is only a 1 percent chance of its truth and a 99 percent chance of the truth of A. This seems to violate our normal sense of what counts as the strongest evidence. It seems to rule against empirical evidence. The objection to James makes it such that nothing is allowed to count against the claim that we should always hold true the belief with the strongest evidence because the best belief to hold true is conflated with the belief with the best evidence. But if nothing can count against it, nothing can count for it. It is vacuous, tautological, non-substantive as claims go resting on a stipulated definition that has little to recommend it.

As William James argues, when we face a forced, living, and momentous option, what he calls "a genuine option," and the consequences of our choices are less than certain (as they always are), our choice may produce our hoped for end. It worked for the United States civil rights movement, Poland's Solidarity, and South Africa's African National Congress (ANC). Had they not hoped, they would not have succeeded. Epistemology is, in part, a hope-based initiative. However, hope alone is not enough. Our actions, our intelligent social actions conjoined with and inspired by hope and imagination, can change the world for the better. The reasoning here is James' sentiment of rationality put to work through praxis and practical insight. To use one of James' metaphors, successful action is the cash value of the sentiment of rationality.

Notice that had civil rights workers, Solidarity, and the ANC been filled with trendy cynicism, they would have failed, and we would all be worse off because of it. Herein lies the self-fulfilling prophecy of the sentiment of rationality. Only if you assume, contrary to the overwhelming evidence, that you do not have disease A and that you do have disease B and, thereby, seek treatment, will you live. Only if you maintain in that belief will you improve your chances of survival by improving your immune system's defenses by your positive attitude.

Only if we assume contrary to the evidence that we can ameliorate the concatenation of problems or any other severe problem that confronts us will we succeed. To do so we need to forgo trendy cynicism. We need to ignore the lap of luxury in which we live and the spell of complacency it casts upon us. We will need to become Camus' rebel and practice the great refusal of Marcuse. We need the sentiment of rationality that James recommends.

What will best resolve global warming is intelligent social action. That social action may take the form of a powerful social movement like the civil rights movement or Solidarity or the ANC. It may take the form of the international divestment movement that, in support of the ANC, helped South Africa abolish apartheid. It may take the form of the Danish resistance during World War II that used nonviolent direct action to stop the Nazis in their tracks and save a higher percentage of its Jews than any other country. It may take the form of Gandhi's nonviolent resistance movement that brought down the British colonial rule of India. People who faced tremendous odds and refused to surrender accomplished these actions. Their joint successes evince what Vaclav Havel appropriately called "The Power of the Powerless" in his call for authenticity that echoes the rebel and the great refusal (2009).

Our social actions may be less obvious and dramatic and may take the form of teaching peace or engaging in political lobbying or writing letters to the local newspaper. It may take the form of educating ourselves about serious world problems. It may take the form of informing friends and family of the world situation. It may involve encouraging friends and family to take political action to confront these issues. Many small actions joined together may yield significant results, as it did for the ANC, Solidarity, and the civil rights workers, among others. Hope is contagious, synergistic.

Let me shift gears once again. Herbert Marcuse not only endorsed the great refusal, he warned that we are rapidly becoming "one-dimensional people." We are so satisfied with the status quo, so privileged and pampered within a consumer culture, that we are losing the ability to imagine the world any differently from how it is. We dismiss any suggested change for improvement as utopian thinking by our trendy cynicism. That trendy cynicism not only breeds one-dimensional thought but also serves in the interest of our unearned privilege. It makes us feel justified in ignoring the painful thoughts of present genocides or future famine while we seek the cheap thrills of consumer culture. We become increasingly a republic of consumers instead of a republic of citizens, to borrow a distinction from Nell Irvin Painter (2008). We are willing to exchange the responsibilities of citizenry for the thrill of consumption, our freedom for things. In the United States, we appear to have made that decision a while ago and now we may be about to pay the price.

George W. Bush proclaimed, in his Address to the Joint Session of Congress on 20 September 2001, "the only way to defeat terrorism as a threat to our [American] way of life is to stop it, eliminate it and destroy it where it grows"

(CNN.com). The "way of life" was not the citizen culture of freedom and responsibility that he had in mind, and not the American Bill of Rights, but the consumer culture of things that run on oil. As an American bumper sticker puts it, "he who dies with the most toys wins." We wage the so-called War on Terror not because a few criminals actually threaten our republic of citizens, for they do not. If we treat them like the criminals they are instead of as if they are members of the armies of legitimate nations, our Bill of Rights and democracy will stand as strong. We fight to protect our right to buy great quantities of goods that we neither need nor want once we have them and that quickly end as pollution in the air or in the landfill as soon as the next gadget comes along. We fight to protect our right to buy these goods with money we do not have, we fight to feed the growing $10 trillion national debt. We fight to protect our right to ignore the fact that our privilege is merely fortuitous rather than deserved.

Meanwhile, intellectuals claim to merely describe incidents of misfortune, not to make value judgments—they claim to describe situations objectively. Such an approach implicitly sanctions the status quo. To merely describe without critique, to forego value judgments such as espousing genocide is wrong, massacring children is wrong, or taking far more than we need is self-destructive, leaves us without a means to admit or understand our problems. We behave like consumer addicts in denial. We become one-dimensional beneficiaries of our consumer culture without a care for the suffering and misery that makes our privilege possible. Marcuse admonishes us to avoid this self-serving, one-dimensional narcissism. Havel cautions us against this lack of authenticity. Painter forewarns us of this trade of the citizen republic for the consumer republic. What is our alternative?

I ask you to imagine a world that practices positive peace rather than negative peace, as distinguished by Duane Cady (1990). Negative peace exists solely in preparation for the next war. It is represented in the United States by the over $9 trillion military spending since World War II through 1996 (Center for Defense Information, 1996). Negative peace is evinced by the Untied States now spending annually almost as much as the rest of world combined on the military (Stiglitz and Bilmes, 2008). Meanwhile, we have not begun to pay for Iraq War II. Instead we have created a national debt of over $10 trillion plus an Iraq War II debt that threatens to become $3 trillion by the time it is paid down (ibid.). Negative peace sinks a nation's resources in weapons and preparations for the next war rather than in the real problems the nation faces. As our national infrastructure declines, as our inner cities decay, as the median income in the United States continues to decline for the average family, and wealth becomes increasingly concentrated in the hands of 1 percent of the population, the opportunity costs of military spending become apparent (ibid.; Phillips, 2002; P. Krugman, "Left Behind Economics," *The New York Times*, 14 July 2006).

As Albert Einstein observed, the only way to stop war is to stop preparing for war. Preparation for war is itself a self-fulfilling prophecy. We fight wars because we are prepared to fight wars. If the only tool we have is a hammer, then every problem looks like a nail, Friedrich Nietzsche wrote. Because we are prepared and we need justification for military spending, we continually generate an irrational fear of external threats beginning with McCarthyism and extending on down to the War on Terror (Klein, 2008). None other than Condoleezza Rice tells us that we have no permanent enemies. The former Secretary of State said as much in her keynote address to the World Economic Forum International Meeting in Davos, Switzerland, January 25, 2008, when she stated, "well, I can assure you that America has no permanent enemies" (Rice, 2008).

So we alternate between war and negative peace in a condition called "warism." We have moved quickly from a republic of citizens to a republic of consumers, from a republic that values its rights and freedoms to a nation that is willing to trade its rights and freedoms—as typified by the USA PATRIOT Act (Uniting and Strengthening America by Providing Appropriate Tools Required to Intercept and Obstruct Terrorism Act of 2001)—for a life based on the never-ending consumption of goods. As Thomas Hobbes put it, we lead lives seeking desire after desire that ends only in death. Our one-dimensionality prevents us from seeing our inauthenticity in the republic of consumption.

Now imagine a different world based on positive peace where nations work cooperatively, and they do this because it serves their interests. Positive peace is enlightened egoism at work. Nations trade ideas and people as well as goods, accomplishing this through treaties and organizations like the European Union and the Kyoto Treaty. Nations defend themselves with elaborate systems of non-violent direct action called "civilian defense" that make invasion or genocide so costly that neither rogue nor rational states consider invasion or genocide a course worth taking. Civilian defense prepares for national defense as the Danes did so successfully against the Nazi invaders.

Imagine the potential of civilian defense as a means of national defense if a nation really prepared ahead. Imagine that we spend some fraction of the half-trillion dollars we spend annually on the military to develop and prepare for civilian defense. Nonviolent direct action and civilian defense promise to make each nation and the people of these nations' self-sufficient defenders. Nations could defend themselves without the false hope of humanitarian intervention. As the history of genocide after genocide in the twentieth century so aptly evidences, humanitarian intervention occurs, if it occurs at all, when there is an expected benefit for the intervening parties rather than for the victims (Power, 2002). However, the interconnected world of positive peace would also allow nations the international protection of humanitarian economic embargoes and restrictions as well as international pressures from other states. In such a world, we could significantly reduce the frequency and severity of wars and genocide.

You may say that is mere utopian thinking, and if you do then Marcuse is correct, we have already become too one-dimensional to see beyond our addiction to consumer culture. What we fear most is any change in the status quo, any change that would threaten the comforts of our consumer culture, the comforts of our addiction. We live in the denial that the source of our fix will never end while it is clear that the nonrenewable resources upon which the republic of desire runs are rapidly reaching a point where demand will outstrip supply and the cost will forever escalate against the backdrop of overpopulation, climate change, nuclear proliferation and all the other problems we confront.

And yet, I hope that you will not find utopian my claim that we can once again become a republic of citizens. I hope that you will realize that positive peace is in the interest of everyone alike and that we can all expect to benefit from it. Think back to how it is rational to believe and treat for disease B in the previous example even when going against the odds. It is my belief that the real solution to our dark times is to create a world where we no longer engage in warism because it is no longer possible.

The real solution to the concatenation of problems, I believe, is to be found in a smaller, saner world of sustainable development and sustainable communities of the sort that Leo Tolstoy and Gandhi foresaw. Imagine a world of self-governing relatively self-sustaining communities where people value their relationships with other people more than they value their possessions; where individual self-sufficiency is more highly prized than greed; where the ideals, if not the means, of Adam Smith and Karl Marx merge into one. We can imagine these communities in the countryside and in the city. (Mckibben, 2008; Speth, 2008).

In fact, let me suggest to you that the truly utopian belief is that we can spread capitalism globally to create a world of wealthy industrialized democratic nations. Jared Diamond argues that the world has too many people and too few natural resources. The environment will not be able to tolerate the greatly increased production of heat and pollutants that such a world entails (2004). James Speth argues that our way of life is not sustainable for us in the United States, let alone the whole world (2008).

We will return to the smaller, simpler world either by choice—in which case it may be an intelligent and beneficial movement to republics of citizens— or by necessity as the modern world disintegrates.

I ask you to consider as our moral ideal a world of positive peace. Such a world is comprised of self-sufficient communities of citizens who are mutually self-supporting and who cling to one another rather than become nothing at all. The cost will be the end to the republic of consumption, the end to life on a treadmill chasing things you do not need with money you do not have and worrying about how to pass that baton to your children. I offer you an end to measuring yourself by what you own rather than by the happiness you are, an end to the constant sense of being homesick that pervades modern life and in its place the possibility of authentic community.

Let me leave you with a plea for hope. This is not mere utopian thinking. This is old-fashioned American common sense: go to the root of the problem rather than attempt to put a Band-Aid on a major, infected wound. We need to return to good, old American common sense and re-imagine the image of Edward Hicks' *The Peaceable Kingdom* that represented the social ideal of our ancestors and invigorated them with hope in the American experience. We need to remember the Populist Movements of the past two centuries that gave America back to its citizens, if only for brief periods of time, for true change only comes from the grassroots. We need to remember the great success of the Marshall Plan that turned a Europe destroyed by two world wars into a land that approaches positive peace and repaid itself many times over through the economic trade it generated. Most of all we need to overcome our trendy cynicism and rediscover the power of hope.

Two

THE VULNERABILITY THESIS AND THE PEACEMAKING VIRTUES

Robert L. Muhlnickel

1. Introduction

My topic is the virtue of care and the place of care among the virtues. I favor a theory of care coherent with the perfectionist consequentialist theory of moral rightness. However, I hold that care is the central virtue, the most important of the virtues that promote the human good. I shall not discuss theories of the good in this paper, but refer to the good or pursuit of the good.

My view differs from the ethics of care as espoused by Carol Gilligan (1982), Nel Noddings (1984), and Michael Slote (2007). Each of them argues that care is central to morality or the basis of moral theory. I do not think that care is the basis of moral theory generally or the best explanation of common-sense morality. However, my debt to feminist thinkers who advocate various care ethics will become evident when I argue that care deserves the central place in accounts of virtue rather than courage, which many think is the central virtue.

I will proceed in three parts. First, I state a fundamental but complex fact about human beings. We are biological beings and the biological processes that underlie our physical and mental life are vulnerable to failure. While we are vulnerable to failure, we are also disposed to develop strengths that prevent or ameliorate those failures. Because we are both vulnerable to failure but enjoy developed dispositions that protect us against failure, we should accept these developed dispositions as virtues. This is the basis of the vulnerability thesis.

The vulnerability thesis asserts that virtues are powers that persons are biologically disposed to develop in favorable social and cultural settings that provide them with the ability to prevent failure and ameliorate its effects should they occur.

Second, I argue that the family of virtues under the heading of care includes what I call the eductive virtues. Eductive virtues are the virtues by which persons promote other persons' development of virtue. I will describe the eductive virtues and show that they can be instrumental in peacemaking.

Finally, I will contrast eductive virtues with the dominative virtue of courage. I will argue that philosophers' preoccupation with courage indicates a failure to recognize that the eductive virtues are more important to well-being than the dominative virtues.

2. The Vulnerability Thesis

To be vulnerable is to be susceptible to failure. Someone who is vulnerable is passive in relation to what threatens. Thus, "susceptible" is more apt than "capable," which is somewhere between passivity and activity when describing vulnerability. To fail means someone's physical or psychological functions suffer some harm that reduces their scope, efficiency, or power. To be susceptible to an event means our nature or condition is such that the occurrence of that event is likely. Involuntarily failure is a kind of harm. Susceptibility is a disposition to failure due to the design of some function.

As an example of susceptibility to failure due to design, consider a human walking upright on two feet. If the evolutionary scientists are correct, our feet and legs evolved for walking, while bent over and the upright walking customary in human cultures is a function for which our limb design is flawed. The result is a susceptibility to breakdown in the physiological processes of our feet, backs, and lower limbs.

Vulnerability extends beyond physical functions resulting from evolution. Our pursuit of the good leads us to use our bodies and minds in ways for which they are imperfectly designed. Biological processes, both physical and psychological, require training for us to engage in our pursuits, and they require restoration or repair to remain usable to pursue the good. Training begins early in life. Adults' efforts that teach upright walking train toddlers to use their feet, limbs, hips, and awareness of balance to move toward things, to pursue them. Adult efforts that teach infants to sleep are the first steps in training infants to do what is necessary for the restoration of physiological and psychological processes during sleep.

I cite these mundane and seemingly unremarkable facts because they indicate the pervasiveness of our vulnerability, and our vulnerability is the basis of the virtues. These facts indicate the pervasiveness of the eductive virtues, which adults exercise when they teach children to walk and to sleep. These facts are reminders that failure is a constant threat to our pursuit of the good. Call the failures to which we are vulnerable threats and call the state of being vulnerable to failure being under a threat. Threats have varied sources and natures; consequently, they figure differently in moral psychology and moral theory.

Just as individuals can suffer setbacks to their interests according to Joel Feinberg's well-known analysis of harm (1984, pp. 31–33), they can also suffer failure in their power to pursue the good. A failure in powers is harmful, just as setbacks to our interests are harmful. Focusing on vulnerability makes our biological nature central. Liberal theorists, such as Feinberg, argue that satisfaction of interests is central to well-being and setbacks to satisfaction of interests are central to harm, thereby making individual self-interest central to well-being.

Liberal theories fail because they omit consideration of a central fact to which any theory of the virtues must attend: that we are vulnerable beings susceptible to failure. Human beings are neither mere pursuers of satisfaction of interest nor pursuers of a rationally endorsed view of the good. Human beings are bodily beings; bodies are biological entities; and biological entities fail, with great consequence for our ability to satisfy interests or pursue the good. Bodily function is more fundamental to human good than is satisfying interests. It is a necessary condition of persons acting to satisfy their interests.

Being under a threat and being aware of being under a threat are distinctively different states. As Alasdair MacIntyre (1999, p. 4) and Barry Hoffmaster (2006, pp. 41–42) point out, we are not aware of as many threats as actually confront us. Awareness of being under a threat is more complex than mere belief that one is under a threat. Belief that we are under a threat is a disposition to respond affirmatively to the proposition that we are threatened. Awareness is a mental state including belief that one is under a threat and that belief having motivational efficacy and a role in intentional behavior.

Something distinguishes the *fact* of being under a threat from the *awareness* of that threat. We are aware of those threats that are salient to our function, safety, or survival. Lacking awareness of threats to our vulnerability has a protective function. We could not get through our days if we were aware of *every* threat to our selves and our activities. The number of things that actually threaten us exceeds the number of which we are aware. The primary causal factors of threats internal to the organism derive from biological processes. Biological processes fail to occur, misfire, or over-produce with great consequence for the good of the person in whom those breakdowns occur. In addition, individual persons have no control, or limited control, over the frequency, timing, and severity of biological failures.

Biological processes include the psychological processes of sensation, desire, emotion, and cognition. These psychological processes are rooted in our biology and the operations of biological processes are necessary to acts of sensing, desiring, feeling, and cognizing. In ordinary awareness, these mental acts seem to proceed from the self. Though we identify the self with the experience of performing these acts, unaware of the biological processes, a threat that reaches the level of salience brings to awareness the self's constitution by its organism's biological powers. When these powers fail us in athletic, social, or economic competition, we become aware that the experienced self depends on non-experiential biological processes. Awareness that incorporates factual beliefs about our vulnerability includes the belief that we have limited ability to control those processes. Though we are often unaware of it, each of us is under threat of failure in the biological processes that constitute our self.

Many threats lie outside ordinary awareness. Given that we are vulnerable to threats from internal and external alike, sometimes we are aware of what threatens us. That we are vulnerable is constitutive of the biological kind we are.

Vulnerability is constitutive of our biological kind, but the social processes by which we develop virtues are pervasive. Persons and societies organize conceptions of childcare, education, rearing, and training by some set of values whereby values are embodied in practices, rituals, instructional maxims, adages, and images. These practices are the activities by which we express care. This social process of caring for others in ways that promote their ability to avoid failure is the basis of the Vulnerability Thesis:

> The function of the virtues is to prevent the occurrence of threats to common human vulnerabilities or, should those threats occur, to ameliorate their effects.

The Vulnerability Thesis is a general claim about how best to understand the virtues. I will now describe a particular class of virtues that are usually classed under the concept of care.

3. The Eductive Virtues

The Vulnerability Thesis recognizes that we are always under different threats and that we have the ability to develop strengths that prevent those threats from occurring or to ameliorate their effects should they occur. It is realistic and hopeful: realistic about the human condition insofar as it accepts our susceptibility to breakdown and hopeful insofar as it indicates the means by which a good human life is possible, given our condition.

Because we are vulnerable and because we are capable to develop virtues instrumental to our well-being despite being vulnerable is the fundamental underpinning of the virtue of care. I adopt Christine Swanton's (2004) concept of the virtue of care, which occurs during interpersonal interaction. It comprises the skills by which agents interact with others, the recipients. These interpersonal relationships are marked by regard for the recipient and aims to promote the recipient's good. The level of intensity of regard between caring agent and recipient ranges from professional detachment, in which the agent provides a specific service, to the sort of intimacy associated with interpersonal love.

Caring is the process by which dispositions get developed into virtues that make the recipients of care less vulnerable. Swanton's conception of care indicates the wide range of activities that can fall under its scope; these include the eductive virtues.

Consider this first-person account of an aid worker among refugees in east Africa. The aid worker operates a center that assists refugees to develop small businesses by which they can support themselves and their families. The author, James Martin, describes his morning routine:

> When I arrived at the Mikono Centre, the sun already blazing in the clear sky, there were normally a dozen or so refugees, waiting for me on the shady porch, mostly women, some nursing children, many bearing crafts

they had carried that morning on the *matatu*, others holding letters request-ing a small business grant. (1999, p. 106)

Martin spent most of the morning meeting with the refugees. Some needed ad-vice on their projects—keeping books, dealing with landlords and merchants, resolving arguments, finding new markets—and most requested some financial assistance to help them through a rough time. He met with the refugees in a small room furnished with simple wooden chairs and a low table where we could talk freely, sometimes in Swahili, sometimes in French. In this way, he felt as if we were all working together toward a common goal:

> The time we spent together, I soon realized, was one of the most important things I could give the refugees. All of them had been for much of their lives forced to wait and wait and wait in endless lines—in the camps, in the U.N. offices, in government offices, in jails, in hospitals. And when in those places they were finally ushered in to see this or that official, they were typically treated shabbily and dealt with as quickly as possible. So I was happy to sit with them and listen as carefully as I could to their con-cerns. (Ibid.)

Martin describes typical attitudes, ends, and values of an agent exercising the eductive virtues: interpersonal relations and interaction undertaken with the aim of developing the recipient's strengths. The aim of the action is the recipient's good; the time spent with the refugees indicates their worth. He describes typical afternoon activities:

> In the afternoon, I visited the refugees in the slums. . . . I wanted to check up on them, to see how they were working together and if I could offer any advice. Usually, I would be asked to adjudicate a dispute, talk to a truculent landlord, or investigate a broken machine. And so my afternoons usually consisted of long drives through the hot city to discover a woman sitting forlornly in a fish-and-chips shop, where she would shake her head and tell me how very slow business was. Or to a woman's home where a new sew-ing machine sat idle . . . for lack of business. On these occasions, I would sit with them and simply listen to their frustrations and problems. For my part, I tried to listen carefully and offer whatever practical advice I could. (Ibid., p. 109)

This aid worker displays three eductive virtues: imaginative empathy, intentional non-dominance, and motivating experimental hope.

Imaginative empathy signifies the agents' ability to imagine the circums-tances of recipients from the recipients' perspective, and conceive of what the recipients construe as their own good. Imaginative empathy is instrumental to the intrinsic goods of companionship and achievement. Aid workers' imaginative empathy is the means by which they are aware that time spent with the refugees is valuable to them as an experience of companionship, and by which they can offer alternative actions and plans that the recipients find attractive. The aid worker takes time to learn about the crafts, styles, and circumstances of the refugees' lives.

The end of the aid workers' efforts is to strengthen the refugees so they are less vulnerable: incomes, work for which they are esteemed, and valued activities make them less vulnerable to despair and exploitation. Imaginative empathy need not drip with emotional intensity. The caring agent's imaginative empathy can take the form of counterfactually conceiving of alternatives, a cooler form than the intense imaginative experiences of artistic creation.

Caring agents offer alternatives instead of imposing them. Intentional non-dominance is the agent's ability to offer alternatives in ways that recipients are free to reject or change them. Agents intentionally adopt this attitude of non-dominance toward their proposals and toward the recipients, being intentional in both its senses. In the first sense, "intentional" means with the agent's intention. In the second, "intentional" means the capacity to represent or be about something other than itself. In the representational sense of "intentional," the agent who offers alternatives in a non-dominant way represents to the recipient of care that the recipient is free to take up what is offered, alter it, or reject it.

This method enables recipients to own the alternatives they chose. The eductive agent can be a peer, a subordinate, or a superior in relevant social or institutional hierarchies. While the aid workers' social status differs from that of the refugees, it is distinct from an interpersonal attitude of intentional non-dominance. Motivating experimental hope is caring agents' ability to motivate recipients to believe that they can do what is required for them to carry out an alternative. I distinguish experimental hope from utopian hope.

Utopian hope is hope that our circumstances will be changed so fundamentally that our agency will not meet any barriers in our circumstances. Experimental hope is hope that attaches to the actions of courses of actions that can be tried, the results observed, the results evaluated, and new courses of actions tried. Experimental hope accepts that the barriers in our circumstances will not be removed, but can be altered, avoided, or ameliorated.

The eductive virtues of imaginative empathy, intentional non-dominance, and motivating experimental hope are central to s the helping professions: health care, social work, and education. Excellent health care professionals exhibit imaginative empathy toward their patients, offer alternatives to patients, who retain the right to determine whether to implement them, and instill experimental hope. Excellent educators can imaginatively empathize with students' frustrations and joys engendered by the material being taught; they can offer alternatives to students for learning the material, and instill experimental hope.

Although the eductive virtues are often identified with the helping professions, this should not obscure their pervasiveness in our lives. Even outside the conventionally recognized and institutionalized professions, people interact with each other in ways that develop the virtues necessary for them to pursue the good. These relationships occur in families, businesses, voluntary associations, and self-help groups. Yet despite the pervasiveness of the eductive virtues and their necessity for any of us to pursue the good, they are not a central topic of philosophical discussion. I will return to this point in the last section. For now, I consider the eductive virtues as a viable means to resolve violent conflict.

4. The Peacemaking Virtues

Among the activities James Martin lists as resolving conflict are resolving arguments and adjudicating disputes. The threat I will consider here, which can be ameliorated by eductive virtue, is that of violent conflict. When violent conflict occurs, we can aim the eductive virtues toward peacemaking.

People resort to violence when they believe they have no alternatives to it, when they bear ill will or hatred toward another, and when they believe they will not be prevented from doing violence to the other. The preventive factors might be located in the object of violence, as when the other is not powerful enough to prevent the agent from doing violence. The preventive factor might be located in a third party, who lacks the power to deter the agent from doing violence. Epistemic, emotional, and situational factors all contribute to violence. I hold that imaginative empathy, intentional non-dominance, and motivating experimental hope serving the end of peacemaking.

Peacemaking agents can have imaginative empathy for conflicting agents who do not believe they have alternatives to violence. They are able to imagine alternative solutions that the conflicting parties cannot imagine or conceive on their own. The peacemakers' intentional non-dominance toward destructive agents' ill will and hatred communicates to the conflicting parties that alternatives to ill will and hatred do exist. Even if peacemaking agents cannot prevent the destructive agents from carrying out their destructive intent, they can communicate a significant potential response to the destructive agent. They convey that they do not fear the destructive agent and respond to the destructive agent's intent without threatening to use violence in turn. Thomas Merton describes the effect of the peacemaking agent's intentional non-dominance is "to clear the atmosphere so that men can understand their plight without hatred, without fury, without desperation, and with a minimum of good will" (1980, p. 23). Finally, peacemaking agents motivate experimental hope when they persuade destructive agents to attempt something of other than destructive intent.

Martin Luther King, Jr. exemplifies the peacemaking virtues. Ralph B. Levering describes King's approach to nonviolent conflict resolution (1986). He shows that King effectively addressed White's fears, desires, and emotional responses to displays of Black resistance. King communicated Black's aspirations to Whites, making nonviolent direct action respectable to the White majority.

King also imaginatively empathized with Blacks who feared the threats of violence by which Whites had historically enforced the norms of Black subordinate status. King's nonviolent tactics offered solutions to both Whites and Blacks. Whites were unlikely to conceive of a nonviolent solution without some compelling impetus and found new respect for Blacks who embraced nonviolence. To Whites, this nonviolence offered an alternative way of accepting Blacks as legal equals without prompting violence. To Blacks, practicing nonviolence offered a means of asserting self-worth consistent with religious beliefs that King reinforced in his preaching.

Historically, Blacks had been barred from legal equality had been motivated by shame at the threat of arrest and imprisonment. King's teaching transformed this shame by persuading Blacks that accepting imprisonment for a worthy cause was a mark of honor. The cause of achieving legal equality, regaining a more accurate estimate of self-worth, and demanding and receiving treatment reflective of personal worth transformed what had been shameful into a source of pride.

5. Care and Courage: Eductive and Dominative Virtues

Let us return to my claim about the centrality of care. If the virtue of care is central to developing the strengths by which persons prevent the failures to which they are vulnerable or ameliorate the effects of those failures that do occur, then moral philosophers central to Western philosophy have failed to appreciate a phenomenon of great importance by failing to give care its due place among the virtues. My view comes close to that of contemporary feminists who argue that because many have identified care with women's activities in reproduction, rearing, and domestic life, it has been invisible to moral philosophy or given a less important role than it deserves.

Since Aristotle, moral philosophers have identified the virtues with the strengths required for participation in public life. The abilities associated with reproduction and with women who had primary responsibility for reproduction functioned as a component of the infrastructure that supported the public virtues. The primary virtue of this conception of the good life is courage. For this reason, it will be helpful to consider the way courage differs from care.

Care and courage are are compatible; persons can have both virtues. But they serve different ends in the moral life. The end of care is to strengthen, so that the individuals receiving care are less vulnerable as they pursue the good. The end of courage is to dominate, so that what threatens does not cause harm or prevent the pursuit of the good.

These ends are pertinent whether care or courage is directed reflexively at the agent or directed at someone other than the agent. The agent who exercises self-care directs care toward strengthening pursuit of the good. Agents who care for another direct their care toward strengthening the others' pursuit of the good. Courageous agents can direct their dominative power toward their own dispositions to harm or fail to pursue the good. Alternatively, courageous agents can direct their dominative power to prevent others from doing harm or preventing the pursuit or maintenance of the good.

This difference can be illuminated by considering different forms of courage. Military courage necessarily involves dominating another person who threatens the good life of the political community the soldier defends. The modern forms of courage (moral courage or intellectual courage), necessarily involves dominating parts of the self that would motivate cooperation or agreement. The internalized courage of modern thinkers requires self-domination, so that the morally or intellectually courageous person endures the loneliness of isolation for the sake of correcting a wrong or rejecting the common wisdom to assert an unwelcome truth.

Amelie O. Rorty has shown that philosophical theories of courage necessarily involve the end of domination, either of an enemy or some part of oneself (1986). Rushworth Kidder's popular work on courage emphasizes dominating some impulse, desire, or need originating in the self because it is unworthy of the end that courageous action serves (2005). The concept of domination is inseparable from the concept of courage.

In contrast, the caring agent strengthens rather than dominates. In the interpersonal sphere, the caring agent strengthens the Other. The caring agent uses the eductive virtues to draw from the recipient strengths they have not yet developed, making the recipient better able to pursue the good.

My point is not to deny that courage is a virtue. I do not deny that there are circumstances in which the dominative end is the good the agent should pursue. I do deny that courage is central to the good life as it is found in the tradition that conceives of the virtues as the strengths necessary for combat, public life, and political achievement.

These theories of the good human life and the virtues that promote it omit or devalue the remarkable virtue of care that pervades our lives, without which there is no pursuit of the good at all. Further, by failing to think about care and the necessity of the eductive virtues, personal and public decisions get distorted from what promotes human development and peace.

Furthermore, care and courage can be combined in complex chains of action. For instance, Blacks who followed Martin Luther King's non-violent teachings required courage to accept imprisonment and violence. The end of courage in that instance is to dominate our self-preserving disposition. To tolerate the impulse to respond to violence without resort to violence, the courageous non-violent resister must dominate the disposition to use violence. To accept imprisonment as a mark of honor, non-violent demonstrators must dominate their learned interpretation of imprisonment as a sign of shame. To the extent that

Blacks adopted King's message of love for Whites, they could be said to exercise courage for the further end of caring for those Whites. However, this does not lead me to deny that the more proximate end of courage is the dominative one.

My final point derives from my claim that even though care is central to the pursuit of the good life, it has been obscured from our view by our acceptance of the conception of the good life as the public life. The public life is closely associated with the dominative virtue of courage. The task for philosophers is to reconsider and work to understand the homely and unremarkable facts about our vulnerability and the practices of care by which the strengths to respond to threats are developed. This reconsideration is a necessary step toward rethinking the virtues needed to educate for peace.

Three

GANDHIAN NONVIOLENCE AS NOT PRESUPPOSING HUMAN GOODNESS

Sanjay Lal

1. Introduction

Critics typically chastise advocates of nonviolence for taking a naïve and simplistic view of their opponents. A ubiquitous justification of violence, ingrained as a conventional common sense understanding across the globe, is that our opponents are so evil that only violence is effective in dealing with them. Alternatively, nonviolence appeals to moral sensibilities. Its application is viable only when dealing with those who have moral consciences.

Mohandas K. Gandhi regards the method of nonviolence not only as the most effective method for instituting change, but also as capable of transforming even the hardest of hearts. While Gandhi's unyielding faith in the goodness of humanity is well known, the question of whether such faith is required for adopting and applying a philosophy of nonviolence is worthy of consideration. If the plausibility of the moral method of nonviolence hinges on a positive view of humanity, then the method's viability is open to serious doubt.

In what follows, I will first explain the place a positive view of opponents has in the application of nonviolence as a method for instituting change. I will rely on the Gandhian concept of *satyagraha* (soul force), which is most often interpreted as the foundational concept behind nonviolent or passive resistance. Given the success that Gandhi achieved in instituting change and the overall influence he has had on effective nonviolent movements, his ideas represent perhaps the best case that can be made for the philosophy of nonviolence.

2. Gandhian *Satyagraha*

Gandhi founded the concept of *satyagraha*, a term derived from the Hindu words for truth (*satya*) and force (*graha*). By revealing truth to our opponents, we thus institute change in, our opponents. Gandhi believed that neither coercion nor purely rational argumentation is able to institute significant change in our opponents. Coercion produces untruth since it leads opponents to act in ways contrary to their understanding.

A fundamental Gandhian precept holds that actions must be in harmony with the actors' inner states to be pure (a necessary though not sufficient condition). Only pure actions can lead to the realization of Truth. This follows since the realization of Truth requires one to believe in the Truth that is realized. Reason, on the other hand, is limited in its ability to change since it can only have impact on the intellect. What is required is a willingness to suffer for our convictions. Gandhi states:

> I have come to this fundamental conclusion that if you want something really important to be done, you must not merely satisfy the reason, you must move the heart also. The appeal of reason is more to the head, but the penetration of the heart comes from suffering. It opens up the inner understanding in man. (Gandhi, 1948 p. 189)

By willingly suffering for her convictions a *satyagrahi* causes opponents to examine the justification of their behavior and thus awakens the opponent's moral conscience. According to Gandhi, no one is without such a conscience. "There is an inmost center of us all, where Truth abides in fullness. Every wrongdoer knows within himself that he is doing wrong" (*Young India* July 1931). When opponents' moral conscience is awakened, genuine change can be instituted.

3. Gandhi's Faith in the Goodness of Humanity

Let us consider what is, perhaps, the crucial difference between Gandhi's understanding of opponents and how more conventional disputants understand them. Typically, people assume that opponents are so lacking in a moral conscience that changing them is outside the realm of possibility. They believe that their very survival depends on stopping opponents from inflicting suffering. On the contrary, Gandhian nonviolence espouses that we must believe our opponents have a moral conscience. Gandhi proclaimed, "no human being is so bad as to be beyond redemption" (Ansbro, 1982, pp. 137–138). He also stated, "[belief] in nonviolence is based on the assumption that human nature in its essence is one and therefore unfailingly responds to the advances of love" (Homer 1956, p. 340). Only one who is convinced that moral force can sway opponents would be sincere in responding to those opponents with nonviolence in the attempt to institute change. Hence, the philosophy of nonviolence requires us to have a positive view of our opponents.

Achieving a positive view of opponents is a genuine obstacle to the adoption of Gandhian methods because the world has no shortage of evil and brutality. To imagine that those who find pleasure in inflicting the most unspeakable kinds of horrors could somehow be swayed by a moral method that derives its morality mainly from a willingness to receive but never deliver suffering appears as extremely naïve to many. They conclude that only violence could eradicate the source of evil actions and thus institute change.

4. Exploring and Refining Gandhi's Premise

Now let us explore Gandhi's basis for believing in the goodness of humanity. Ultimately, he sees nonviolence as an attribute of ultimate reality (*atman*), which is everyone's True Self, which is manifested in the attraction, cooperation, and order (aspects of the True Self) that underlie the everyday world. *Atman* is also manifested in the moral consciousness of human beings. Since *atman* is the True Self, Gandhi reaches the conclusion that human beings, at their core, are good.

Such is Gandhi's basis for concluding that everyone ought to practice nonviolence, not just those who are inclined toward it. He writes, "I am certain that nonviolence is meant for all time. It is an attribute of the *atman* and is, therefore, universal since the *atman* belongs to all" (Iyer, 1986, p. 430). We read:

> Scientists tell us that without the presence of the cohesive force amongst the atoms that comprise this globe of ours, it would crumble to pieces and we cease to exist; and even as there is cohesive force in blind matter, so must there be in all things animate, and the name for that cohesive force among animate beings is Love. We notice it between father and son, between brother and sister, friend and friend. But we have to learn to use that force among all that lives, and in the use of it consists our knowledge of God. Where there is love there is life; hatred leads to destruction. . . .

> Though there is enough repulsion in Nature she *lives* by attraction. Mutual love enables Nature to persist. Man does not live by destruction. . . . Nations cohere because there is mutual regard among individuals composing them. . . . I have found that life persists in the midst of destruction and, therefore, there must be a higher law than that of destruction. Only under that law would a well-ordered society be intelligible and life worth living. (Gandhi, 1955 p. 16)

> The fact that there are so many men still alive in the world shows that it is based not on the force of arms but on the force of love. Therefore, the greatest and most unimpeachable evidence of the success of this force is to be found in the fact that, in spite of the wars of the world, it still lives on. . . .

> Hundreds of nations live in peace. History does not and cannot take note of this fact. History is really a record of every interruption of the even working of the force of love or of the soul. (Gandhi, 1956, p. 111)

Given the behavior of so many throughout history, it is difficult to agree with Gandhi's belief that everyone's True Self is good. However, the persistence of life in spite of so much destruction and the prevalence of moral sentiments in human beings appear to provide some basis for Gandhi's premise. Perhaps if we take Gandhi to be speaking of human beings in the general sense, we can see his premise as more plausible. In the remainder of this chapter, I will develop implications for this revised understanding of Gandhi's premise.

5. The Inhumane as More Separated from the Truth Within

Given the prevalence of moral sentiments in normally functioning psyches, it is plausible to conclude that those who seem to lack such sentiments have some kind of malfunction and are abnormal. Such individuals, in Gandhi's worldview, could be even more separate from the ultimate Truth within. The presence of *atman* is less apparent in such individuals. Thus, rather than providing the basis by which we generalize about all of humanity, we should see them as exceptions.

Moreover, all such individuals must rely on the cooperation of more normal individuals (who can be persuaded by moral force) to accomplish their objectives. While such cooperation is often achieved by fear and imposed by force, only limited cooperation can be achieved that way. Eventually, the cooperators must be convinced of the rightness of a cause for the cause to succeed; the iron fist cannot be present at all times when cooperation is needed.

When confronted with the pure innocence of practitioners of organized nonviolence, being convinced of the rightness of an evil cause becomes virtually impossible for the rank and file regardless of how much fear and force is imposed. Therefore, unless we assume that all who participate in evil systems are without a moral conscience, we must not rule out Gandhi's approach too quickly when confronting opponents.

6. *Satyagraha* as Effective When Reaching the Reachable

When we consider the success of nonviolent movements, we see how that success lay precisely in the ability to reach the convertible masses. No matter the brutality of particular individual leaders, the rank and file members of their societies have shown a remarkable ability for moral growth. When the moral understandings of such members are awakened, the evil systems their actions have perpetuated no longer continue.

The normalized relations Allied countries now have with Germany and Japan are examples of moral growth among rank and file members of those societies for which only violence was regarded as an appropriate response (to the rank and file and their brutal leaders). Given their proven propensity to change, regular members of societies whose leaders have been among the most brutal quite likely would have been moved by a nonviolent method. Had organized nonviolence been the response to the evil regimes under which they lived, the taking of life from those who were blameless and unwilling to die (for example, victims of Hiroshima) might not have occurred. The morality of those responding to, say, Imperial Japan, would have remained all the more preserved.

Later, I will address the question of whether a nonviolent response would have been conducive to survival. However, the larger point should not be lost—once the rank and file have been swayed, the leaders can no longer perpetuate their brutality.

7. Significance of Rank and File Cooperation

At this point, we should keep in mind that every evil system needs social architects with organizational talents and ideological reliability—for example, such as Adolph Eichmann was to the Nazi regime—to keep things like the trains running on time. In addition, evil systems need indifference, which amounts to tacit consent, from bystanders as well as crops of recruits from the general—and morally reachable—population. Furthermore, as Arendt has shown, depicting Eichmann as a sadistic monster is fundamentally wrong (Arendt, 1963, p. 193). Instead, it is more accurate to see such people as uninspired bureaucrats who simply thought they where doing their jobs.

Given the changes that have occurred among the members of German society, to depict Eichmann or the greater German population as beyond moral persuasion would be equally wrong. While it may seem that such persuasion could only have been realized by the violence that was inflicted on Germany by the Allies, the changes themselves would not have been lasting unless the members of the society underwent some kind of inner transformation. Nonviolence has not been shown to be less effective in initiating such transformation than has violence. Indeed, it is plausible to think methods akin to nonviolence (for example, those that change hearts and minds) were most responsible for this mass moral transformation.

8. Being Good versus Having a Capacity for Good

While it may appear awkward to consider those who participate in and cooperate with the most horrendous of evils as being fundamentally good, we must keep in mind that all have shown a great capability for good. Indeed, merely this capability for good, which the general population at large has exhibited throughout history, and not the inherent goodness of human nature, a more controversial supposition, is all a *satyagrahi* must be committed to show that such a method is viable.

Eichmann and typical Germans, for instance, showed a remarkable capability for being just toward members of their own families. This indicates a great potential for good that was realized when Germans people extended their justness to include a greater population.

Indeed, demonstrating to such people that the victims of their evil were not fundamentally different from their own family members is what lay the groundwork for moral transformation.

9. *Satyagraha* Eradicates Presumed Distinctions

The Gandhian method of *satyagraha* is ideal for conveying to oppressors and bystanders that the Other is not fundamentally different from those to whom the oppressors and bystanders have already shown regard. Willingly accepting suffering without any hint of hostility or bitterness toward those who are inflicting the suffering makes it difficult for the general population (if not oppressors themselves) to harbor ill will or indifference toward the victims of oppression. This point is in evidence in the successful nonviolent movements in history. A lack of antipathy and apathy among perpetuators of evil systems makes it all the more difficult to maintain the impression that another group is so fundamentally different from our acquaintances and relatives that we find it acceptable to treat them in immoral ways.

Whenever we treat the Other in ways in which we are not willing to be treated, we presume a distinction between them and us, and thus feel justified in our treatment of them. The perpetuation of distinctions that enable persons to feel no presence of a moral conscience when observing or inflicting evil on the Other ultimately requires ill will or indifference toward the ones who are being distinguished. Their sentience is either denied or deemed irrelevant.

Furthermore, the dignity, strength of spirit, and innocence exhibited by *satyagrahis* leaves those who observe and participate in the systems that oppress them with the impression that the victims are morally superior to (and not merely similar to) those closest to their oppressors and bystanders. Once this impression is cast, it becomes easier (if not inevitable) for the participants in evil systems to sympathize with their victims.

The pure innocence of the sufferers, moreover, has such an appeal to moral conscience that it becomes impossible to remain indifferent toward their plight. Since it is typical for any group of human beings to also regard themselves as blameless, the innocence of *satyagrahis* ultimately shows others that they too could be victimized (and thus eradicates any sense of separation one may feel from the sufferers).

10. Nonviolence and Individual Evildoers

Some may argue that none of these arguments are helpful in dealing with acts of evil that flow from individuals or acts that are not the result of oppressive systems. In that regard, we can ask whether violence is justified to deal with the individual psychopath, who does not rely on the consent or cooperation of the uninspired bureaucrats who have shown a great capacity for good.

All of us, regardless of how lone we may be in our actions, need cooperation from others to subsist. Even wretched serial killers, for example, must rely on others to enable their existence. They have needs that can only be met by others doing their part and when these needs go unmet, their life as they know it is threatened. Once such cooperation is withdrawn, it becomes impossible to continue much less to continue perpetuating evil.

Systemic and institutionalized support is never consciously given in support of the lone psychopath's acts and such an individual never poses a threat to group survival. In addition, there exists universal acknowledgement of the moral superiority of the psychopath's victim. Thus, the case for nonviolence may be even more viable with regard to individuals than it is with regard to oppressive systems. In the case of individual evildoers, hearts and minds are already on the side of the sufferers. Once one moves beyond thinking the continuation of one's own life is the supreme good, genuinely abandons self-interest, and gives moral superiority primary importance, the viability of the nonviolent response becomes all the more clear.

11. Nonviolence and Willingness to Die

When our primary objective is survival, adopting Gandhian methods of nonviolence appears to be questionable (if not immoral). By willingly suffering and dying, do not practitioners of *satyagraha* jeopardize their group's very existence regardless of whether their methods are ultimately conducive to moral transformation? Such reasoning leads many to conclude that violence is necessary to ensure a group's continuance.

Gandhian philosophy calls for a detachment from our individual life. For Gandhi, genuine nonviolence requires individuals' willingness to die for their convictions. Such a notion is not as radical as it may seem, since the selflessness entailed by the willingness to die for a cause is widely regarded as a virtue among the violent and nonviolent alike.

Inevitably, the means we adopt influences the ends that are established. Pure ends can only be realized by pure means. Thus, Gandhi had a strong commitment to use only moral means, such as the refusal to kill, to realize and reveal Truth. Since Truth is the only good and can only be realized by moral means maintaining moral superiority is, for Gandhi, of primary importance. When elaborating to Europeans about how to combat Nazism, Gandhi stated, "in the end I expect it is the moral worth that will count. All else is dross" (Homer, 1956, p. 338). Similarly, he called the acts of the South African resisters he led who were willing to die rather than sell their honor for personal comfort "*ahimsa* (nonviolence) in its active form" (Gandhi, 1971, p. 147).

A key distinction exists between desiring the survival of one's group, which is more other centered, and the more self-interested desire for individual survival. Desire for the survival of a group is conventionally regarded as morally outweighing the desire for individual survival.

I will show that nonviolence is not antithetical to group survival, but is a viable response even when individual survival is at stake. Gandhian nonviolence can be accepted on consequentialist grounds. Though Gandhi calls for disavowing consequences, consequentialist considerations (such as group survival) can nonetheless help establish *satyagrahas'* practicality, and thus its viability to everyday concerns.

Considering the multitudes of the violent that have died for their cause and the penchant for violent responses to escalate violence, history provides no reason for assuming that resorting to violence will assure survival, individually or collectively. Thus, the problem of advancing survival remains also for a proponent of violence.

However, nonviolence not only includes a willingness to die for a cause but also an unwillingness to kill. Thus, it does not compromise the morality of a cause. By maintaining a superior moral stance, the nonviolent method is capable of transforming and moving others and thus gaining support for a group's own survival. Only the most committed proponents of violence would think that killing off one's opponents is ever a viable, realistic, or satisfactory solution to resolve conflict.

At some point, hearts and minds must be changed for a campaign to have ultimate success. No prima facie reason exists for assuming that violence is more effective than nonviolence in reaching such aims. Furthermore, we cannot assume that the nonviolent method would not engender those aims in time to ensure a group's survival.

Many groups have responded to evil with nonviolence (from the members of Indian society who followed Gandhi, to the Serbians of the late twentieth century, who were influenced by Gandhian ideas). The continuance of such groups has remained intact. Either outside onlookers (for example, the overall international community in the case of the Serbians) or the oppressors themselves (for example, the British leaders of Parliament who honored Gandhi formally on his 100th birthday) will be won over by the nonviolent method and will be compelled to not cooperate with or engage in evil doings.

12. Conclusion

Typically, many offer the rationale that our opponents are so evil that only violence is effective in responding to them. This argument can be countered without strongly assuming all human beings are inherently good. The apparent lack of a moral conscience in some should not be taken to deny the general goodness of the population at large or the capacity for goodness that virtually all human beings have exhibited.

Keeping such features in mind along with the virtue of selflessness (entailed by the willingness to look beyond one's personal survival) and the importance of moral superiority make it easier to see the viability of nonviolence as an adequate response to evil acts and institutions. Adopting a philosophy of nonviolence does not entail an unrealistic or simplistic attitude toward human beings.

Four

NONVIOLENT RHETORIC IN GEOPOLITICS

William C. Gay

1. Introduction

For several years, I have been seeking to articulate within philosophy and within Peace Studies a language of positive peace and a practice of linguistic nonviolence (Gay, 1998; 1999a; 2004). While we hear a lot about nonviolent action in peace and justice studies, we hear much less about the supportive role of nonviolent communication in general and the increasing success of nonviolent rhetoric in geopolitics in particular. Several recent works outside of philosophy and outside of peace studies advance the significant role that nonviolent communication and nonviolent rhetoric can play in the establishment of peace. In this chapter, I will appropriate some of this work as providing empirical support for and useful terminology in developing a language of positive peace and a practice of linguistic nonviolence.

I will first draw particular attention to the work of Marshall Rosenberg and the work of Ellen Gorsevski, showing how they advance peaceful resolution of conflicts from interpersonal through international levels. The integration of Rosenberg and Gorsevski's concepts of nonviolent communication and nonviolent rhetoric into the theory and practice of nonviolent action can broaden and strengthen efforts to avoid violent conflict and war on the international level. On a practical level, I will note a related effort to promote nonviolence by the Tanenbaum Center for Interreligious Understanding. Finally, I will address the ethics of nonviolent rhetoric.

2. Nonviolent Communication and Nonviolent Rhetoric

Within psychology, Marshall Rosenberg has written extensively on nonviolent communication. Through his work with Carl Rogers, Rosenberg became inspired to stress how success in communication is likely to lead to success in relationships. One of his best-known books is *Nonviolent Communication: The Language of Life* (2005). Rosenberg also has established the Center for Nonviolent Communication in Albuquerque, New Mexico, which offers training on how to practice his techniques of nonviolent communication. For my purposes, however, I will focus initially on his distinction between Giraffe language and its opposite, Wolf language. The language of peace is similar to Giraffe language, while the language of war is similar to Wolf language.

Giraffes have long necks that give them great overviews. Giraffe language refers to the ability to express a larger perspective on discussions and conflicts. We can use Giraffe language when we wish to listen to feelings and values that others are trying to express. The goal is to make contact with the other and reach a solution with a common basis.

We know about the aggressive behavior of wolves. Those who are filled with judgments that they hold ferociously use Wolf language. Because those who use Wolf language criticize, blame, and scold the other, and insist on proving their position to be right, the outcome may be conflict resolution through violence or war rather than through mediation and diplomacy.

Rosenberg's distinction between Giraffe language and Wolf language has some parallels to what Carol Gilligan calls an "ethics of care," which is oriented to relations, and an "ethics of justice," which is oriented to procedures (1982).

Care ethics is a relational approach to morality that avoids generalization in favor of particularity and connection. Not surprisingly, those who favor care ethics are more inclined to use Giraffe language. The tradition of care ethics holds a prominent place in contemporary ethical theory. Thinking about care and caring is connected to the central theme of care (*Sorge*) in Martin Heidegger's *Being and Time* (1962) and can be found in a variety of subsequent philosophical theories, such as Hubert L. Dreyfus's *Being-in-the-World*, especially Chapter Fourteen, "The Care Structure" (1990).

Gilligan picks up on this tradition of care ethics and develops it in her own specific manner, especially by stressing the web of relations within which we find ourselves and how we tend to and show care for these relations. She developed her alternative moral voice while working as an assistant to Harvard psychologist, Lawrence Kohlberg, who drew heavily on Kantian ethics. She challenges many of the Kantian assumptions in the dominant moral theories of the West which typically are based on an ethics of justice rather than an ethics of care.

"Justice ethics" represents the approach traditionally favored in philosophy: a morality based on abstract principles and moral concepts. Kant stressed the concept of duty and an a priori commitment to the categorical imperative. Those who stress justice ethics may be inclined to use Wolf language.

The main differences between Kohlberg and Gilligan relate to concepts of connection, particularity, and emotion. In this regard, Gilligan's position and Rosenberg's position have some striking similarities. Gilligan stresses connections among people and the relationships they establish. She views the individual as entangled in a web of dynamic relationships, not all of which are freely chosen. She believes moral action requires knowledge of particular others and their circumstances, not universalized cases. Her approach embraces feelings as a moral capacity that facilitates an ethical response. Emotion, then, has a significant role in creating connection and motivating action. Further, we could say that it constitutes a large part of what makes us human beings. Care creates and sustains connection.

In *Nonviolent Communication*, Rosenberg explores the fundamental aspects of human needs, desires, judgment, and empathy. He explains why techniques of nonviolent communication are effective in achieving good interpersonal relations. He argues that the key technique is the use of empathy, because when those in conflict with you feel that you understand them and are trying to feel what they feel, they are more likely to speak honestly with you to resolve conflict.

Gilligan's concept of care and Rosenberg's concept of empathy go hand in hand. In my judgment, the language of positive peace would benefit from incorporating these concepts and practicing the techniques of Giraffe language and care ethics. I will return to this point in my final section.

While I find Rosenberg's position to be rather straight forward, I am more impressed by the position Ellen Gorsevski has developed within Communication Studies. In her book, *Peaceful Persuasion: The Geopolitics of Nonviolent Rhetoric*, she challenges the emphasis within geopolitics on violence, militarization, and retribution (2004). She contends that nonviolent rhetoric, though largely overlooked by most scholars, can support the transformation from frequent threats of physical violence to more regular discussion of nonviolent options in the approach to conflict in contemporary political communication. To redress the neglect of nonviolent rhetoric, an important initial step is to overcome misconceptions about nonviolent communication. These misconceptions are similar to those regarding pacifism.

Critics ridicule and marginalize nonviolent communication, presenting it as cowardly, utopian, unrealistic, and ineffective (Gorsevski, 2004, p. 10). Such criticisms are similar to ones leveled against pacifism. Duane Cady, for example, has explained how pacifism is easily dismissed because of distorted characterizations of it (1989). Critics imply that nonviolent communication amounts to the passive acceptance of abuse and injustice. Many feel that violence must be fought with violence. In fact, nonviolent communication is not passive; instead, it seeks to actively build peace and justice and resist oppression without resorting to violence. In *A Force More Powerful*, Peter Ackerman and Jack DuVall elucidate that the twentieth century provides examples in each decade and on every continent (except Antarctica) of successful nonviolent struggles (2000).

Gorsevski holds that nonviolent rhetoric is intended to make the oppressor acknowledge the importance of our views. In all instances in which a population is oppressed by a totalitarian regime, the power of the oppressor over the oppressed is effective in large part by the cooperation of the oppressed. Nonviolent communication seeks to undermine the power of rulers through the deliberate withdrawal of consent and cooperation. In this regard, Gorsevski's position is like Gene Sharp's view that nonviolent means of persuasion are effective because they remove the underlying acquiescence of the populace, thus removing the support for the oppressor that is required for the oppressor to maintain power (Sharp, 1992). Nevertheless, Gorsevski draws from models of rhetoric and presents her view of nonviolence as a way to reconfigure rhetorical studies and social movement strategy.

In part, Gorsevski uses a case study approach. For example, she examines the pragmatic nonviolence of Macedonian President Kiro Gligorov and the visual rhetoric of Nobel Peace Prize winner, Aung San Suu Kyi, in Burma (Myanmar). Gorsevski also addresses how conflicts can be understood, prevented, managed, or reduced through the use of peace-minded rhetorical techniques. In this regard, she makes use of The Seville Statement on Violence, originally published in 1986 and reprinted in 1990 (Adams, Barnett, Bechtereva, et al., 1990). She says that the world-renowned scientists who wrote this book "maintain that language and culture are the reasons for war, not 'natural' biological makeup" (Gorsevski, 2004, p. 193). For this reason, she stresses the need for theorists of peace and conflict studies and of rhetoric to examine the role of language in culture. In my terms, Gorsevski is calling for a move from the dominance of the language of war to an increased use of the language of positive peace to transform the culture.

The nonviolent rhetoric that Gorsevski proposes: (1) empathizes with the opponent; (2) eschews violent metaphors; (3) relies on feelings, facts, and history of mutual agreement; (4) is culturally respectful and aware; (5) relies on a sense of community and mutual responsibility; (6) practices stubborn non-cooperation with unjust actions or systems; (7) displays the ethos of being an underdog; (8) shows care for the earth's ecosystems and creatures; and (9) portrays all people as deserving of human rights, equality, and respect (ibid., p. 164).

Obviously, Gorsevski initial emphasis on empathy parallels the positions of Gilligan and Rosenberg, as do several other characteristics of nonviolent rhetoric. Many of these characteristics are taken from Mahatma Gandhi. In part, nonviolent rhetoric works by melting the hearts of the oppressors by conversion or persuasion (Childress, 1972). It allows the oppressors to perceive the oppressed as being human beings. This aspect, to have the oppressors recognize those they oppress as human, occurs because of the voluntary suffering of the oppressed, which moves the oppressor to acknowledge them as human. In this sense, nonviolent communication operates on an emotional level to let the opponent know that all people share the same humanity.

An important aspect of nonviolent rhetoric is its propaganda. Although propaganda is normally seen as language used dishonestly by the oppressors in society, Joan Bondurant (1988) suggests propaganda is an integral part of nonviolent rhetoric. In this instance, nonviolent propaganda is used to educate one's opponents, the public, and those who participate in nonviolent rhetoric. Nonviolent propaganda is intended to promote awareness and understanding of the issues. Gorveski writes:

> The nonviolent text, as written, spoken or enacted, is reflexive; the opponent, as audience, is also a participant, and must be instructed on how to

engage; the opponent must be trained, in a sense, to read the text, the discourse, or the actions as rhetoric. (2004, p. 180)

Gorveski gives as an example Dr. Martin Luther, Jr.'s "Letter from a Birmingham Jail," where he addresses the misconceptions of his adversaries and educates them on the strategies of nonviolent action (King, 1964).

Gorsevski reviews how nonviolent communication was a vital feature of several significant events of the twentieth century, including Gandhi's rhetoric of nonviolence, Martin Luther King, Jr.'s "I Have a Dream" speech, and Nelson Mandela's Inaugural Address (Thonssen, 1964; Mandela, 1994). In these and other key world events, the aims of nonviolent communication include trying to prevent or reduce the potential for destroying life on earth, enhancing the potential for improved human coexistence, and fostering greater respect for human and ecological diversity on earth (Gorsevski, 2004, p. 8).

Are these techniques effective in producing peaceful change? In several significant global events of the twentieth century, the techniques have been effective: the collapse of British colonial rule in India; success of the Civil Rights movement in the United States; the fall of the Iron Curtain in East Germany; the end of apartheid in South Africa; and the peaceful development of the Republic of Macedonia among the violent civil wars that racked the remainder of the former Yugoslavia (ibid., p. 159). Through these world events and the examples of Gandhi, Martin Luther King, Jr., and others perhaps less well known, these techniques do contribute to peace and to a nonviolent culture.

3. Nonviolent Rhetoric and Practice in the Resolution of Religious Conflicts

While these theoretical works are helpful, we can also learn at the level of practice from the work of those who are committed to nonviolence. One excellent treatment of such examples is provided in *Peacemakers in Action: Profiles of Religion in Conflict Resolution* (Tanenbaum Center for Interreligious Understanding, 2007). This book was a project of the Tanenbaum Center for Interreligious Understanding, which is a not-for-profit, nonsectarian organization dedicated to providing practical programs that prevent the growing problem of verbal and physical conflicts based on religion. It presents twelve case studies that illustrate how religious leaders, while putting their lives on the line, have succeeded in using nonviolent conflict resolution. The cases are drawn from places such as Afghanistan, Bosnia, Kosovo, Sudan, Sierra Leone, Israel, and Palestine. They include efforts by Christians, Jews, Muslims, and others. The book suggests that these grassroots efforts can provide valuable lessons, even for diplomats and government officials.

Sheherazade Jafari further develops this theme in her essay, "Local Religious Peacemakers: An Untapped Resource in U.S. Foreign Policy" (2007). Jafari notes the traditional separation of church and state can lead to problems when it neglects the role that religious leaders can have in resolving conflicts nonviolently. One example she gives is that of Sakena Yacoobi, a religious peacemaker in Afghanistan. This Muslim woman has stressed how Islam is to provide key protections for woman. To convey this message, she ran secret underground schools that taught girls and women literacy, leadership skills, and the importance of human rights. Jafari contends that Yacoobi was able to reach individuals who government officials and diplomats cannot reach. Since some of these individuals are key players in creating a stable Afghanistan, Jafari believes that the efforts of people such as Yacoobi should be showcased. In more general terms, she suggests a first step is "to acknowledge the powerful role that religious peacemakers can play, and then to pay more attention to them" (ibid., p. 125).

Of course, some peacemakers working at the grassroots level, while respecting local religious practices, are not operating as representatives of a religion. One of the most notable figures in this regard is Greg Mortenson. In his *Three Cups of Tea: One Man's Mission to Promote Peace One School at a Time*, Mortenson recounts how, over the last decade, he has build over fifty schools, especially for girls, in remote regions of Pakistan and Afghanistan (2006). Interestingly, his publisher subtitled the original hardback edition, "One Man's Mission to Fight Terrorism and Build Nations . . . One School at a Time." While his publisher regarded that subtitle as more "marketable" in the post-11 September 2001 environment, he insisted that if the book went into a paperback edition, the subtitle must be changed to stress the constructive and nonviolent aspect of building schools. This book illustrates an effective alternative to military action in the region. Infant mortality rates are lower among Muslim women educated in basic health. The number of young men who become terrorists is reduced when educated women refuse to support their sons' commitments to jihad.

4. The Ethics of Nonviolent Rhetoric

My position is that, generally, linguistic violence can be avoided. However, changing discourse is difficult because of the relations of power in society. Discourse cannot be separated from the relations of power in society, and such relations are unequal in every society. In my work on linguistic violence, I trace a continuum that stretches from subtle forms, such as children's jokes, to grievous form, such as totalitarian and genocidal language (Gay, 1999b). In addition to numerous abusive forms found in racist, sexist, heterosexist, and classist discourse, this continuum also contains the language of domestic politics and geopolitics. While I have previously addressed public policy discourse (Gay, 2004), I see nonviolent rhetoric extending to geopolitical discourse as well.

Various writers have addressed how, despite the power and violence of language as a system, the active speaking subject can find modes of expression that avoid the constraints of the received system (Gay, 1980). Hence, we can speak and write in ways that model alternatives to linguistic violence. The work of Rosenberg and Gorsevski provide useful models for changing discourse in ways that make nonviolent outcomes more likely in conflict situations— especially in geopolitics. These models also provide ethical implications for nonviolent discourse.

In *Embodied Care*, Maurice Hamington argues that feelings such as compassion, empathy, and care need not remain solely in the female realm (2004). In this regard, his extension of Gilligan fits nicely with what I have been saying about empathy in Rosenberg and Gorsevski, and lets me bring out the ethical dimension of their arguments. Hamington contends that gender should not be a barrier to an empathetic response; otherwise, care becomes a concern for women alone. In rejecting a gender-based ethical dichotomy. He states:

> Care is richly possible for embodied beings no matter their gender. . . . A woman who has a child is in a better position to empathize with a woman who is pregnant because of their embodied knowledge, but that does not preclude a man from caring and using embodied resources to inform that care. (Ibid., p. 20)

By stressing the biological similarity of males and females, Hamington intends to erase the gap between the genders. He proposes an ethics of care that applies to all human beings. When such gender-inclusive ethical discourse also includes nonviolent communication and nonviolent rhetoric, I maintain that we have a language of positive peace—an attainable ideal that we should strive to achieve.

Five

WILL KYMLICKA AS PEACEMAKER

Joseph M. Betz

1. Introduction

Will Kymlicka is Canada Research Chair in Political Philosophy at Queens University, Kingston, Ontario, Canada. He published *Multicultural Odysseys: Navigating the New International Politics of Diversity* at Oxford University Press in 2007. I was part of the three-member 2007 Book Award Committee for the North American Society for Social Philosophy. It was our task to choose the winner of the award from among the nineteen books nominated by publishers and Society members. We unanimously and enthusiastically chose *Multicultural Odysseys* for our prize.

I had known that Kymlicka was an important political actor in reshaping Canada's relations with its indigenous tribes and its large francophone minority. The title of his 1998 Oxford University Press book, *Finding Our Way: Rethinking Ethnocultural Relations in Canada,* suggests both the problem and that he aided in crafting a successful solution. The term he has come to use to name this successful approach is "liberal multiculturalism." This refers to the recommendation that a liberal democracy confronted from within by complaints from significant sub-national minorites best answers these complaints by granting the minorities extensive group rights. Among these rights, with some variation for circumstances, are territorial autonomy, acceptance of the group's language, religion, quasi-legal system and courts, control of its homeland's natural resources, and traditional ways of making a living even when they are outside the nation's market economy. This has worked well in Canada, and what Kymlicka proposes in *Multicultural Odysseys* is that this recommendation, extended to three new and different sorts of state/sub-national minority conflicts, is one of the world's great hopes for avoiding wars.

2. The Breakdown of the Nation-State and Rethinking the United Nations Charter

The world seemed determined, after World War II, to avoid future wars. The outcome of this determination was the creation of the United Nations in 1945. Though allowing a nation military self-defense against actual attacks, the United Nations Charter prohibits the aggression of one nation against another, and requires that member states refer conflicts involving or threatening aggression to the United Nations Security Council. The intention of the Charter is to give the Security Council a near-monopoly on the right, responsibility, and means of waging war.

The Charter assumes that, for the most part, wars occur between its member's nation states. These nation states exist in the Westphalian model, one strengthened by the outcome of World War I, a model in which each significant national group has its own state. France has been the best example of this, a culturally pure and homogenous national group inhabiting its historical homeland. However, today, insistence on the pure nation-state model is the source of enormous trouble in the world. The successful modern state is not exclusively the property of one national or ethnocultural group. For if it tries to be, it invites continual conflict. Canada, for example, is a successful modern state because it has granted significant autonomy to its minority (1) Quebecois, (2) indigenous peoples, such as the Inuit, and (3) more recent immigrants, especially from Asia.

When a contemporary nation-state of the old sort refuses to accept the tolerant liberal multiculturalism Kymlicka recommends, there is conflict often leading to wars. Such conflicts have been some of the world's most troublesome breaches of the peace for the past twenty years. Think of state/sub-national minority conflicts like those between the majority Serbs and minority Muslims in the former Yugoslavia, between the majority Sinhalese and minority Tamils in Sri Lanka, and the majority Hindus and minority Muslims in India's Kashmir.

The nation-state, or Westphalian sovereignty, assumed by the United Nations Charter means that each state is autonomous in settling its own internal problems, especially its majority/minority conflicts. This means that external military intervention in a member state's internal national affairs is prohibited. The Charter thus does not explicitly deal with state/minority conflict and war, only nation/nation wars.

Hence, during 1995, horrifying internal slaughter occurred as the Rwandan majority Hutus slaughtered more than 800,000 minority Tutsis. The United Nations watched passively because Rwandan sovereignty meant that the United Nations would not intervene. In my view, this is a morally unsatisfactory situation.

However, in several passages of the United Nations Charter, world powers can easily find a right and duty to intervene in sovereign nations' internal conflicts. It gives the Security Council the responsibility and the power "for the prevention and removal of threats to the peace . . . or other breaches of the peace" (chap. 1, art. 1, sec. 1), and the "primary responsibility for the maintenance of international peace and security" (chap. 5, art. 24, sec. 1). In this new world order, internal conflicts have serious, adverse, external consequences for other nations. The Rwandan slaughter created enormous and continuing problems for neighboring Congo as guilty Hutus sought refuge there. Neighboring Burundi was also affected. Burundi was under serious threat of destabilization because its majority Tutsis and minority Hutus reversed the Rwandan social relationship.

This African case suggests an international duty to intervene that was not followed. However, when state/minority conflicts have erupted in Europe, the duty has been recognized, for it more closely coincides with the national self-interests of important world powers. Thus, the United States and the North Atlantic Treaty Organization (NATO) intervened militarily against Serbia in the Bosnian conflict and forced the peace of the 1995 Dayton Agreement. This militarily attained peace was not a peace based on justice, for it rewarded territorial seizure with ethnic cleansing that particularly benefited the Serbs.

Kymlicka's experience with liberal multiculturalism, beginning in Canada, has inspired him to influence international actors to intervene peacefully and justly in state/minority conflicts to solve them as permanently as possible. Kymlicka's hope is that he can convince national majorities to abandon the old model of the nation-state and to create for themselves the new post-modern state that grants its minorities extensive rights.

3. Kymlicka's Human Rights Bases

Kymlicka's liberal, multicultural approach has met the consequentialist success that a utilitarian, like John Stuart Mill, or a pragmatist, like John Dewey, would demand. But it also has the deontological warrant that Immanuel Kant or a human rights theorist would require.

Kymlicka notes that World War I ended with group rights centrally accepted. If possible, each cultural group should have its own nation. Because the Nazis so egregiously violated the rights of stateless national minorities who were individuals within the German state, such as individual Roma (Gypsies) or individual Jews, World War II ended with a focus on the individuals' rights within their state. Thus the United Nations, in 1948, created the Universal Declaration of Human Rights (UDHR).

Then issues of the violations of group rights returned to center stage. After all their suffering in the states of other nations, the Jews asserted a group right to their own state. In addition, since the Allies fought the Germans for extinguishing the sovereignty of France, Poland, Czechoslovakia, and of almost all of the nations of Western and Central Europe, the Allies could no longer act, in their overseas colonies, against the principle that states have the right to their own sovereign self-determination. Hence, the European powers were morally and situationally compelled to decolonize. New nations in the Middle East, Far East, and Africa came into being as a matter of group rights. With them came the group rights problems of the minority groups within these new nations.

Kymlicka's liberal multiculturalism results from the realization that the just peace after World War II demanded that national groups have the right to their own autonomous states. This resulted in new states, and even old states realizing that there was not justice or peace in their own, internal, state/minority relations.

So the solution was in the doctrine that true, liberal democracy, should recognize strong and extensive new rights for their national minorities.

Kymlicka thus holds that the UDHR demands supplementation by the development of similar universal declarations of the rights of minorities. He has been an important actor in the international and regional development of many such declarations and conventions. There are nine examples in his book's index (2007, p. 373), under "United Nations conventions" and "United Nations declarations," including the 1992 Declaration of the Rights of Persons Belonging to National, Ethnic, Religious, and Linguistic Minorities. The reasoning for the extension of the United Nation's UDHR is that if protected individuals are truly free and protected in the development of their potentialities, those individuals must be guaranteed the right to such development according to their own language, culture, religion, and customs of group governance and dispute settlement. Only with group autonomy—this often means territorial rights—can individuals realize their autonomy.

This approach to minority autonomy guarantees a satisfactory answer to the objection of moral relativism. That is, it is supposed that these autonomous minority groups will create islands of tyranny over their own members and outsiders within their regional jurisdiction. However, this will not be the case, because the right to form such autonomous regions derives from the UDHR. These new sub-governments must respect the individual rights under the UDHR as the condition of their formation. Women's rights, the rights of minorities within this new minority region, the rights of children, and rights like those in our Bill or Rights are guaranteed. The successful cases of granting sub-national groups this autonomy are mostly among Western democracies with robust constitutional protections in their civil and criminal laws.

4. Kymlicka on the Adoption of Liberal
Multiculturalism in the Four Kinds of New States

Kymlicka's great achievement begins in the distinction of four kinds of new states in the present world, the reasons liberal multiculturalism is adopted in some but not others, and the history of international organizations attempts to get it adopted in the others. Where liberal multiculturalism has not been adopted, Kymlicka has experienced-based suggestions on how to change this. To get liberal multiculturalism adopted in problem states is to prevent incipient wars, or settle actual wars. Hence, Kymlicka deserves our admiration as a peacemaker.

The first of the four kinds of new states are the former English settler-colonies of the United States, Canada, Australia, and New Zealand. These nations have long been, practically speaking, independent states. They are liberal democracies with strong legal protections for individual human rights. They officially cherish freedom and joined in World War II to stop Adolf Hitler from oppressing minorities. They were then forced to realize that, after the war, continuing their oppression of their own minorities would be inconsistent.

Thus did the United States eventually repent of what it had done to minority groups, including Native Americans, African Americans, and women. Some groups were happy to settle for equality and the chance at assimilation. However, indigenous peoples had suffered from attempts at forced assimilation, and almost all wanted tribal, territorial autonomy. The United States government began a long and complicated experiment of trying to grant this autonomy.

Something like this is true of the way the United States has treated the Amish, a cultural and religious minority not attached to any one American homeland. They do not want territorial autonomy, but they enjoy the autonomy of determining that their children are schooled only through the eighth grade, they are—as members of a peace church—all exempt from the draft, and they do not participate in our Social Security system.

The United States is blessed in not having any dissatisfied national minority that wants to rejoin the neighboring state to which they once belonged. The United States has abandoned its traditional white and Northern European-biased official immigration quota systems, but we have not discovered the right liberal, multicultural way to treat illegal Mexican immigrants, or many other immigrants, especially Muslims.

Thus, the United States has a good but far from perfect record in liberal multiculturalism, as do Australia and New Zealand. Canada's record is better (perhaps thanks to Kymlicka), but not quite perfect. Immigrants and issues of immigration are the main problem in all four of these formerly English settler-states, but there is no great threat of war within these states.

The second of Kymlicka's four kinds of new nation-states are the older Western European nations. To varying degrees, they were once typical nation states, with policies like: France for only the French and Germany for only the Germans. But they have all been forced by history into more acceptance of the post-modern multicultural state. The moral logic implied in fighting Hitler forced them to free their external colonies after World War II. The same logic forced them to internal decolonization, and so non-territorial minorities such as the Roma were treated better. Western European nations had no indigenous peoples as America did, but they did have troublesome sub-national minorities because the breakdown of empire and other state boundaries after World War I did not give all members of one national group the same territory. For instance, there were ethnic Germans outside of Germany. There were German minorities in Belgium, Denmark, and Italy who were denied strong autonomous rights because the majority nationals worried that the Germans would have a cross-border loyalty to Germany in the event of any national conflict. However, the situation changed with the creation of the European Union and, especially, NATO. These effective movements toward transnational unity created alliances whereby the neighboring state and its ethnic group's members—including minorities within another state's borders—were no longer a threat to the security of the host state. More liberal treatment from the majority followed.

Even older national minorities could be given more freedom as the logic of liberal multiculturalism demanded. Thus, the once-conquering English gave more autonomy to the Scots and the Welsh. With nothing to fear from one another as committed democratic peoples, autonomy did not destroy the desire for the advantages of federalism.

In addition, these Western European nations had long had immigrants from their colonies who, mostly, wanted assimilation, not autonomy, like Pakistanis in Great Britain. However, the British and American reactions to the terrorist attacks of 11 September 2001, especially in waging war on Iraq, partly changed this, and Muslim immigrants in Great Britain are no longer handled liberally. Thus, for these Western European nations, liberal multiculturalism fares well except, perhaps, as in the United States, with many immigrants.

The third of Kymlicka's four kinds of new states are the states of Eastern Europe that came into existence with the demise of Communism and the USSR. Liberal multiculturalism is partly achieved in them since the old Communist central governments in the former USSR and Yugoslavia did allow nationalist groups to secede and form their own nations, usually on the old nation state model. Thus, Catholic Croatia separated from Orthodox Serbia and the rest of the old Yugoslavia while Estonia separated from Russia and the old Soviet Union. Unfortunately, the newly separated and autonomous nations now refused to treat the minorities they included from the original nation liberally. Thus, Croatians ethnically cleansed their new nation of some Serbian enclaves, and Estonians treated their Russian minority with great hostility.

Why? In Western Europe, the attractive new unity of the European Union and NATO was a safeguard before them, guaranteeing majorities no fear of minorities. However, in post-Communist Eastern Europe, coerced unity was behind them and a safe new unity was not achievable for some nations. Hungary and Poland achieved it by joining the European Union and NATO on the condition that they must treat their minorities well. But Croatia was disqualifying itself from such memberships by treating its minority Serbs badly. In Estonia, its ethnic majority was in a vengeful mood toward the Russian minority because those Russians represented the recently ended oppression of the Soviet Union. The Russians within Estonia also were seen as a threat to security because their cross-border loyalty to Russia was greater than any internal loyalty to Estonia. Finally, seeking safety in NATO would be an enormous provocation to Russia.

Minorities present in post-Communist states are, or are perceived as being, too much of a threat to the new state to be granted autonomous respect. Consider the present situation with Georgia. In becoming independent of the former USSR, Georgia lost a golden opportunity to create internal harmony by extending the benefits of liberal multiculturalism to two border minority enclaves within Georgia. These regions are Abkhazia and South Ossettia.

Not only did the new Georgian government fail to respond to minority complaints from these two regions, but also, from the Russian perspective the United States became overly friendly with Georgia. The United States provided Georgia with military arms and training, and Georgian soldiers even went to Iraq to be part of the American-led Coalition fighting there. The United States promised Georgia quick NATO membership, a promise repeated even after Georgian and Soviet troops had attacked one another. When the Abkhazian and South Ossetian complaints went unheard by Georgia, and struggle began in those regions, appeals from the dissident minorities to Russia caused Russia to send its military—as protector and peacekeeper—across the border. The result has been the large-scale Russian invasion and occupation of the two regions and little hope that the Russians will soon leave.

The sad truth about the new post-communist states of Eastern Europe is that they could become strong democracies, but only if they were overwhelmingly homogenous, like Poland and the Czech Republic. As democracies, these states would tend to favor liberal multiculturalism in treating minorities, but are only democratic because they have no significant minorities. New post-communist states with significant sub-national minorities do not become strongly democratic and are therefore not inclined to liberal multiculturalism. Kymlicka thus has the difficult task or trying to convince these states that they can only become stable and prosperous by becoming democratic and treating their minorities liberally.

The fourth type of Kymlicka's new states are those states in post-colonial Asia and Africa. Often these states began as autocracies, so the democratic background prompting them to extend autonomy to minorities did not exist as the required democratic precondition of liberal multiculturalism. Dictators in these states oppress everyone except their own thugs.

However, neither is it the case that these states are simple examples of state majority/minority conflicts. For many African states resulted from colonizers' lines being drawn around areas containing many tribes or ethnic groups, none of which are a majority. The new state thus has no alternative but to adopt the colonial language to achieve unity, for there is no common tribal language. The problem is to create a democratic state, and then to extend human rights considerations to all tribal, ethnic, religious, and cultural groups.

Iraq is a Middle Eastern post-colonial state which was formed by drawing arbitrary lines around an area that happened to include, on both sides of its borders, perhaps 60 percent Shiites (others in Iran), 20 percent Kurds (others in Turkey), and 20 percent Sunnis (others in Syria). Kymlicka would here warn that the majority Shiites must be very tolerant and careful. The government might grant territorial and/or cultural autonomy to each group to encourage federation under a tolerant, wealth-sharing, national government. However, group rights are non-existent until individual rights are secure, and Iraq has a long way to go until they are secure.

Under colonialism, colonizers frequently chose a tribal minority for the favored role of helping the colonists govern. The Belgians utilized the 10 percent Tutsi minority to help govern the 90 percent Hutu majority in Rwanda. No wonder that, after independence and Belgium's withdrawal from Rwanda, the Hutu majority wanted revenge on the Tutsi minority.

According to Kymlicka, many reasons explain why liberal multiculturalism has not worked for many post-colonial states (ibid., pp. 252–264). In summary, these are: (1) The precondition of accepting and protecting human rights, especially for women, is often missing. (2) Too often, every neighboring country is considered an enemy that appeals to cross border minorities to cause instability. (3) Western insistence on good treatment for minorities follows a patently insincere double standard. For instance, the United States might complain about a Muslim majority nation's mistreating Christians, but not about NATO ally Turkey mistreating Kurds. (4) Western generated standards seem designed to sustain Western hegemony. (5) Western colonists made minorities the instruments of oppression. After decolonization, those minorities are now distrusted, even hated by the majority of the population. (6) Post-colonial states do not have ethnic majorities and minorities in the Western sense, for all groups are minorities, often being of diverse tribes.

5. Will Kymlicka's Importance in Remedying these State/Minority Conflicts

Finally, what is Kymlicka's advice to the various nations of the world? First, he advises that nations try the best practices of liberal multicultural states. Second, Kymlicka would suggest recognition and understanding of international agreements on human rights norms. Sure to be among these is Article 27 of the United Nations International Covenant on Civil and Political Rights, which allows every member of a minority the "right to enjoy one's culture" (ibid., pp. 200–201). Kymlicka also explains the importance of defining generic norms for all minorities and targeted norms for particular minorities. Third, with different varieties of norms failing, Kymlicka talks of international interventions to stop resulting conflicts, to achieve security if not justice.

When Kymlicka discusses a norm that is not being observed, he always distinguishes levels of possible observance. Thus, the Organization for Security and Cooperation specified in Europe's 1990 Copenhagen Declaration that every minority group has "a right to effective participation" in public affairs. Kymlicka distinguishes a three-step range (from minimum to maximum) of what effective participation might mean (ibid., pp. 239–246). The first level would mean that minority members face no discrimination in standard political activities like voting, advocating, or running for political office. The second level would mean that the minority achieves some degree of representation in the legislature. The third level would mean that the minority achieves some form of power sharing with the majority, even if its representatives in government remain a minority. Kymlicka's aim in such analyses is to induce majorities to grant minorities at least a minimum of effective representation, a minimum that can, with persistent cajoling, be quietly nurtured to its fullest potentiality.

Kymlicka's practical peacemaking often depends on carefully developing sequenced lists with which to negotiate the improvements of a minority's standing. He tries to be effective by inducing national majorities to consider this list of typical national minority demands, given in ascending order of strength (ibid., p. 194). These demands include: (1) minority-language street signs; (2) minority-language elementary schools; (3) official language status; (4) collective rights; (5) veto rights; (6) minority-language higher education; (7) territorial autonomy; (8) democratic secessionist mobilization; (9) secessionist violence/terrorism.

The point of the careful sequencing is that the first is not so hard to allow, and the second is not much different from the first. The continuation of this reasoning gets the minority almost everything that it wants with (7) territorial autonomy. The point of listing the eighth and ninth steps is to warn the majority that these state troubles will logically follow unless the majority grants all of the first seven sorts of rights.

Six

SYSTEMIC CONSTELLATIONS AND THEIR POTENTIAL IN PEACE WORK

Anna Lübbe

1. Introduction

Modern wars tend to be atrocious, complex, and protracted. The division between friend and foe is often along ethnic lines (Kaufman 2001; Münkler 2002; Smith 2004). The results of third party efforts to conciliate such conflicts are meager. We need a multidimensional approach that encompasses methods to address the unconscious dimension of the conflict and to develop realistic, sustainable, and culturally sensible solutions.

This chapter discusses Systemic Constellations, a technique to simulate social systems, as a potentially useful additional approach in peace work. The method can give quick access to unconscious dynamics in complex social systems. I will first describe the characteristics of ethnopolitical conflicts and the need for new approaches in dealing with them. Then I will discuss the Systemic Constellations method, its development, execution, and open questions. Finally, I will outline the method's potential for working with conflict parties and for consulting professionals in the field of peace and development work.

2. Ethnopolitical Conflict and the Need for New Approaches

"Ethnopolitical" does not mean that ethnic difference would be the cause of conflict. It means that the friend/foe division follows ethnic lines. Ethnicity is not biologically determined. It is sufficient that members of an ethnic group share a feeling of connection with each other and of separation from other ethnic groups by specific cultural characteristics, such as a common name, language, rites, or symbols. Crucial for the ethnic identity is a common narrative of the group's history that answers the question "how did we come to be what we are?"

Ethnic groups have a shared story of their origin, triumphs, and travails, or, in the terminology of Vamik Volkan, of the glorious and the traumatic chapters of the common past (1999; 2007). In that sense, ethnic groups are *Schicksalsgemeinschaften* (communities of fate) (Lübbe, 2007). With the image of the group's history, specific fears and desires are connected—fears of repeating past collective trauma, such as displacement, genocide or forced assimilation, and desires for the reestablishment of past greatness, the return to a territory of origin, or for a compensation for a once suffered humiliation (Kühner, 2003).

In times of peace, the ethnic identity is weakly pronounced, the group permits ambiguous membership, and the ethnic affiliation coexists with numerous other affiliations of the group members (Sen, 2006). In times of tension and uncertainty, all of that changes. Factors promoting tension and uncertainty include sparse resources (especially when unjustly allocated), a weak national identity (often caused by state structures superimposed on tribal traditions), and political destabilization. People then tend to move together in more archaic communities, in *Schicksalsgemeinschaften*, while other affiliations abate. The collective hopes and fears become salient and political leaders exploit them to gather the group behind them (Kaufman, 2001; Volkan, 2007).

Even if the initial conflict concerned actual resources, it will soon revive an unsolved past dimension of ancient traumas and claims, and the conflict will be about dignity, truth, revenge, identity, and ultimately about the right to exist. As the conflict escalates, propaganda suggests that the time has come to put right everything that has ever gone wrong in the ethnic group's history, and that "the Others," inhuman by nature, must be annihilated. From this, mass killing may appear to be a necessary self-defense, or, in very asymmetrical conflicts, a necessary cleansing to get rid of something evil (Lübbe, 2009). When violence finally breaks out, another collective trauma is added to the fate record, ready to serve as another psychopolitical hot spot in further conflicts.

Such ethnopoliticized conflicts cannot be mediated as a simple distribution conflict could be. They tend to be complex and protracted, especially when mutual atrocities have already happened. The ethnic groups and their leaders become entrapped within a dynamic of violence and counter-violence. Split images of "Us" and "Them" obstruct the path to cooperative relations (ibid.). International peace endeavors underestimate the fatal power of this socio-psychological background to conflict.

If we want to find sustainable peace processes for such conflicts, instead of teeth-gritting control of violent outbreaks, we need a multidimensional approach encompassing methods that allow the unconscious dimension of large group relations to be addressed.

3. The Systemic Constellations Method

A. Roots and Development

Systemic Constellations have their roots in systemic family therapy. Moreno's Psychodrama, Family Sculptures after Virginia Satir, and the multigenerational approach of Ivan Böszörményi-Nagy are relevant predecessors

(Franke, 2004). The systemic view considers the interaction dynamics and mutual influences within the social system of which a person or collective is a part to find a solution for what, at first sight, is the person or collective's problem alone (König and Vollmer, 1999; von Schlippe and Schweitzer, 2000; Simon, 2004).

In Germany, the Systemic Constellation method has been developed to its present form and made widely known by Bert Hellinger (2005). Today, Systemic Constellations are established in psychosomatic therapy there. The method is also widely used in management consulting, coaching, and supervision, and is beginning to be applied to political issues. Still, the method is young and open questions remain, in both theory and practice.

B. The Procedure

Systemic Constellations are executed in a group setting led by a trained facilitator. The group members are clients with a private or professional concern—depending on the workshop theme—with which they will deal in a constellation. In some workshops, interested professionals participate as observers. A client is selected and presents an issue. After a short exploration of the issue by the facilitator, the client is asked to select group members to represent those parts of the client's system that seem relevant to the issue in question. It is also possible to represent entities of a system that are not persons, but things or collectives.

When the representatives are chosen, the client positions them somewhere in the room, according to the client's inner picture of how these system parts might stand in relation to each other. The client does this intuitively instead of following some preplanned concept. Once the representatives are moved into place, the client sits and the facilitator gives the representatives some time to tune into the resonance of the constellation field. The facilitator then asks the representatives what they perceive as they stand there—not what they reflect, but what they perceive or sense. Usually they report emotions or physical sensations that emerge as the representatives are positioned in the field; they might have desires to move, bodily sensations that they did not have before, or emotions concerning other represented parts of the system.

The representatives' perceptions, as reports of experiences from many constellations indicate, are relevant to understanding the client's system and its dynamics. What emerges in the constellation are apparently not the affectivities of the representing persons, but something concerning the represented system parts. This is called the phenomenon of "representative perception." Usually the problematic issue initially reported by the client is confirmed by the picture of the represented system and the statements of the representatives. Interesting for the clients is that also emerge unconscious and otherwise barely accessible aspects of the represented system and its dynamics that cast a light onto the issue in question.

When the problem is thus present in the room, the facilitator induces changes in the respective positions or verbal exchanges between the representatives, following hypotheses developed from the constellation picture or from what the representatives say. This process is repeated until, judging from the representatives' feedbacks, the problem is solved and every part of the system feels more resourceful and peaceful. Often the clients themselves are taken into the constellation at some point, in exchange for the person who represented the client thus far. In this way, the clients can feel and experience the solved system and themselves in it. This experience and the information that arises during the constellation, about where the represented system was disturbed and what the system parts needed, will modify the clients, their attitudes, and their behavior within their system. In the systemic view, such a change within the client will influence also the system he lives in.

C. Discussion

On one hand, the Systemic Constellations method quickly enjoyed an enormous clientele. On the other hand, it initially attracted quite a lot of criticism in the media, centered upon the personality, attitudes, and assumptions of Hellinger instead of upon the method itself. As to the method itself, the fact that we do not know how the representatives come to have their perceptions is disconcerting from a scientific point of view. If representatives start to feel numb or hateful, or start to shake, for instance, and this stops as soon as they quit the constellation, we have no satisfying explanation for the occurrence.

Nonetheless, we should continue research on constellation work. According to the short and long-term first-hand feedback of many clients, constellations have helped to clarify and resolve their issues. Few systematic evaluations have been conducted so far, but those that have been done confirm that constellations are significantly helpful (Höppner, 2001; Kohlhauser and Assländer, 2005; Mraz, 2006; Ruppert, 2007). Also, the participants of constellations experience their perceptions not as a role-play or something they make up, but as something that happens spontaneously. Participants or facilitators, even witnesses of constellations, have a strong intuition that what is going on is something healing. Constellations apparently are a systemic healing approach. They integrate the excluded and let each system part find a good place in the whole, or more precisely, they create a picture of that possibility.

The method is especially helpful in solving what we call "transgenerational legacies." It is probably not astonishing that the method developed to its present form in Germany. Germany is full of family systems that one or two generations before included Nazi perpetrators, or persons who suffered displacement, early loss of relatives due to war, war associated rape, fleeing, or families torn apart. Families and organizations also profited from the property of exiled or killed Jews or from forced labor. From constellations, we can learn that this past is an influential part of today's social systems. All of this causes wounds in the systems that usually do not heal in the same generation, but are taboo, creating entanglements in later generations. These entanglements unconsciously influence the lives of descendants. Systemic Constellations show that the past members of a system—ancestors, the dead, exiled, disappeared, victims, and perpetrators—belong to the system. Opening this dimension and acknowledging what there is and was is often necessary to bring peace into the system.

D. An Example

This example is one from a family constellation workshop facilitated by Hellinger together with Hunter Beaumont, a psychotherapist who supported Hellinger in English-speaking countries. In this workshop, the clients had psychological or somatic problems. The client in question suffered from a commitment phobia (Hellinger and Beaumont, 2007).

After a short exploration, the client chose representatives for his parents, his brother, and himself, and positioned them in the room. All four faced the same direction. The facilitators asked at whom the representatives might be looking. The client replied that it might be his paternal grandfather. The client did not know much about his grandparents. They were from Romania and Austria, and they emigrated as children by themselves, but the client could not tell why. He then found out by making phone calls, that both of his grandparents were refugees. The family of the paternal grandfather had been in an especially difficult situation. The family had been exposed to violence and killings. They had taken the chance to send the client's grandfather, who at that time was ten years old, to the United States, where a relative already lived. With this information, the constellation was resumed.

Representatives for the grandparents and several representatives for those relatives victimized in Romania were introduced into the constellation. All of the former representatives felt an enormous change they described as pressure or energy coming from the Romanians; the father-representative wanted to shield his "family" from this. The client, who meanwhile had been taken into the constellation in exchange for his representative, felt ashamed and wanted to hide before his "ancestors."

The turning point for the client came when the representative of his father was told to take the client by the hand, lead him to the "Romanian ancestors," and present them to each other: "This is my son—this is my father." The client was profoundly touched and he and his grandparents' representatives hugged. Further moves were made to enable the client to turn toward the future and step into his life. According to the feedback of the representatives, he now had his Romanian ancestors with their now-acknowledged fates as a supportive power in his background, instead of a blank inhibiting his commitment to life.

4. Applications in Peace Work

A. Working with Conflicting Parties

The capability of the Systemic Constellations method to shed light on unresolved past could make it a helpful addition in any kind of dialogue project
or problem solving workshop. Such relational work is usually done at the
micro level. But attempts have been made to bring a deeper relational work—
a work with what is unconscious in the relation—into the meso and macro
levels of leadership.

An example for a dialogue project on the micro level is Dan Bar On's
"To Reflect and Trust" groups (2008). Bar On brought descendants of holocaust perpetrators and descendants of holocaust victims together in storytelling projects. He found that they were all suffering from unresolved holocaust issues. Later he brought in Palestinians, believing the holocaust to be a
relevant collective trauma in the unresolved past background of the Middle
East conflict.

Similarly, at the meso level, Vamik Volkan applied his "Tree Model," a
large group psychoanalytical approach, in the conflict field of Estonia versus
Russia (2004). Herbert Kelman and others did informal diplomacy work with
political leaders on higher levels (Fisher, 2002; Kelman, 2002). Finally, Stuart
Kaufman suggests an approach including the media and the language of symbols to working with leaders in ethnopoliticized conflicts to help them escape
from the "leader's trap" (2006). Could it be useful to integrate Systemic Constellations into these kinds of peace projects?

Systemic Constellations render the unresolved past dimension of the
conflict visible and treatable. When we open this dimension, we meet the perpetrators, victims, disappeared, and profiteers in the parties' past. To see and
acknowledge this will help to bring peace into the system and to set the system parts free for their present and future.

Access to this unresolved past is possible because representatives do not
avert emotions that, for the parties involved, might be inaccessible, too overwhelming, or too shameful. Thus, the clients can see their often-emotional
issues from a perspective outside themselves, maintain a healthy distance, and
emotionally detach from their distress.

When such work is shared in the presence of members of both, or several conflicting parties, it will become apparent that pain, needs, and love
exist on all sides. That will re-humanize the image of "the Other" and lead
all concerned back to the common ground of humanity that gets lost in ethnopoliticized conflicts.

Often, to bring together all the relevant conflict parties is not possible,
especially extremist groups or spoilers. In Systemic Constellations, their part
can be made present through representatives, and must be, because they belong to the system. According to the systemic view, every part of a system, as

destructive as it may behave, must be integrated into the solution. Such constellations might transform only the party present, but a change in one party's attitude will influence the whole conflict system. The Systemic Constellations method is based on an integrative, holistic approach.

For work not only done at the micro level, with individuals and their individual backgrounds, but also with group leaders and other office holders, the Systemic Constellations method allows us to deal with prototypical attitudes, since it makes possible the introduction of representatives for collectives, such as a tribe or a minority group.

Finally, some peace projects fail because the methods applied by the intervening party are not culturally acceptable for one or several of the conflicting parties. The Systemic Constellations method might be inter-culturally acceptable or might be integrated into hybrid conflict transformation approaches that embrace native approaches. Often, satisfying the ancestors, dealing with the dead, and practicing systemic healing techniques are lost in Western culture, but appreciated in other cultures.

B. Consulting Intervening Parties

The Systemic Constellations method can also be used as a clarification instrument for a third party's peace or development cooperation project, especially when a project is stuck for unknown reasons. Such a deadlock may have many reasons, since development and peace work professionals move in complex fields. Reasons may include latent conflicts within a third party's team, differing objectives of cooperating subsystems, opaque motives of the intervening party, the exclusion of an essential system part, or the failure of the project design to fulfill a hidden need of one of the parties.

The problem can also lie at different levels—as in the personal backgrounds of clients, at the level of their organizations, or at the collective level of large group relations. Constellations show that the difficulties of third parties to successfully intervene are often caused not only by the problematic relations between the conflicting parties. The relation with the intervening party may have, on its own, an unresolved past dimension that inhibits the success of peace projects if not taken into account sufficiently.

An example of the latter kind is the neo-imperialism problem, which appears in constellations of professionals in the peace and development fields (Lübbe, 2007). The representatives of Third World countries sometimes are not interested in sustaining the projects of an intervening country and wish to find solutions for themselves. Such constellations often reveal an unconscious relational problem between the conflicting or developing country and the intervening party.

Typically, such projects are initiated by countries belonging, in a simplified global classification, to the West, while poor and conflicting parties often belong to Third World countries, or in a politically incorrect term expressing the global devaluation of these countries, the "Rest" (Francis, 2004). Countries in the "West" are typically former colonizers and the current advocates of globalization. Countries that make up the "Rest" are typically former colonies that are currently losers of globalization. The legacy of this unresolved past is unconsciously active and yields relational problems in the present interactions between "West" and "Rest" countries (see Figure 1).

"The West"	"The Rest"
• Former colonizers • Globalization winners	• Former colonies • Globalization losers
• Concept imperialism • Hidden agendas	• Resistance • Distrust

Figure 1. The Neo-Imperialism Problem

The collective trauma of colonization is reactivated when Western countries want to help Third World countries in an unconscious attitude of "You have problems—we have solutions." Such projects are likely to meet resistance and distrust. Western countries have caused and continue to cause many of the Third World countries' problems. They also have vested interest in these interactions, typically hidden beneath the official goal of assistance. These interests are not always so obvious as natural resources, sales markets, or strategic allies. Even the wish for peace might not be as candid as it seems. Peace favors those who profit from the status quo, for instance from present economic structures. For the losers, fighting for structural change and redistributing justice might sound better.

When all this relational background is made conscious in a constellation, patronizing attitudes on one side and passive resistance on the other side both end. The initial dynamism of the intervening party's representatives yields to a sense of temporary cluelessness and concernment. The representatives of the Third World countries feel perceived, understood, and on equal grounds for the first time. This more respectful contact opens a space wherein the co-operative and creative development of hybrid solutions becomes possible, joint solutions to problems which, ultimately, are joint problems. In the systemic view, the distinction between conflicting and intervening parties in last consequence becomes doubtful.

5. Conclusion

Anwar el-Sadat is credited with saying that the "psychological barrier" between Israel and Egypt constituted 70 percent of the problems between the two countries (Volkan, 1999, p. 22). We should acknowledge the power of unconscious relational deadlocks, of split images of self and "the Other," of unresolved past, and of detrimental perceptions and constructions of reality in peace work. Such psychological factors are substantial not only in individual but also in large group relations. To reveal this dimension of difficult large group relations is a first step to deconstruct its entrapping power.

The Systemic Constellations method has been shown to have potential to deal with unconscious entanglements within social systems in family therapy and other fields. The method allows us to depict the actual condition of the system in question, unfold the underlying dynamics, configure a way out, and end with a more peaceful image of the system. All this can be seen and felt by the participants, and the experience will change their perceptions, attitudes, and behavior within the system.

Systemic Constellations thus may help to modify fatal constructions of reality (Wendt, 1999). To add them to the toolbox of conflict transformation might be worth the effort.

Seven

PEACE EDUCATION: A SYSTEMIC FRAMEWORK

Joseph Rayle

1. Thinking Systemically about Education

As a social institution, the American education system is in a position to facilitate the kinds of cultural changes necessary to promote peace (Tozer, Senese, and Violas, 2007). Social transformation has always been a major impetus for American education (Cremin, 1990; Tyak and Cuban, 1995), although the nature and sources of this social transformation are not always clear (Gatto, 2008). American education represents a cultural change in and of itself. It began as a social movement and has been characterized by the three-fold aim of inculcating morality, citizenship, and self-sufficiency (Gatto, 2006). The project of implementing these simple goals is revolutionary in that it has never before been tried on such a large scale in any society.

This effort can be highly contested, as any philosopher who has tried to bestir a little doubt in the minds of sophomores knows. Indeed, public education is something of a cultural battlefield of competing values. Educational critics from George S. Counts (1978) to Sebastian DeAssis (2003) have argued that American society can be transformed through changes in the educational system. As school integration, Title IX, and other transformational, sometimes controversial, changes demonstrate, public education can have an impact on the values of our society. Efforts at promoting peace education in American education have a similar potential to impact American values with regard to the promotion of a peaceful culture.

The way to educate for this transformation, of course, is not always easy to determine. Reform in American education aimed at creating social change is full of dead ends, often characterized by recurring curricular changes, merit schemes, and other initiatives designed to improve education to achieve produce better results (Ravitch, 1983; Tyak and Cuban, 1995). Initiatives involving multiculturalism, social justice, environmentalism and peace have made their way into the curriculum (Au, Bigelow, and Karp, 2007), although they often take a back seat to the "basic skills" emphasized by the No Child Left Behind Act (NCLB) (Kohn, 1999). Oftentimes what passes for peace education tends to teach students skills for conflict resolution and to teach teachers effective classroom management skills. These efforts ignore social and cultural forces that maintain the status quo and do not critically examine the social processes that re-create the culture of violence in this society. This should come as no surprise given the tendency in schools to use curricula that draw few connections between subjects and that do not encourage much critique of the culture (De Assis, 2003). This disconnection reflects a cultural orientation that is largely reductionist in that it is concerned with the "bottom line," instead of the complex relationships that underlie these things (Capra, 1997). The curriculum and approach to American education ignores the insights of complex systems theory, which takes as its starting point the intricate connections that must be a part of the understanding and amelioration of problems of peace education. In other disciplines, such as the physical and biological sciences, this approach is commonplace.

Peace in education cannot be considered just another topic to be taught in isolation from other ideas. Further, we need to better define peace before undertaking the work of integrating it into public education. Once, in a talk with a local peace group, I asked the participants, much to their annoyance, what "peace" means. A rather roundabout discussion with no satisfactory conclusion ensued. Despite efforts of writers such as Jonathan Schell, contemporary American culture does not have a clear conceptualization of peace (2003). Consequently, we have no particularly useful way to talk about it or to teach it.

Reflecting the problems caused by the confusion around the conceptualization of peace, the changes advocated by reformers tend to be limited. Henry A. Giroux (2003) and Counts for example, argue that the class system in the United States is to blame for a host of social problems, and both authors point to the role of educational institutions in the creation and reproduction of these inequalities. While Counts' approach reflects traditional Marxist thinking about education and its reproduction of the social class system, Giroux's emphasis is on translating individual concerns into the public sphere. This reflects the influence of such post-modern thinkers as Zygmunt Bauman. Both approaches provide a reductionist analysis of public education.

Counts and Giroux are aware of the issues of social structure. Giroux's exploration of the role of popular culture is particularly salient. However, both critics appear to lay aside the highly complex nature of the problem of education, only focusing on particular facets and not the interdependency of the factors that create the class system and relegate many social problems to the individual.

Education has been made worse by past attempts to fix it (Ravitch, 1983). A systemic analysis is useful in dealing with situations that have been exacerbated by past attempts to fix complex problems, which need to be understood by a wide range of actors and problems that affect many things and whose solutions are non-obvious (Rayle, 2007).

The myriad people involved in forming and executing educational policy need to understand it and how it affects many other social institutions and individuals. Because people have written about and critically analyzed education in this society almost since its inception is evidence that the solutions for educational problems are not obvious. As many government and university reports, media stories, and political speeches elucidate, education affects the family, government, religion, the economy, and the political system. Entire sub-disciplines exist to study educational problems. This is sufficient proof that the solutions to these problems are elusive. Therefore, we can conclude that education is a social institution that needs a systemic or ecological analysis, allowing for an explication of the complex relationships that make a social system such as education possible.

Liberal and conservative critics alike decry the state of contemporary education in terms of learning outcomes, funding, and teacher preparation (Kohn, 1999; Ravitch, 2000; Rochester, 2002; Spring, 2005; Kozol, 2005). Issue groups focus on and promote their causes without regard for education as a whole (deMarrais and LeCompte, 1999). Given the layers of politics, bureaucracy, and organizational inertia facing any would-be educational innovator, this is rational behavior. However, this is usually self-defeating because the impact of any change brought to the educational system in this way is either distorted or extirpated by unaccounted for currents within the educational system (Capra, 1983).

At my academic institution, no fewer than three different centers aim at addressing problems in education. Education has been said to affect everything from economic productivity to public morality (Berliner and Biddle, 1995).

In the same way as the criteria for justifying a systems theory approach apply to education in general, they also apply to peace education in particular. The danger of moving toward the incorporation of peace education into the curriculum lies in the potential for peace to be reduced to a disconnected set of skills or ideas taught in isolation from other aspects of the curriculum. This would trivialize the meaning of peace education and reduce its effectiveness to produce the changes necessary for the development of a culture of peace. The skill-oriented milieu of contemporary education might emphasize going through the motions of peace as opposed to creating the lasting changes required to sustain peace.

2. An Ecological Approach to Peace Education

Education is potentially a useful vector for creating a culture of peace. An ecological or systemic approach can be useful in two ways. One is to frame peace as a phenomenon, explicating the highly interconnected nature of cultures, societies, and groups. One of the many contemporary criticisms of education is that what gets taught fails to incorporate the critical perspective necessary to examine alternatives to the dominant narrative. James Loewen provides a particularly compelling example in *Lies My Teacher Told Me* (2007). Although his analysis mainly concerns American history and its passive, vaguely triumphal presentation with emphasis on the memorization of disconnected—often inaccurate—facts and dates, similar criticism can be brought to bear on practically the entire education curriculum.

An ecological framework allows students to draw interdisciplinary connections that make concepts more salient and interesting (Bain, 2004). This could serve to mitigate chauvinism toward "other" cultures, which is currently a feature of American education and culture. Further, it undoes the "disciplinary violence," in which students are prevented from drawing significant and meaningful connections among the various subjects they are taught.

Our culture has its roots from disparate sources. Students need to understand that many aspects of "mainstream" culture in the United States have their origins in distant lands and times and that the divisions between "us" and "them" are not as great as they are taught to believe (Linton, 1936). By drawing connections between disciplines, we can come to understand on a deeper level the highly constructed (and contested) nature of knowledge. This perspective on knowledge and learning can further serve as a catalyst for synthesis and innovation.

Another key aspect of the ecological approach to peace education is that it allows instructors to help students understand in a direct and salient manner how they connect to, and have a stake in, a culture of peace. Many have lamented that we live in a culture in which self-centeredness is the norm. Arguably, the modern college campus is a monument to this phenomenon. One look at the ever-growing list of amenities that make the contemporary college experience increasingly like a youth resort catering to every whim and need says it all. Nevertheless, one way to overcome student resistance to threatening ideas dealing with race, class, gender, peace, or religion is to appeal to students' self-interest.

This approach involves indicating to students what they lose, how they are controlled, and how their freedom is limited or threatened by a violent culture. I have argued that working in the context of anti-racist/sexist education helps students (usually undergraduate teacher education candidates) see what they (as individuals) have at stake in efforts to eliminate racism and sexism from our society (Rayle, 2008).

First, students must understand that the loss of human potential in a racist society limits what technological, cultural, and other innovations they have in their daily lives. Teachers can illustrate this through a historical study that points to technological and cultural innovations made by African Americans prior to the desegregation of American schools. Such contributions happened in a system explicitly designed to deny African Americans education. Had all members of this society been able to develop their potential, one might well wonder where we might be today.

Further, I point out the myriad ways in which Whites, and to a lesser extent, minority groups, are manipulated and controlled through the pervasive racism in our society. Loewen shows how unscrupulous real estate dealers manipulated Whites into selling their homes at very low prices in response to the relocation of middle class African Americans into traditionally "White" neighborhoods (2005). Consequently, Whites lost money on the sale of their homes and then paid inflated prices for homes in "nicer" (read "White") suburbs. Unrealistic fears of violence from minorities (usually African Americans) limits where people—in the majority and the minorities—live, eat, shop, worship, socialize, and recreate, which then limits the quality and quantity of these experiences. This approach also opens the possibility of a discussion about the violence that racism does to human dignity and teaches that everyone's humanity should be respected.

Finally, I suggest to students that the "culture of fear" makes it possible for those in positions of authority to frighten citizens into giving up their basic rights, particularly those involving unreasonable search and seizure (Glassner, 1999). The nature of bureaucracy comes into play here as well. Bureaucracies tend to grow over time, and they often expand into areas of life beyond the purview of their original mission (Peters, Connor, Pooyan, and Quick, 1984). In a society characterized by multiple state-run security agencies, we should be alarmed by this.

John Taylor Gatto notes that the actual number of terrorists is low, and the ability of individuals to engage in sustained terrorist activity in this society is limited by a number of social factors (2008). If the general population no longer has the essential elements of support and compliance necessary for would-be terrorists to engage in sustained campaigns, their terrorist enterprise could be prevented.

Agencies such as the Department of Homeland Security are bureaucracies. Finding little, if any, of the activity they were created to prevent causes them to pursue other activities to justify their existence. As a result, we will encounter ever-greater intrusions into our privacy and freedom.

This approach starts from what students already know about peace and what their motivations might be for learning more about it. Developmental theorists, such as L. S. Vygotsky (1978), argue for a "scaffolding" approach, one where teachers guide students in a pedagogical environment so that the students take on greater independence with regard to the ideas and skills being taught. An effective method is to encourage students to connect with the ideas on a personal level (Palmer, 1998).

This "civic engagement" has been highlighted at my institution; students have been presented with opportunities to engage in "service learning" in the community. This creates in students a sense of civic responsibility and connection with others. But whether students would freely choose to participate in such activities outside of the context of their educational requirements is not clear. Unfortunately, many appears have the attitude, "What's in it for me?"

This self-serving attitude should not be surprising given the culture of narcissism reinforced by mass media messages and the highly rationalistic behavior required of students to negotiate the high stakes (in terms of time, economic investment, and future earning potential) environment of higher education. The result is an attitude of self-preservation, in which students are unwilling to pursue interdisciplinary connections in their learning. They are frequently encouraged by advisors, parents, economic contingencies, and the design of their programs of study to work out how to get through college as quickly and successfully as possible—often at the expense of deep learning. Students have little incentive to examine and change behaviors, patterns of consumption, and other decisions that sustain and further the culture of violence (Bowers, 1997).

Teaching students about their stake in the creation of a culture of peace is the first step in meaningfully engaging them in the project of peaceful action and culture.

3. Systems Theory

Ludwig von Bertalanffy is usually credited for system or ecological theory (1969). It challenges the reductionism prevalent in science specifically and in our culture in general. Reductionist science makes dramatic improvements in technology and living standards possible. But to grapple with and solve complex problems such as peace, we must move from thinking mechanistically about problems of peace education and begin to think about them in terms of relationships (Capra, 1983).

The essential move that systems theory makes is to shift its emphasis from studying individual parts of a phenomenon to attempting to understand the interdependent nature of the elements that make up that problem. For example, one may study a classroom in a school, but from a systems theory standpoint, to do so requires an examination of the manner in which that classroom affects and is affected by other systems. Other systems in this case may be other classrooms, the school, the community in which the students in the classroom live, and the socio-cultural context in which the school is located. Examining a classroom in isolation will lead to an incomplete understanding and solutions to problems in that classroom that are likely to be ineffective or even deleterious as they will tend to be concerned with only one aspect of the classroom. For example, witness the attempts of NCLB to fix public education through a system of high stakes testing, and the resulting "teaching to the test" that has placed constraints on what is being taught in school (McCaw, 2007).

To avoid similar pitfalls for peace education, we must understand and teach peace systemically. Any would-be peace educator must overcome the hurdle of a poorly conceptualized notion of peace. For example, Ghandi's idea of *satyagraha* (nonviolent or passive resistance), based upon the Sanskrit words *sat*, which translates as "being," and *graha*, which translates as "holding firm to," is difficult to render in English, as it encompasses a renunciation of physical violence (but not action), and a rejection of dogma, but not belief (Schell, 2003).

We often conceive of peace as the absence of something such as violence or war, but not as an emergent property of a social and cultural system that adopts behaviors and beliefs that make peace possible. War is driven by numerous causes, although it tends to be presented in an idiographic manner (Bertalanffy, 1969; Keeegan, 1993). Neither war nor peace is really understood in education as emergent properties of social systems.

The creation of a peace-oriented curriculum must simultaneously present peace as a systemic concept and use a pedagogy based upon system theory. It is only by addressing peace education in a holistic manner that peace educators can hope to create the transition to a culture of peace.

Eight

BUILDING BRIDGES TO PEACE: TEACHING TOLERANCE THROUGH THE HISTORY OF ART

Paul J. Parks

Truth is the first casualty of war.
Hiram Warren Johnson in Phillip Knightly's *The First Casualty of War*

The challenge of repudiating war as an acceptable means of solving political, religious, and cultural conflict necessitates the recognition and inclusion of a coalition of varied and viable methods to legislate policy and to mobilize the citizenry and leaders of the world in adopting alternative and pragmatic perspectives and solutions. The process of establishing effective geopolitical guidelines requires that their foundation be rooted in effective instruction and guidance. A collaborative undertaking must be based on an enlightened vision and motivated by a mutual respect and appreciation of our diversity, unity, and shared stake in each other's futures.

Education plays a significant role in achieving this goal. A well-intended diplomatic pledge of nonviolence without a principal core predicated on connection and consequence remains hollow and flawed. Encouraging our global constituency to celebrate its contrasts and affirm its fundamental commonality forms a structure for international policy and fosters the populist support to empower such legislation and partnership.

By teaching tolerance, and inspiring today's public, students, and leadership, we sow the seeds that will bear fruit tomorrow. Jennifer Holladay, Director of the international organization and magazine, *Teaching Tolerance* and winner of the 2007 Periodical of the Year award from the Association of Educational Publishers, confronts this issue:

> If our nation's young people are to embrace equality and justice as values and help transform our world, becoming more tolerant of others is not enough. Students also must come to see, analyze, and work against the structural and social practices that continually create and re-create a world of division. (2007, p. 5)

We have left implementing peace primarily to the dictates of politicians, government officials, and the corporate elite, whose relationship and position often entails a conflict of interest and an agenda that undermines the process and progress of peace. While we focus on these conventional avenues, we neglect a powerful ally in this endeavor.

We would be wise to consider the function and potential of the arts in this effort. Artists, musicians, poets, and dancers are uniquely able to convey the message of peace, speaking as they do in a ubiquitous language that reaches beyond the walls of political, cultural, and religious divides. We should appreciate their ability to connect people through the profound and subtle persuasiveness of creative expression. Carol Rank, senior lecturer at the Centre for Peace Studies at Coventry University, supports this contention:

> The power of the arts to promote peace lies in their emotive nature; the arts can help people feel the pathos and waste of war and help to instill a desire and commitment to end war and work for peace. (2008, p. 1)

The art, music, film, and literature of our time and the invaluable gifts of the past comprise a potent vehicle for demonstrating the spectrum of human experience and the integrated relationships among all human beings. The arts provide a forceful agent for awakening these untapped sensibilities.

Cooperative cultural programs and exchanges have attained remarkable success in bringing people together despite divisive political and religious partitions. Such projects and events unite seemingly disparate parties in an emancipating experience, which resonates in a way that no judicial mandate can. The transforming results are not only true for participants in these projects, but also for audiences and viewers who witness the promise the arts confer in building bridges.

A telling example is the West-Eastern Divan, a group of fifteen to twenty-five-year-old Israeli, Palestinian, Lebanese, Syrian, Jordanian, and Egyptian musicians enrolled in a challenging program of classical music. Founded by the noted Israeli conductor, Daniel Barenboim, and Palestinian scholar, Edward Said, in 1998, this "Orchestra of Coexistence" facilitates dialogue between embattled neighbors. It promotes understanding and paves the way for peaceful resolutions. In the process of rehearsing and performing together, the musicians acquire a deeper awareness of each other's lives and attitudes. From personal interaction, the indoctrinated stereotypes of sustained adversarial conditioning begin to dissipate. Participating musicians return to their home countries with a greater feeling of respect and kinship.

The orchestra has performed throughout the globe, even in Israel and the Palestinian territories. Their harmonizing chords suggest the possibility within our grasp. Barenboim professes this unlikely advocate's impact:

> The moment you have music, everyone is equal, and therefore the project has been successful. Before a Beethoven symphony we all become equal, whether you are Israeli, Palestinian, or Syrian. (2006)

The resonant appeal of the arts engages and compels these audiences to embrace the human achievement in the music, its uniform lexicon, and our nobler aspirations beyond the futility of war.

A film by Paul Smaczny about the orchestra, entitled *Knowledge is the Beginning*, won the Emmy Award for best documentary related to arts of 2006. Addressing the assertion in the title, Barenboim says, "It's not that I believe (music) can resolve issues. It is not a peace orchestra; it is an orchestra that speaks out against ignorance" (ibid.). That very ignorance feeds countless misconceptions that fan the fires of violent confrontation.

A notion of the Other often fuels war, a marginalizing rift is drawn between one faction and a dehumanizing stereotype of the Other. The propaganda of the Other is perpetrated through a detachment and ignorance of the world outside and its viewpoints. Educating our citizens about the exceptional variety of cultures, religions, and advancements emanating from our diversity is vital in overcoming that ignorance and refuting the myth of the Other.

For the past eight years, students in the Modesto, California, school district have been part of a novel curriculum requiring them to complete a world religions class in grade nine. Modesto teacher, Yvonne Taylor, discusses the underlying reason for this initiative. "When you don't know about something, you fear it—and when you fear something, you become more likely to strike out against it" (Kilman, 2007, p. 41). Researchers interviewed students before, during, and immediately after the semester, and again six months after the course ended. They found that students had become more accepting of other religions and more willing to protect the rights of people of other faiths.

The visual arts offer a productive tool for conveying the history, achievements, and beliefs that form the inimitable identities of differing societies, while concurrently illustrating the pervasive elements they share. Utilizing art to inform and enlighten while promoting diversity and peace is a method that can be applied to a broad range of students and audiences.

One such enterprise, the Global Art Project for Peace (GAP), founded in 1994, was nominated for a 2002 United Nations Educational, Scientific, and Cultural Organization (UNESCO) Peace Prize for tolerance and nonviolence. Nearly 100,000 participants of different ages have been asked to create works of art expressing their hope for solidarity. The works are exchanged internationally and are organized into exhibitions, books, performances, and slide presentations, involving community groups and organizations in this action. According to director Katherine Josten:

The mission of the project is to spread world peace by promoting tolerance and nonviolence through art. Focusing on the value of the arts as a
pathway to understand the world as it is and to imagine how it might be.
The Global Art Project exemplifies in concrete form that we can be different, yet act together as integral members of one living organism. (2007)

Teaching the history of art of Asia, Africa, and the Americas for the
State University of New York has allowed me to incorporate this approach
and attest to its benefits. Over the term of a semester, students analyze an as-
sortment of works of art and architecture from an extensive and divergent
selection of regions and countries featuring distinct concepts and localized
representations. Confronting such multiplicity challenges them to consider
unfamiliar and often contrary artistic standards outside their own societal aesthetic norms. Employing an incisive and equitable examination of these dis-
similar criteria and portrayals prevails upon students to advance beyond their
habituated notions of the formal qualifications and subsequent applications of
art. Supplementary probing of the arguments in the philosophical debate over
a universal sense of beauty, essential to modern aesthetic theory, is facilitated
through an accessible and informed engagement in course material and discussion. Students witness and weigh a brilliant and intriguing display of imagery and form, noting each culture's complexity and dignity, directed
through an array of mediums that exhibit the highest degree of intelligence
and imagination.

The visual arts equally permit students to viscerally assess the active exchange of information and artistic styles across time and territory, as evident
in the synthesis of influences that many works of art feature. Through these
examples, they can tangibly decipher the juncture of various cultures and their
stylistic characteristics and signature. Students also discern that these independent components can successfully integrate into a harmonious unit, rendering a poignant metaphor. In his classic text *The Mythic Image,* Joseph
Campbell explains this didactic and elemental dynamic:

Mythic forms, that is to say, may be regarded either as pointing past
themselves to mysteries of universal import, or as functions merely of
local ethnic or even personal idiosyncrasies. Universals are never experienced in a pure state, abstracted from their locally conditioned ethnic
applications. It is, in fact, in their infinitely various metamorphoses that
their fascination resides. And so, while it has been my leading thought in
the present work to let sound the one accord through all its ranges of his-
toric transformation, not allowing local features to obscure the everlast-
ing themes. The wonder of the revealed accord should not diminish our
appreciation of the infinite variety of its transformations. (1974, p. 11)

While acknowledging the capability of myriad disciplines to educate and influence, my experience as an instructor in the history of visual media well qualifies me to address its particular affects and implications.

The history of Islamic art presents an instructive testament to the eloquence with which art embodies the essence of a religion or culture. The context of Islam in our current political landscape provides an extended resource to debunk uninformed assumptions. Students are introduced to Islamic art with Arabic calligraphy. The organic and fluid forms of the serpentine characters, coiling and entwining in a graceful ballet, initially captivate them with their beauty and energy. Students subsequently learn the crucial relevance of the Arabic language to the Qur'an and Islam itself, enhancing their perception by studying the doctrine of aniconism (opposition to the use of icons or visual images to depict living creatures or religious figures) in the Islamic faith. The restriction placed on religious imagery serves to further highlight the ingenuity of these artists and their versatile accomplishments in design, architecture, and the utilitarian arts.

Islamic art, as with many other categories of art history, allows students to distinguish the mixture of sources from remote locations that assimilate within various mediums. Analyzing from a wider historical vantage, students are instructed to realize how distant quarters have traded ideas, goods, and artistic innovations for millennia. The decorative arts in the Islamic realm display an explicit example of this relationship. Motifs from Hellenistic Greece, Imperial Rome, Byzantium, and China, all make their appearance in the ceramics, metalwork, and textiles of Asia Minor and Persia. These ingredients were adapted and synchronously meshed into singular and captivating art forms of their own.

The distinctive classical landscape brush paintings of the Song Dynasty in China (tenth through thirteenth centuries) substantiate the philosophical and spiritual precepts of Confucianism, Taoism, and Chan Buddhism in a concise and evocative manner. Students grasp how their intrinsic concepts of structure and balance, harmony with nature, flexibility, and spontaneous expression, play themselves out in the skilled hand of the trained master. The bold and flowing lines that define this school of painting, articulate the tenets that helped mold China in a graphic and direct format. A material projection of their metaphysical principles allows students to comprehend these abstract observations in intuitive and meaningful terms.

Chinese art history also affords an opportunity to consult semiotics and examine universal iconography produced in the region. The emblematic shape and design of the Chinese pagoda depicts an archetypal form, mirrored in the Hindu *ratha*, Buddhist *stupa*, Cambodian *wat*, Mesopotamian *ziggurat*, Mayan pyramid, and the two-dimensional heavenly chart of the Tibetan *mandala*. All are adaptations of a comparable structure and diagram mapping the progressive stages to the symbolic "center" and analogous higher spiritual level, as well as a conduit between the celestial and terrestrial spheres equated as a metaphorical mountain. Examples such as these let students ascertain the affinity of numerous cosmological ideologies in addition to the interplay and modifications of endemic deities and the attributes that denote them.

The same dual reflections are applicable to the history of illuminated manuscripts. Medieval manuscripts are replete with symbolism and renditions of venerated figures. Canonical and inspirational passages are complemented by colorful decorative patterns in the borders and bodies of the texts, reinforcing the written word with visual reference. These iconic works evolved over centuries into a sophisticated and radiant medium directly associated with the Christian gospels. Nevertheless, stylistic derivations from Islamic epic poetry of Western and Central Asia, India's ancient religious parables, geometric configurations in East and Southeast Asia, and European monastic artisans blended together within the pages of these heralded relics of the Western tradition—another vivid example of the cross currents of interdependence that shaped human history.

We can examine numerous artistic idioms throughout the globe and trace their transcontinental network. Despite geographical, cultural, and political boundaries, the visual arts have vigorously maintained a continuous and open reciprocity. As a critical link across time, the arts have often furnished a lone sanctuary for free, innovative thought—supplying and diffusing an enriching flow of scholarship and nurturing the development of our world. The eminent art historian, Herbert Read, in his essay "Art and Society," states, "society as a viable organic entity, is somewhere dependent on art as a binding, fusing, energizing force" (1969). The existing model bestows on us a long established and successful means of creating new cross-cultural relationships and discourse.

In the process of studying the history of art, students who have chosen to explore the subject come to relish the variety of visual expressions from around the world while simultaneously recognizing aspects of themselves in these pieces. They gain a new and liberating voice while discovering a bond of fellowship. After exposure to works of Western and non-European art, students acknowledge a wide-ranging benefaction of aesthetic interpretations, valuing each creation as a unique contribution to their communal endowment. Embracing a sense of inheritance fosters a desire to cherish and conserve this collective bequeathal as entrusted custodians. Moreover, it highlights the need to preserve the local and indigenous groups who produce this enduring legacy.

Students learn how war historically and currently affects the art and communities caught in the crosshairs of battle, decimating precious lives and valuable artifacts. This is no more apparent than in the present occupation in Iraq where thousands of irreplaceable antiquities from ancient Mesopotamia, the "cradle of civilization," have been demolished, plundered, or sold on the black market as a direct repercussion of military combat and the instability that accompanies it.

On 25 September 2008, the United States Senate voted to ratify the "1954 Hague Convention for the Protection of Cultural Property in the Event of Armed Conflict," premised on its preamble statement that "damage to cultural property belonging to any people whatsoever, means damage to the cultural heritage of all mankind" (Hague Convention, 1954). In the case of the war in Iraq, many stolen artifacts have been recovered, but countless more remain missing, most likely disappeared from the public domain forever. The eradication, damage, and theft of these icons of ancient civilization represent one of the greatest single losses to humanity's cultural and historical repository and its vital contact with the fabric of the past.

Crystal Lyon, a New Media Design major in the Bachelor of Fine Arts program at State University of New York College at Cortland, and student in my course, "Art beyond the West," addresses these issues in her recent solo thesis exhibition "My Moksha." Incorporating the Hindu term for enlightenment and nirvana into the title reflects her interpretation of these core beliefs. Lyon's exhibition statement says:

> I am a woman of the West, hardwired in its traditions. I have been bound by the ideas of my upbringing, blind to other cultural traditions that only existed for me as stories about far-away places. Higher education opened up a new world for me. Now they became tangible and real. I find myself striving to understand ideas that are outside of my own normalcy. New ideas began influencing my thinking process and my art. The works of art deal with my introduction to and understanding of Indian and Eastern ideas through a "Western lens." "My Moksha" deals with these concepts, capturing nature's movements through video installation, creating a peaceful environment for meditation, building a bridge between Western and Eastern influences. "My Moksha" is a launching pad for my life long research and artistic developments dealing with these ideas, building bridges of understanding, interpretation, and inspiration, through art. (2009)

Art history students come to know that when war destroys societies and their artistic treasures, a part of us is diminished. This realization provides additional impetus to resist war and cultivate a climate of cooperation. Perhaps as they move on to positions of authority in the twenty-first century, this knowledge, insight, and outlook may well provide a fruitful path toward peaceful coexistence.

Nine

ANTI-WAR WAR FILMS

Dennis Rothermel

1. Introduction

It is difficult to believe that it should ever be necessary to acknowledge the horrors of warfare. Nevertheless, an undeniable glorification of war and war-like virtues lies embedded in the literature and culture of Western civilization. Treatments of the horrors of war in the arts are equally old. Cinema that promotes the honor of soldiers in war does so mostly in the obligatory context of how a particular war is justified. The tendency of such films is to glorify war, warriors, and war-like virtues generally. The alignment with imputed justness of the cause ameliorates qualms about how shallow the warrior's allegiance is to any cause.

Few individuals, particularly among those who have had direct experiences, would encourage the experience of combat in war as something unequivocally desirable for its own sake (Rose, 2008, pp. 45–60). The legacy of war films—especially those produced in Hollywood—engenders the expectation for war films to glorify war, to encourage the virtues of warriors, and to justify the particular wars depicted. It should take nothing more than to show war for what it is to evoke a countervailing message. How well a national audience is prone to hear and understand that countervailing message may suffer from the common expectations that the legacy of war films has inculcated into the national culture.

This countervailing message underscoring the experience of warfare will also be a message generally constrained to lie beyond the discourse concerning whether engagements in particular wars were justified, or whether war generally is ever justified. This kind of message will contribute to the assertions that particular wars or war generally are fraught with horrible consequences, but without relying upon such assertions. The anti-war war film will have significance for philosophical stances regarding war that encompass a broader spectrum than that of pacifism alone, however inclusively that may be defined.

A long tradition in the culture and in the history of cinema commemorates the glory of those who suffer and sacrifice in combat for the sake of national purposes. That legacy of glorification establishes a concomitant need to stress the obvious horrific aspects of combat. The anti-war war film simply asserts the obvious. The inspiration for such works often comes from the film's director having directly experienced or witnessed combat in war. Robert Altman, John Ford, Sam Fuller, Howard Hawks, Lewis Milestone, Jean Renoir, George Stevens, Oliver Stone, William Wellman, and Fred Zinnemann have made films reflecting their wartime experiences. The sole overriding intent in these examples is to show the experience of the soldier in war for exactly what it is—without glorifying it to justify a national political agenda, and without exaggerating it to trivialize the heroism, mutual care, and reliance among soldiers that engender loyalty, solidarity, gratitude, and sacrifice.

Sometimes that careful balance avoiding jingoism and trivialization will result in a mixed message. Some war films that glorify war also include anti-war elements, even if the mixture of contrary meanings is not intentional. Some examples of films with this sort of mixed message that still show the horror of the soldier's experience are John Ford's *They Were Expendable* (1945), David Lean's *Lawrence of Arabia* (1962), Lewis Milestone's *Pork Chop Hill* (1959), William Wellman's *Story of G.I. Joe* (1945), Robert Aldrich's *Attack* (1956), Francis Ford Coppola's *Apocalypse Now!* (1979), Samuel Fuller's *The Big Red One* (1980), Clint Eastwood's *Letters from Iwo Jima* (2006), and Edmund Goulding's 1938 compromising remake of Howard Hawks' *Dawn Patrol* (1930).

Showing war for what it is focuses upon depiction of the experiences of soldiers. Sam Fuller asserted that no stronger opponent to war exists than the ordinary soldier who has endured combat. Fuller, a war veteran, also asserted that we have no genuine way to translate the soldier's experience to a movie audience other than to fire weapons at them from behind the screen—not just for show but hitting a few here and there (Dombrowski, 2008, p. 46). How actual experience differs from how cinema can depict it will be salient for any experience where the contingencies of the experience are of consequence to the person having that experience. That difference, however, may not necessarily entirely close off the possibility of empathy even without having had direct correlative experience.

Some have found the experience of combat energizing and some find it alluring. Those mostly deeply enthralled in the culture of militarism will find encouragement in any depiction of warrior action, and perhaps even reveling in the depictions clearly intended to show the transgressions of humane behavior that combat requires (Swofford, 2003, pp. 6, 64). The anti-war war film such as I characterize it will be something other than propaganda meant singularly to influence an audience to accept a certain opinion.

The reception of cinema that shows war for what it is provides a litmus test of the cultural and political health of a nation. It is one question as to what a film, a book, or a painting may mean and another as to how a public variously perceives it. Both issues will have their separate relevance, but we should expect to exclude as inherently suspect answers to the first question that are based upon evidence relevant only to the second, for the simple reason that popular reception may fall far short of careful comprehension.

It will also be important here to understand the importance of fiction film in delivering the anti-war message. We expect documentary cinema to photograph and record without having staged or influenced actual events and testimony, but we absolve fiction film from adherence to actual events. A fictional narrative, on the other hand, can construct the immediate thoughts and experiences of soldiers, which can remain elusive to a documentary account.

Showing war for what it is presumes authenticity of the conditions, weaponry, materiel, tactics, locales, and events of the war depicted. Fastidious adherence to historical fact and sustained verisimilitude, however, do not guarantee capturing the soldiers' authentic psychological experience. Engendering comprehension of their confrontation with horror is more important than adherence to historical detail.

Military music inspires military virtues and emotions. Jean Renoir's *The Grand Illusion* (1937) contains one scene devoted to this power. French officers, prisoners of war, watch from an upper-floor window of a guarded fortress, where they prepare costumes for their Christmas pageant. Below, youthful German soldiers drill in the vast stone courtyard. Outside the gates, two diminutive elderly women, clad entirely in black, watch the soldiers marching and drilling. One wrings her hands and says, "*Die arme Jungen!*" ("The poor boys!") as she nods her head gently. The old woman's sympathy derives from seeing the young men endure marching and drilling, and likely from anticipating their fate.

The older French officers—Boeldieu, Maréchal, and Rosenthal—gather at a window high above the courtyard. They become increasingly entranced by what they see and hear in the courtyard below. Boeldieu remarks upon the paradoxical contrast of the young men playing at soldiering below and the seasoned soldiers engrossed in children's celebrations above. They discuss their reasons for wanting to escape the prison camp, none of which includes a desire to return to the fight. Maréchal complains that the sound of the marching feet is emotionally captivating. As this noise and the fife-playing increase in the soundtrack, Boeldieu mutters his abhorrence of fifes. Obviously, both men remain emotionally affected, even as they resist it. It disturbs them how much the marching and music that works so well to inculcate military regimen in boys still affects them. Ironically, when later the prisoners stage an escape they will use the cover of a penny-whistle riot, with Boeldieu becoming the one sacrificed. The escape begins with a musical parody of the drum and fife military regimen that we know he abhors, and ends with his conscious sacrifice so that Maréchal and Rosenthal may escape.

Maréchal and Boeldieu resist the disquieting power of music employed to tug at passions that young boys harbor for glory. Those fixations will not automatically subside as they grow to manhood. Pyotr Ilyich Tchaikovsky's *1812 Overture* (1882), with its climatic duel of national anthems, pealing of church bells exulting victory, and actual canon fire indulges that power unabashedly. By contrast, there is no stronger musical rendition of what expe-

riencing war means than Benjamin Britten's *War Requiem* (1962). The pin-
nacle moment of the *Requiem*, which captures the soldier's fear and despair,
comes in the fifth movement when the orchestration for the liturgy of the day
of wrath features a repeated series of four riveting, syncopated, *sforzando*,
percussive orchestral chords:

> *Dies illa, dies irae, calamitatis*
> *et misereriae, dies magna et amara valde.*
> *Libera me, Domine, de morte aeterna,*
>   *in die illa tremenda.*
> (O that day, that day of wrath, of calamity
> and misery, a great day and exceeding bitter,
> Deliver me, O Lord, from death eternal,
>   in that fearful day.) (Britten, 1991)

These clasps out of time and out of rhythm may evoke the explosions of
a bombardment. The emotive side of the sequence imparts the terror of random annihilation, when it is not possible to stifle the thought that without
warning life may terminate in an instant—perhaps this instant, or the next, or
the next, or the next. Abject fear and sublime relief alternate, without either
having the time to register completely. Only for an instant is fear gone before
the cycle repeats.

The two musical examples of the *1812 Overture* and the *War Requiem*
define an axis aligning opposing inclinations. Maréchal and Boeldieu struggle
with these conflicting draws on their emotions as they listen to the fifes and
the sounds of the marching feet. Is the effect more than one can resist, or is
how it entices so easily that troubles us? Is there also music that will reverse
the tug of the military march? The depiction of the soldiers' struggling with
the easy pull on their emotions lays bare the ease with which cinema, like
music, toys with the emotions of its audience, and how easily those emotions
can be marshaled on behalf of the glorification of war.

Anti-war war films include portrayals of soldiers struggling with those
passions. They relate those experiences of war that horrify while avoiding an
enveloping dramatic structure designed to elicit the audience's emotional
identification with a heroic protagonist, to elicit catharsis in the resolution of
combat, to moralize loss and sacrifice, or to build antagonism toward a vil-
lainous enemy to be expiated in vicariously gratifying violence.

Renoir explained that his intention in making *The Grand Illusion* about
soldiers in a prison camp was to avoid the bipolar clichés of war films, either
to wallow in the mud and gore of combat or to pander to stereotypes of heroism, gallantry, and the conquest of evil (1973, p. 145). He identified Lewis
Milestone's *All Quiet on the Western Front* (1930) as the only film that
showed what the experience of war was for soldiers. The bombardment sequence in *All Quiet on the Western Front* surely does not elicit visceral attrac-

tion. The soldiers sit huddled together, coping with the anticipation of the next explosion coming near enough to bury them in their underground bunker. Importantly, we do not see the explosions in this scene. Not showing explosions might be how to avoid their visual allure. In relying instead upon the dull thunder of the earth reverberating around and above the bunker, Milestone is able to render the horrifying sensations of living through a bombardment.

Similarly, an early scene in Milestone's *A Walk in the Sun* (1945) depicts two soldiers, safe in a ditch, listening to enemy aircraft bombard the ships that just brought them to their beach landing. They cannot see the action, which lies just beyond the sand dunes in front of them. Then one explosion registers loudly enough to indicate a hit. Soon deep black clouds of smoke billow up into the sky and the two soldiers mourn for the sailors in those ships. The oddly graceful and sensual billowing clouds signal how quickly danger turns into loss, and how warfare dispenses its fates dispassionately.

The advent of intelligent technology, particularly with an animated computer graphics interface, in contemporary warfare and in the representation of war in film and video games, renders the experience of warfare as interchangeably virtual for the real soldier and the video-game player.

In utilizing these interfaces, soldiers sometimes experience real danger and killing in warfare only as mediated by an interface similar to what the game player or moviegoer enjoys as engaging and pleasurable. That removal into virtual experience saves the soldier from the direct, visceral experience of horror such as Milestone depicts in the bombardment scene in *All Quiet on the Western Front*. The experience of combat—real and as captured in film— loses its power to impart the accompanying horror. Furthermore, the advent of technology that removes soldiers from a space in which devastation and horror occur undermines the creation of a powerful anti-war sentiment impossible, as Bernd Hüppauf has argued (1995, pp. 96, 120). That combat has become interchangeable with playing computer games, however, has not been borne out in the experiences soldiers have had in warfare in recent years, particularly in Iraq and Afghanistan. Donovan Campbell's chronicle of an officer's experiences in combat in Iraq demonstrates that soldiers still experience these horrors and their aftermath (2009a).

Victor Perkins criticizes David Lean's *The Bridge on the River Kwai* (1957) for its elicitation of audience's sympathy with the combatants and its creation of the audience's catharsis in the climatic combat action. Those dramatic elements suffice to obliterate the anti-war sentiment elaborately woven into Carl Foreman's script (1972, p. 149). The escape sequence in *The Grand Illusion* shows some of that same tension between the over-arching anti-war message and the catharsis in the valiant escape from the prison. A similar complaint could be launched at Renoir were it not for his ironic employment of the penny whistles and Boeldieu's rejection of prison commandant Rauffenstein's insistence upon a shared affiliation with aristocratic class and devotion to military honor.

Few war films deliver an anti-war message without some complexity of message, as mentioned above. In some cases, this will arise because of influences on the production not entirely under the control of the director. The best examples of complete and undiluted efforts may be Milestone's *All Quiet on the Western Front* and Terrence Malick's *The Thin Red Line* (1998). As well, Stanley Kubrick's *Paths of Glory* (1957) and *Full Metal Jacket* (1987) situate anti-war elements within Kubrick's continued meditation on humanity's deeper proclivity for destruction. Kubrick dismissed Renoir's assertion that one cannot depict warfare cinematically without making it attractive. He noted that the experiences soldiers actually have would mix horror with courage, loyalty, and exhilaration (2001, pp. 176–188). The next section of this paper will include detailed treatment of the important aspects of these four films that construct that message that derives from the depiction of the experiences of soldiers in combat.

These four films, though hardly exclusively, comprise sufficient demonstration of how war films can deliver an anti-war message rooted in the depiction of the experiences of soldiers. Gleaning traits found in those war films that contribute to the anti-war message, we can identify thirteen successful strategies that the filmmakers of these four films employ. Importantly, this collection constitutes an expandable and versatile list of strategies for imparting an anti-war sentiment, evident in films by other filmmakers as well. Other strategies are indeed possible. Hence, there is no point to attempting to compose a comprehensive typology. The essential trait that defines effective anti-war war films is intelligent invention that invites intelligent comprehension. It is exactly in that way that the effective anti-war war film contrasts to the automatic emotional responses that non-anti-war war films ordinarily indulge. Identifying general traits to define a film genre applies only to the lesser attempts—those that assimilate mainstream formulaic fare. The strategies listed below are not so much the genre-defining common traits of anti-war war films as they are rather specific strategies that exemplified in some intelligent and intentionally anti-war war films.

Consistent in this set of strategies is the opportunity for a filmmaker to imbue a film with structures of meaning that require careful, detailed observation and ultimately engage the audience in exercising intelligence in interpreting the film. We should always expect the endeavor for peace to rest upon engaging intelligence. This will be particularly important for the task of teaching peace, to include using films that teach peace.

2. Thirteen Anti-War War Film Strategies

Strategy #1: Depict war as experienced, by soldiers who endure fear, horror, doubt, terror, panic, loss, horrific injury, and particularly confrontation with death. Trucks deposit soldiers at the front in *All Quiet on the Western Front*. As they march away toward their positions on the front line, one by one, the soldiers turn around to steal one more glance at the departing trucks, each look loaded with the innocent wish still to be on one of those vehicles. Milestone repeats the image at the end of the film, superimposed on a wide view of a vast graveyard—every single one of the young soldiers in the earlier image has died.

Beleaguered troops march to landing craft waiting to take them to the departing troop ships at the end of *The Thin Red Line*. They pass a graveyard, already filled with long rows of white crosses. Sprinklers water newly planted sod as if it had always been there. One by one, they steal glances, silently counting the number of men they knew who now lie interred somewhere beneath that immaculate lawn. It could easily have been any of them.

The night before a planned attack, two soldiers in *Paths of Glory* debate which is worse in anxious whispers: death by machine-gun bullets or by bayonet. Both are a matter of cold steel ripping through flesh, but which death is better? This goes to prove, the one soldier says, that we fear pain more than death. That wry discovery paradoxically gives the man solace.

Strategy #2: Broach the thin distinction between heroic bravery and pointless sacrifice. Pvt. Reese in Don Siegel's *Hell Is for Heroes* (1962) assumes initiative for the sake of preserving the survival of his squad. He devises measures to fool the enemy into thinking his squad consists of a full regiment. He becomes convinced that he needs to preempt an enemy attack. So Reese schemes ingeniously—but, as it turns out, unnecessarily—to destroy the enemy machine gun emplacement, only to see all his men killed during the treacherous approach through a mine field. Despairing in the recognition of his folly, and mortally wounded, Reese completes the assault and sacrifices himself, carrying explosives into the enemy bunker, just as reinforcements surround the bunker, making its conquest moot.

Pvt. Witt in *The Thin Red Line* volunteers to scout ahead with Cpl. Fife and Pvt. Coombs, convinced that these two green soldiers will surely succumb to the enemy advance in force that he correctly anticipates. Witt sends the wounded Coombs and Fife back to their company to report what they have seen, while he provides distraction to impede the enemy advance. Witt successfully diverts the advance and finds himself surrounded in an open field. Witt is convinced that people see into divine light upon dying. He refuses to surrender, instead raising his weapon knowing that doing so he will die, and see the light.

In *Full Metal Jacket*, an enemy sniper inflicts a soldier with a wound strategically placed to disable him and elicit his cries of pain without killing him outright. The wounded man's cries attract other soldiers to fall under fire while trying to rescue him. Though one of the squad understands this tactic and orders a withdrawal, the others refuse to leave him there. Two more will perish before they find and kill the sniper.

In *The Thin Red Line*, a soldier writhes, screaming in agony, midway between enemy soldiers and the location where his commander and squad gather in the cover of a ditch. He is surely dying, but his agony compels an effort to relieve his suffering, which amounts to benevolent euthanasia. Enemy fire kills one man, a medic, who attempted this task. Another man finishes the job, though foolishly putting himself at risk, and luckily escaping with his life.

A standard trait of the war-film genre depicts acts of individual courage and heroism that promote the valorization of warrior virtues and endorse the articulated purposes of the side of the conflict for which the warrior hero fights. Without that context of purpose, the valorization will lack legitimization of the audience's engagement worthy of justifying loss and sacrifice. Careful interpretation of a film uncovers to what degree the absence of reasonable purpose is intentional. A close reading of the film as a text is crucial to grasp clear hold of the filmmaker's intentions, and to acquire more than willfully subjective impressions of meaning. It is only when the construction of meaning in a film is vague that a depicted act can be interpreted as heroic or pointless with equal cogency.

Strategy #3: Show how random victimization is inherent to warfare. An American assault upon a Japanese bivouac in *The Thin Red Line* begins with soldiers advancing nervously through a thick mist. Bullets whistle past, and then the encounter begins. Malick's disorienting flash montage shows us the moments of death only: a man bayoneted, a man felled by a bullet, a Japanese soldier or American interchangeably. Alternately, we see each soldier's sustained terror and moments of becoming lifeless. There are no heroes or cowards, good men or bad, enlisted men or officers, Japanese or American—just men running, firing weapons, killing, and dying.

As troops climb up out of the trenches to advance in *All Quiet on the Western Front*, enemy machine-gun fire mows them down in a row. Milestone's camera tracks the length of the line, showing the men falling like dominoes (Kelly, 2005, pp. 23–29). A scene in Peter Weir's *Gallipoli* (1981) repeats this instantaneous massive slaughter of World War I trench warfare nearly exactly.

Kubrick captures his long-take traveling shot from a crane in *Paths of Glory* as soldiers advance through a desolate no man's land. The terrain is unlike any recognizable on earth—deformed into the unnatural contours of bomb craters and littered with remnants of trees, wire, fence, and war materiel. The men clamor and crawl over this terrain. Bombs and bullets kill them randomly and mercilessly, scattering their organized formations into desperate individuals struggling to traverse the alien terrain (Nelson, 2000, p. 46).

In *The Thin Red Line*, troops rise up out of the wind-swept tall grass to continue their charge, knowing the enemy lies hidden within range and ready to attack. Explosions and bullets decimate the command. Men fall flailing, blown this way and that and into each other, without ever seeing their attackers.

In Danis Tanovic's *No Man's Land* (2001), soldiers rig an enemy soldier taken for dead with a booby trap meant to kill his comrades who will arrive eventually to remove the body. He awakens and learns of his predicament, which not even a cease-fire can alleviate. His comrades cannot defuse the explosive, nor can the ones who placed it, nor the United Nations peacekeeping troops. He lies at the bottom of a wide trench—prone, silent, calm, and clutching a tattered photograph of his family. He awaits either deliverance from immanent death or the inevitable. Finally, all abandon him. He is no longer anyone's soldier, but not yet a casualty.

Strategy #4: Show the brutal logic and tactics, borne of necessity, serendipitously unmasked through confrontation with an enemy soldier-representative of one's self. Among Pvt. Train's voice-over lamentations in *The Thin Red Line* is how the humiliation and terror of defeated prisoners shows the conquering soldiers what might just as easily have been their own fates.

In a crucial scene in *All Quiet on the Western Front*, Paul Bäumer becomes isolated during an assault across no man's land. He watches from his hidden vantage point in a deep bomb crater as advancing French soldiers leap over him and then back again in retreat. One of them falls into his crater. Bäumer pounces on the man, stabs him once with his bayonet, and then covers the man's mouth with his hand lest his cries attract the attention of the retreating French troops. That second action by Bäumer betrays his difficulty with having taken the life of another man. That man is a stranger and an enemy, but he is a soldier like him. Killing the French soldier would have been a more effective way to render the man quiet. What he has done in an instant he instantly regrets.

The two men remain trapped in the crater by machine gun fire for the remainder of the day and night. Bäumer draws close to the man, declaring that he wants to help him. He offers him water to drink. Later, delirious from the noise and terror of the unending barrage of machine gun fire and explosions, Bäumer begins to curse the Frenchman, condemning him to die, before reverting to remorse. When the French soldier dies, Bäumer asks the dead man's forgiveness, declaring that if he were to jump into this crater again he would not kill him. He mourns what the war has done to both of them. As Bäumer extracts the Frenchman's identity papers and looks at the photo of wife and child, he promises to write to the man's wife and family, and to make restitution to them. This scene in the bomb crater exposes Bäumer's loss and retrieval of his humanity, which will disprove Hüppauf's criticism that Milestone's realization of the novel fails to capture Bäumer's immutable transformation from having endured combat (Hüppauf, 1995, p. 110).

Strategy #5: Show that every soldier—every officer—objects to the brutal logic imposed by hierarchical command, but then acquiesces, becoming the instrument of that logic. Gen. Broulard visits his old friend, Gen. Mireau, in the initial scene of *Paths of Glory*. Broulard brings news that general staff wants an attack on a German stronghold named the Ant Hill. Mireau protests that his men are in no condition to mount such an attack. Broulard mentions a second issue, which he insists disingenuously is unconnected—a pending promotion for an aggressive field officer such as Mireau. In what passes as a gently choreographed *pas de deux*, the Generals Mireau and Broulard meander about the ornate Baroque palace hall that Mireau occupies as his officer quarters. They play out a predictable, polite debate replete with subtle reversals. By the time their circumnavigation of the vast room returns to its starting point, Mireau avers finally that he will not allow Broulard to impose constraints upon the courage and capabilities of his men.

Mireau and Col. Dax share virtually the same conversation in Dax's command post in a dingy underground bunker along the French trenches. They exchange the two sides of the point somewhat more frankly, and Dax relents to lead the attack on threat of being relieved of command, lest some other officer lead his men indifferently to slaughter. Without revealing his thoughts, Col. Dax explains the attack to his officers, who politely reiterate exactly the same points he had made to Mireau, which Dax now does his best to counter, although unenthusiastically. What he does not share are Mireau's non-sanguine calculations of casualties far in excess of the majority of the attacking force, calculations that Dax did not dispute, and which his officers must be calculating silently on their own.

In his recently published accounts of his experiences in Iraq from June 2003 to June 2004, Ricardo Sanchez, Lt. Gen., ret., explains this very same duality of not being able by office to criticize the decisions in the chain of command, and yet choosing to remain in command as the best servant to the men under command. Very much like the French attack on the Ant Hill in *Paths of Glory* the executive political leadership underestimated the strength of the insurgency in Iraq, Sanchez's troops were ill equipped and ill trained, and they were put at increased risk on behalf of the political needs of President George W. Bush to secure reelection. Though, like Dax, he had threatened to resign, Sanchez decided to remain in his position lest he put his troops at greater risk under the command of individuals with less comprehension of the exigencies of the conflict in Iraq (Sanchez, 2008b).

Similarly, in his memoirs of service in Iraq from March to September 2004, Lt., ret., Donovan Campbell explains that caring for the soldiers under command may seem to be the principle concern, but engaging the enemy and maintaining communication with higher command are what "the grim logic of combat dictates." This account, too, reiterates what Dax contends with (Campbell, 2009, p. 5).

Shown in celebrated long-take, wide-angle, and deep-focus tracking shots, Dax traverses the trenches just prior to the attack. His seething anger is just beneath the surface of his countenance. From his subjective view, we can count off the men knowing, as Dax surely does, what percentage will perish horribly within the hour: maybe this one will die, this one will be wounded, and this one may survive the day.

The attack is an abominable failure, which Mireau blames on the cowardice of the men. He insists upon court-martialing and executing 100 of his soldiers. Broulard and Dax negotiate that number down to a randomly chosen three, one from each company. Of course, given the odds, a betting man among the French soldiers would calculate that there is considerably less risk in refusing the charge on the Ant Hill than in joining it.

The Court martial is concluded prejudicially. In spite of Dax's spirited and intelligent defense, the court convicts the three soldiers of cowardice. The night before their scheduled execution, Dax shares information with Broulard about Mireau's order to an artillery captain to fire on those troops who had not left the trenches during the attack. Broulard refuses to commute the court's judgment, but he does use Dax's testimony to discredit Mireau, setting him up as the person to take the blame for the failed attack. Broulard then offers Mireau's job to Dax, who angrily refuses. Broulard is incredulous, having supposed the promotion to be Dax's ambitious intent. He is aghast that Dax truly wanted to save the three men from execution. Broulard declares his disdain for what he takes to be Dax's naïve devotion to the welfare of his men. Dax declares his pity for the man who has lost the capability for human compassion. Dax and Broulard are passionately contemptuous of each other. Their outlooks are mutually incomprehensible. This exemplifies the dramatic contrast between the logic of sacrificing lives from the viewpoint of looking up to authority and from looking down the chain of command.

Dax's *sotto voce* despairing retort is caught in a dark, grainy, shallow-focus close-up shot, separating this one moment out from the deep-focus, wide-angle ornate and luxurious terrain where Broulard's logic rules unchallenged. Broulard is astonished at Dax, but he is unconcerned—there will be no dearth of ambitious officers to fit his needs. Dax is profoundly chagrinned—his confrontation with Broulard reveals the upper reaches of the underlying casual indifference of the war, the military, the nation, and the continent, toward the humanity of the people who succumb to the war's insane slaughter.

On a troop ship, Brig. Gen. Quintard wants to know how much Col. Tall wants victory in *The Thin Red Line*. "As much as I have to," he replies. Tall's plan of attack places the company under Capt. Staros at the center of a frontal up-hill assault. Staros prays at night for the strength not to forsake his men. He explains the attack plan to his incredulous sergeants, who transmit instructions to stone-faced squads. Enemy fire decimates the attacking force. Sgt. Walsh's angry confrontation with Staros gives Staros the fortitude to defy Tall. Tall relents but will want to know later how many of his men Staros is willing to let die—one, a few, twenty? Staros has no answer and Tall eventually relieves him of command for being too softhearted. Staros, like Dax, refuses to continue to administer the brutal, calculated logic of warfare. Tall, like Broulard's reaction to Dax, finds Staros' contrary way of thinking incomprehensible and unsuitable to an officer in battle command.

Strategy #6: Show how soldiers lose or never acquire a clear sense of purpose in the conduct of the war that engulfs them. In *Full Metal Jacket*, a news crew interviews soldiers, inquiring about their perceptions of the purpose of the war. With the exception of their sardonic aping of official purposes in the war, not one soldier cites a reason consistent with national foreign policy.

In *The Thin Red Line*, after the annihilation of his entire squad, Sgt. McCron picks up handfuls of dirt and grass. Letting the dirt then fall through his spreading fingers, he pronounces that that is all they are—his soldiers, himself, and all the rest of them—just dirt. Sgt. Walsh bitterly surmises that this battle and the entire war are over nothing more than property, grander in scope perhaps than the dirt they now stand on, but still just so much property to own and control.

Strategy #7: Show how the culture of a nation contributes to the eagerness that young men exhibit for war and warlike virtues. Lewis Milestone begins his adaptation of *All Quiet on the Western Front* in a German schoolroom. A schoolmaster whips young men in his classroom into a frenzy of nationalism. He quotes a sentiment he attributes to the ancient Romans: *"Dulce et decorum est pro patria mori"* ("It is sweet and fitting to die for one's country") (Horace, Odes III.ii.13), while his pupils dream of heroism, adventure, glory, and adulation. This film evoked demonstrations and virulent denunciations from the leadership of the burgeoning National Socialist Party when it was first released in Germany in 1930. The schoolmaster's dreamy patriotic militarism juxtaposed blatantly to his pupils' childish susceptibility to that ideal proved incompatible with Nazi sentiments (Imhoof, 2008, pp. 186–191).

The young men in the schoolroom talk excitedly of the medals they will earn. They celebrate their collective commitment to join the army by throwing their books and papers in the air, gleeful that there will be no more classes for them. Later in the film, having experienced war and life in the army, these same boys struggle to come to terms with the purpose of the war, unable to state any purpose that they can align with their own. The allegiance they have left is for their immediate comrades, to help each other simply to survive.

Strategy #8: Show how soldiers suffer moral degradation, as conditioned in training and as un-suppressible response to horror and loss. A soldier in *The Thin Red Line* delights in taunting captured enemy soldiers and in extracting gold teeth from their dead. Later, he breaks into uncontrollable weeping at his own moral degradation. Sgt. Welsh initially lectures Pvt. Witt that no one man is anything by himself, and, a moment later, that it is necessary to close oneself off from the rest of the world and its horrors and suffering.

Paths of Glory elaborates upon *All Quiet on the Western Front* in depictions of trench warfare and assaults across the cratered terrain of no man's land. *Full Metal Jacket* draws upon other elements that are spare and brief in Milestone's 1930 film. Kubrick's elaboration of the deliberate sadism of the drill instructor in training camp and the arrangement of the training barracks circumnavigated in long, slow dolly takes have precedents in Milestone's film. The self-consciously absurd explanations by soldiers of the causes and reasons for the war in which they fight, the progress of a squad of soldiers as they experience the first shock of a death among their comrades, and how they soon become inured to that occurrence also connect the two films (Naremore, 2007, pp. 90–92). The confluence of images and moods in the boot camp barracks demonstrates how that very carefully designed training conditions young men to be willing and ready to kill. Psychological conditioning of a predisposition to kill emerged subsequent to World War II. Investigation of infantry performance in that war revealed the predominant incidence of "nonfirers," soldiers who could not bring themselves to aim a weapon at an enemy soldier and then to fire with intent to kill. (Grossman, 1995, pp. 249–280; Rose 2008, pp. 66–68).

The narrative of *Full Metal Jacket* follows the experiences and development of the one character, Pvt. Joker, who links the two segments of the film. Patricia Gruben explains how Kubrick sustains characterizations that— in the European style of cinema narrative—subvert an audience's emotional identification with the personality and plight of the film's main protagonist. Kubrick assiduously avoids building Joker to become the protagonist in whom the audience commits its emotional and moral attachment (Gruben, 2005, pp. 25–29). Kubrick's intent was to tell a story with greater moral complexity than encouraging the audience to identify with the main character's personality and actions.

When Gny. Sgt. Hartman asks Joker why he wants to be a Marine, Joker declares that he is "a killer, sir!" A subsequent incident of abuse shows Joker's contorted face as he conjures up the courage to respond genuinely to the drill instructor's taunts. A colonel in the field harangues Joker; he wants to know the meaning of Joker wearing a peace–symbol button on his flak jacket while having inscribed "Born to kill" on his helmet. Joker explains it away with as "the Jungian duality thing," a *non sequitor* that baffles the colonel and has only inchoate meaning for Joker. Neither Hartman nor the Colonel ostensibly comprehends Joker's strained ironic retorts.

The recruits in boot camp conspire to punish Pvt. Pyle for having repeatedly caused the whole company punishment. Their carefully planned reprisal stalls only when it is finally Joker's turn to administer his blow. Joker hesitates, frozen in place, moved only by the angry urging of the man who holds Pyle down. Joker's contorted facial expression betrays his struggle to muster the will to inflict harm. He then strikes the man hard—harder than had any of the others—again, and again—each blow harder than the last. His own need to suppress his inability to do harm willfully animates the verve with which he does finally inflict that harm on Pvt. Pyle, redirecting his own internal torment. As the punishment concludes, Joker falls into his bunk immediately below Pvt. Pyle who cries out in agony and humiliation. Joker closes his eyes and places his hands flat against his ears, shutting out what he might see or hear. These gestures insulate Joker from his shame and fortify his suppression of empathy.

Joker's avowed aspirations to be a manly, killer-warrior grate against his nature. His frustration at that disparity emanates aggressively as excessive, punitive violence against a defenseless man whose sin was not being able to be a good soldier.

Strategy #9: Show how soldiers become alienated from the world where they may live in peace, and from the world shared with women. In *The Thin Red Line*, Pvt. Witt spends his AWOL escape from the war in a Melanesian village, with a woman and her children, lingering in the simple peace of love and play with youth and innocence. Pvt. Bell had refused a deployment overseas as an officer, to avoid separation from his wife. Because of that refusal, he loses from his officer's commission. He is then drafted into the army as a foot soldier, which takes him away to the Pacific theater of the war. He dreams of the times spent and yet to be spent with his wife. Susie Walsh details how time Bell spent in erotic dreaming and reading her letters provide him with the ballast to sustain his equilibrium in the buffeting storms of the war (Walsh, 2005, pp. 306–312).

The sole escape Bäumer and his colleagues enjoy in *All Quiet on the Western Front* begins when he and Kropp dream in front of a theater poster of a young woman. Milestone captures their reverie in an uninterrupted long take, with the two men reflected in the mirror beside the poster on the tavern wall, putting them side by side with an image of their fantasies. The sustained shot underscores how little it takes the men's thoughts to wander far away from the war and then to stay far removed.

Inspired by this reverie, they bathe in the nearby canal, where three young French women offer them bread and sausage to share. To join the women, the men must swim across the canal at night, naked and undetected in their momentary escape from the war and the army. After sharing the meal, they start a record playing on the phonograph, but the three couples retire to bedrooms before the song has played out.

"*Pauvre garçon*" ("poor boy"), Susanne says to Paul, tenderly kissing the palm of his hand, and showing the same spontaneous sympathy for young soldiers destined to war as the old women in *The Grand Illusion*. The French officer's tunic she gives Paul to wear shows the absence of men that the war has exacted upon the household, similar to Elsa's home in *The Grand Illusion*. Paul notes with disdain that it is an officer's tunic, but makes nothing of wearing the uniform of his enemy. He tells Susanne that all the world of the war has fallen away during his time with her. As the men leave, peacefulness and gentility imbues their actions and demeanor, replacing the agitation and anguish that had prevailed before.

In *The Grand Illusion*, Renoir has his camera track back slowly, capturing the prisoners' captivation, one by one, at the sight of one of them dressed in drag. The pageant they have organized and rehearsed celebrates the happy community of men and women much as they had known it before the war. After their escape, Maréchal and Rosenthal linger long at Elsa's farm in the remote Bavarian Alps, forgetting war and duty.

The concluding scene of *Paths of Glory* solidifies the film's anti-war sentiment. The scene derives from Kubrick's realization, since it has no connection with the literary source for the film. Col. Dax returns to his headquarters, pausing when he hears an enormous din emanating from the café next door. The café owner has corralled a young German girl to entertain Dax's men. The German woman is the sole female role in the film. They shout, whistle, cheer, holler, and stamp their feet in anticipation.

Kubrick's montage of soldiers' faces in close-up here provides stylistic counterpoint to the tracking, wide-angle, deep-focus and long takes that otherwise dominate the film's style. The explosion of the men's behavior into unrestrainedly aggressive, juvenile lust bespeaks their emotional need for release beyond what would ordinarily derive from romantic and sexual deprivation. Not an hour after the gratuitous execution of three of their brethren to mask the foolhardy machinations of the army generals, the three executed soldiers are far from the minds of their fellow soldiers. This demonstration of the easy forgetfulness of human conscience among his men sinks Dax into irrepressible anger, which is palpably visible in his expression.

The young woman in the café is fearful and apprehensive standing before this aggressive crowd. The café owner declares suggestively that she has no talents other than her natural beauty, but she can sing like a bird. The men become even more aggressively vociferous in demanding a song. Demurely, softly, and reluctantly, the young woman begins to sing, though terrified by the soldiers' aggressive and dehumanizing behavior toward her. Tears stream down her face as she continues. However, no one can hear her sing over the men's loud shouting and whistling. One soldier shouts for her to sing louder, and in reflexive response, the men begin to cease their noise. They begin to hear the song she sings in German, an old folk song, "*Der treue Husar*," ("The Faithful Cavalryman").

Known since 1825, this is a gentle singsong melody about a soldier who receives news that his beloved is dying of illness (Naremore, 2007, pp. 95–96). The soldier flees his post to be with her as she dies. Kubrick's staccato montage during the first part of the scene gives way to a slower rhythm of individual images of the men. The soldiers begin to listen intently to the song, one they must all know. As their mood changes, they cease their shouts and jeering. The woman now sings with nothing but silence to accompany the song as she slowly regains her composure. The men sit silent, motionless, and morose—lost in thought. One by one, they begin to hum along and to weep—their faces approximating the singer's tear-stained visage. The woman's spirit begins to pick up as the men's humming and singing grows. The turn in the soldiers' reactions buoys her. She directs her singing toward them individually, as their own thoughts turn inward and away from her.

Kubrick's montage of men's faces now repeats, but with a succession of sad, weeping soldiers lost in contemplation of the loss of love, wife, family, and home. What they long for is a world and an eternity away from the realm of death and horror that instigated their boisterous harassment of the woman only moments before. Their tears finally settle her initial fright. She now sings passionately, joyfully, and without apprehension. Her face remains streaked with tears.

The explosiveness with which the soldiers' sexual aggression overcame them initially, and the rapidity with which that mood dissipates and alters, offer testimony to their experiences. They cannot harbor thoughts about love in the pervasive gloom of impending, violent death. It does not require very much to reverse that alienation. The example early in the film of Sgt. Bell, who rambles in shell-shocked delirium about never seeing his wife again, offers the only reasonable reaction to that gloom. What Kubrick shows us in this last scene is something important about soldiers subjected to combat: the series of volatile, emotional reactions the soldiers display to the young woman and her song could only emerge from soldiers who have experienced what these soldiers have.

Col. Dax hears this extraordinary transition, which moves him profoundly. Kubrick brackets the concluding episode of the woman singing before the soldiers with close-ups of Dax's reactions at the beginning and end of the scene. Initially he is horrified at their callow disregard for the tragedy of three of their own, and then profoundly moved afterwards by the depth of their suppressed suffering. Kubrick elevates the episode by ending with Dax's reflective contemplation to encourage the film's audience to attend to that same reflective contemplation.

The song episode delivers, in purely cinematic narrative, the film's philosophical message about what it is like to be a soldier. Dax can indulge this pause and wrenching emotional turn no more than a moment before his staff sergeant informs him that the regiment has been ordered back to the front. He instructs the sergeant to allow his men a few more moments of respite before conveying the orders, and then steps briskly into his headquarters.

The exit music recapitulates the tune the German girl had sung, but rearranged ironically into a bright military march over a montage of major characters in the film. The montage imitates the concluding heroic tribute to soldiers featured in the war film genre. However, in this instance, the series of close-up vignettes orders the characters in the story without any hint of judgment: the victims of the summary executions, the conniving generals, the shell-shocked sergeant, Col. Dax, and others variously revealed to have been brave or cowardly. Kubrick's ironic concluding images emphasize the opacity of soldiers' suffering beneath the impositions of the representational culture that summarily glorifies war.

The penultimate scene of *Full Metal Jacket*, which depicts the killing of a Viet Cong sniper who has killed three men of a squad on patrol, derives from two separate scenes in Gustav Hasford's novel, the source for Kubrick's script. As happened also with *Paths of Glory*, there is little hint in the novel, however, of Kubrick's final emotive construction of the scene, which underwent several revisions before Kubrick settled on a final version (Naremore, 2007, pp. 212–216).

Joker is the first one to confront the sniper, who turns out to be a young woman. As she turns toward him, firing her weapon, Joker hesitates and does not fire. As happened earlier in his confrontation with Pyle in the latrine at the end of the first part of the film, Joker is unable to respond to sudden lethal danger. He falls behind a concrete pillar, drops his weapon, closes his eyes and places his hands flat over his ears—repeating his gesture after the earlier beating of Pyle in the boot camp barracks. The report of the sniper's weapon and impact upon the opposite side of the pillar overwhelm him. His protégé, Rafterman, saves Joker by shooting the young woman repeatedly, inflicting mortal wounds but not instantaneous death. The squad gathers around the fallen sniper. They show neither animosity nor pity, only indifferent curiosity about the young woman dying before them. She whispers prayers in Vietnamese and then beseeches the men, in English, to shoot her. They debate what to do, but the prevailing opinion is to leave her to suffer a slow, agonizing death. Joker insists that they cannot just leave her there, an insistence at first misunderstood by the squad to mean transporting her for medical care.

Taking on the task of executioner, Joker draws his pistol and takes slow, deliberate aim. His face again screws up into a contorted grimace. This is exactly the same expression as he had in his confrontation with Gny. Sgt. Hartman and exactly the same expression he showed just before his culminating vicious contribution to the beating of Pvt. Pyle. His hand begins to shake. Finally, he fires the weapon. From the verbal reactions of the others, we understand Joker to have inflicted a horrific wound. His face slowly uncoils, falling into a solemn visage unmoved by the morbid jocularity of his squad members.

We understand Joker to be a young man who fashions himself as a writer and a killer. Joker's voice-over narratives provide evidence of his literary aspirations. We see how he struggles to become a warrior, how he struggles to acquire the killer instinct that does not dwell in him naturally. Despite regimented boot camp training, Joker is still a soldier who hesitates. The reification of his being "a killer, sir!" that he seeks to find in the painfully deliberate shooting of the woman sniper only verifies the profound difficulty he has with that act. It is not something that he can do naturally—something he can do only by marshalling all of his willpower.

The sniper's inversion of Joker's traits—a beautiful woman, young, slight of build, courageous, coldly effective at killing, and fearless in facing death—inflame his self-conscious inadequacies. Joker is not a reluctant killer; he is a man who yearns to be a killer yet cannot muster it. Killing this woman is his attempt to blot out what he perceives as failure. It will salve his present disquietude more readily than it will change his nature. For the moment, however, he savors his victory over his shortcoming, unaware of his momentary acquisition of what Paul Virillio calls the soldier's "obscene gaze" (Virillio, 1989, pp. 49–50). Kubrick spares us the object of that gaze—the disfigured face of the dead sniper. The subject of the gaze is horrifying enough. Joker's act defiles youth, beauty, and femininity. He transforms the sniper into an object of horror—human debris to fit in with the worthless, ruinous urban terrain in which she and the soldiers have killed and died.

Time will never recoup the spiritual cost of having forced a self-projected heroic image upon Joker's psychology, however much we imagine that he is now capable of killing. That will be the meaning of the concluding images of the film—an array of silhouette ghosts. These young men have become killers, having incurred irredeemable moral and spiritual wounds. Jollily they chant the Mickey Mouse Club theme song, which they had all learned during their childhood from the popular children's television show, as they march into the false sunset of the fires of a burning city set against a smoke-blackened sky. As Naremore explains, through a regression to malleable, infantile urges, these young men have become effective killers—what the military needs from its foot soldiers (2007, p. 216).

The joyful retrieval of a song from their nationally shared childhood is thoroughly appropriate to their arrested moral and emotional development. The intensely desensitizing behavioral modifications of boot camp freeze their maturity at that peak of early manhood when it is easiest to mold post-adolescent anger and violence into a readiness to kill. As Nelson points out, served up this way, Kubrick's set of characters stand even farther away from the comfortable emotional approximation that war films ordinarily invoke (2000, p. 259). These ghosts of men—with their maturity arrested and subverted, carrying weapons and happily chanting a children's song to commemorate having killed and survived—horrify. They horrify us for the sake of what they have done, for the sake of what they have become, and for the sake of how that transformation will plague them forever.

Kubrick's cut to black to conclude the film, while the Rolling Stones' song *Paint It Black* plays, leaves all coy irony aside, in contrast to the outrageous musical irony that concludes *Paths of Glory* and *Dr. Strangelove* (1964). Kubrick has painted the soldiers black, "black as night, black as coal," against a darkened sky, for they are the ones who need to "see the sun blotted out from the sky."

> I see people turn their heads and quickly look away.
> Like a new born baby it just happens ev'ry day.
> I look inside myself and see my heart is black.
> I see my red door and it has been painted black.
> Maybe then I'll fade away and not have to face the facts.
> Its not easy facin' up when your whole world is black.
> (Jagger and Richards, 1966)

These are the thoughts that these ghosts are *not* having so long as they can chant a childish song, with its diametrically opposite sentiment.

Strategy #10: Demonstrate the debilitating forces of horror and terror. Colonial soldiers load canon with chain and other metal fragments, open the fort gates, fire upon on-rushing Indians, and then close the gates again in John Ford's *Drums along the Mohawk* (1939). The colonials pause in the midst of the fight, aghast at the horrifying carnage lying at their feet.

Even more dramatically on the same point, the remnants of the British force at Roarke's Drift in Cy Endfield's *Zulu* (1964) stand surrounded by piles of dead and dying Zulu warriors, who were slaughtered as they delivered the thrust of their attack precisely into the teeth of the arrayed British infantry fire power. The British soldiers and officers stand frozen in their ranks, too stunned to react. They have been victorious, but only a thin sliver of luck has saved them from annihilation in the very moments just past, in which nevertheless they triumphed. These moments of the onslaught align exactly with the time-halting chords of Benjamin Britten's *War Requiem*.

Once Bäumer returns to his own trenches, he confides in his sergeant and protector, telling of his moral ordeal with the French soldier. The sergeant encourages him not to mind the killing, pointing out—unconvincingly—a sniper nearby who exults with every French soldier he is able to catch off-guard. That will be Bäumer's fate as well. He, too, will step unawares into the path of a sniper's bullet.

The students from that classroom in the first scene will all become casualties of the war. Paul Bäumer will be the last to die, taking advantage of the Armistice cease-fire to crawl out of a bunker to reach for a butterfly, his hobby from his previous life, thus exposing himself to a French sniper. We see only his hand, gently extended toward the insect, draw back into a clenched fist with the report of the distant rifle, and then finally relax in death. Milestone provided his own hand for this detail shot that concludes the story of Paul Bäumer.

Strategy #11: Eschew audience emotional investment in single characters glorified or vilified to elicit calculated positive emotional responses to brutality and violence exacted by heroes upon villains. Engaging the cathartic thrust of combat action is the failing of *The Bridge on the River Kwai*. Col. Saito is easily the object of derision and resentment, as is Col. Nicholson. As much as Cmdr. Shears does not want the opportunity to be a hero, the film aligns our sympathies with his heroic efforts. Not until the end does either Col. Nicholson or Maj. Warden engender anything other than sympathetic identification. Similarly, Oliver Stone's *Platoon* (1986) allows deflection of empathy with the soldiers' suffering into allegiance with a good sergeant against a bad sergeant.

In *Paths of Glory*, Col. Dax may elicit strong sympathetic identification, and Lt. Roget's cowardice and perfidy may elicit antipathy. These effects, however, pale by comparison to what happens in the attack on the Ant Hill, in the court martial and executions, and in the concluding scene, with Dax's reflection upon the experiences of terror and release evinced by the soldiers he commands. The extended character development of Joker in *Full Metal Jacket*, particularly in the concluding scenes, distances him much more strongly by comparison.

Though several characters weave in and out of the narrative fabric more than others, the dominant form of characterization in *The Thin Red Line* is one of fragmentary, transient presence curtailed by death and by the flux of military deployment. No single character's nature elicits our identification absolutely. The chaotic attack on the Japanese hilltop position dissipates point of view and continuity of action, rendering American and Japanese soldiers alike as the victims of the frenetic violence that engulfs them, which is an aspect of the scene that Richard Misek analyzes effectively (2008, pp. 116–123).

The interchangeability of Capt. Willard and Col. Kurtz, and the irrelevance of political purpose derived from the logic of the war in Coppola's *Apocalypse Now!* combine to undermine character identification as either good or evil, likeable or detestable.

Strategy #12: *Avoid fixing blame or hate-worthiness upon individuals, nations, or institutions.* In Weir's *Gallipoli*, it is easy to blame the British generals for the pointless sacrifice of the Australian brigade. This focus upon their blameworthiness detracts from the more important dramatic element, Frank Dunne's indifference to the attraction of glory and adventure in war. That indifference builds upon his rational fear of being killed, in contrast to his friends who, deluded by their own youthful adventurousness, talk Frank into enlisting along with them.

Similarly, it is easy to blame the French generals in *Paths of Glory* for the disastrous attack on the fortified enemy stronghold and for the gratuitous execution of three soldiers as scapegoats. Ultimately, the concluding scene of the German woman singing in the café imparts an indelible reflection upon the broader context of soldiers at war that overwhelms these easier targets for moral disdain.

Strategy #13: *Broach the meaning of war independent of the historical context of particular wars, as an arena of behavior that affords us a sobering contemplation on human existence.* In the opening images of *The Thin Red Line*, A crocodile slips slowly and silently into green, algae-filled water, disappearing beneath the surface while an ominous, descending musical cue intones for the first time. That same musical cue repeats later when battle looms. A troop ship glides through still ocean waters, transporting its cargo of soldiers toward Guadalcanal. A wounded and bloodied soldier crawls steadily toward safety. A hatchling fallen from its nest struggles meekly and hopelessly to rise upright. A soldier crawling through deep grassy cover comes face to face with a viper; snake and man weave back and forth facing each other, each looking for a way around imminent danger.

A soldier on patrol with two comrades lies at the base of a tree, paralyzed with fear. Looking up, he sees a large lizard clinging upside-down onto the tree bark a few feet above him. The lizard, like the soldier, remains motionless, presuming to be less vulnerable to looming danger. An owl shifts his head to the side, then up to get a better view of three soldiers who stealthily make their way along a jungle river.

The soldier in command of the patrol looks up to see a wide-eyed bat hanging upside down above him. He then sees a swarm of the bats staring intently at the strange creatures below. Along the jungle river, brush seems to move into the waters. The movement of the brush turns out to be the stealthy movement of a force of camouflaged enemy soldiers.

These instances of pairing soldiers and warships with animals that capture their significance metaphorically are among the elements that Terence Malick imbues in characters, details, and events to adapt James Jones' literary source for the film, *The Thin Red Line* as has been discussed in the commentary on the film (Kline, 2000, pp. 137–144; Power, 2003, pp. 147–159). Another of Malick's contributions infuses voice-over monologues by ten different speakers into the narrative drift of scenes, but mostly unanchored in the diegesis: Col. Tall, Capt. Staros, Pvt. Train, Pvt. Bell, Pvt. Witt, and, briefly, Pvt. Doll, Pvt. Dale, Sgt. Welsh, Marty Bell and an unidentified, half-buried dead Japanese soldier.

James Morrison and Thomas Schur compare Malick's use of character voice-over in this film with voice-over narrative in his previous films (2003, pp. 26–27). The private voices in *The Thin Red Line* intone differently from how their characters speak in depicted action. Their thoughts give us a glimpse into their private reflections, revealing why they act as they do. Col. Tall bristles over his stalled career. He envisions his successful leadership of the assault on Hill 210 as vindication. Tall is ashamed of his son's lack of ambition. He sees an ersatz lineage in the men who serve his goal well, those who are willing to sacrifice all for his sake. Capt. Staros prays that he not fail his men, but Tall's need for redeeming battle victory overrules Staros' dedication to preserving the lives of his men.

Whereas commissioned officers think in terms of the larger picture, sergeants worry about their immediate charges. Sgt. Welsh consoles his inability to save men from dying by repeating thoughts of not caring as a kind of reverse mantra. If he could assure himself of being divorced from attachments, he would not suffer the pain of losing men. At one point, Welsh utters the same bitterly ironic sentiment of Sgt. McCron—that soldiers are just dirt and that the war is about property. This tenuous posture of being beyond caring contradicts the interest Welsh takes in Witt, his intervention on behalf of a soldier taken sick on the brink of attack, and his reckless dash through enemy fire to provide a dying man the release of morphine. Welsh solemnly lectures Witt that only by being a member of something—a community, a company— can he be something, but then concludes the lecture with the opposite view, that one is always alone nevertheless.

Witt tells Welsh that he sees through Welsh's disclaimers, which Welsh does not dispute. Though Witt insists that he has seen an alternative to the world governed by war, namely in the peaceful simple Melanesian village life he had discovered while AWOL, Witt had evidence that men and boys there routinely became embroiled in fighting over small matters. Both men construct philosophical orientations of self and world as means of coping. Each admires the other more than he is able to confess. Each sees the illusion of the other's thinking without gaining that reflective understanding of his own thoughts as susceptible to illusion as well.

Understanding the subtleties in the relationship between the two characters will suffice to avoid Simon Critchley's simplifying interpretation of the film as posing the philosophical opposition between Welsh's belief in there being only physical causes at work in the world and Witt's belief in a spiritual reality (2009, pp. 18–20). The dynamic of hope and despair is one that each man knows from both ends of the spectrum. What they share and acknowledge in each other is the need to explore both ends of that polarity to find answers in the world of destruction that envelopes them both.

Soldiers who face death unavoidably have thoughts about the meaning of life and existence. These thoughts are unattached to historical or situational context. The broader context of strategy and the chain of command fall away as ephemeral and irrelevant. Pvt. Doll ponders the sudden transgression of normal morality once he realizes that he killed a man. Pvt. Dale cauterizes the confrontation with horror by defiling enemy corpses. He's not able to sustain this forced eventually weeping uncontrollably as he discards the gold teeth he's pried from the mouths of dead Japanese soldiers.

The memory of intimacy with the woman he loves sustains Pvt. Bell through the immediacy of death and horror. Pvt. Witt recollects how his mother died. He looks into the eyes of dying men for the glimmer of departure that he might have seen in her passing. This thought explains how Witt would have been inspired to go AWOL and serendipitously discover a simple, peaceful life in a Melanesian village—ostensibly, a place where he would have been content to live out the war and the rest of his days. Witt's yearning for serene passing explains his detached bravery. It also explains how he finally invites his own killing.

Even without the advantage of translation, we have no trouble comprehending the meaning of the Japanese soldier who approaches Witt when Japanese troops surround Witt. The Japanese soldier's anguished speech is meant to beseech Witt to surrender and to implore him not to attack, contrary to Critchley's reading (Ibid., p. 23). Witt contemplates his opportunity, looks up into the light of the sky, and then languidly raises his weapon, knowing that that action will precipitate his death. He chooses to die rather than surrender—not out of aversion to capitulation, but to witness for himself the light for which he searches in the eyes of the dying men he has seen.

Contrary to one reading of Witt, that he would be the man who not only goes AWOL but also thrives as a soldier, derives from the complexity of his character and does not deny the film's anti-war message, particularly if we take Witt as the primary vehicle of that message (Bersani and Dutoit, 2004, p. 141). Whereas Welsh struggles with his inability to let the heinous contingencies of combat suppress his need for fellowship, Witt has no trouble finding meaning in attending to the needs of his fellow soldiers. Both men cope with the stark reality of being soldiers at war with convoluted and illusory philosophical strategies (Michaels, 2009, pp. 69–73). It is Pvt. Train alone who, uninhibited in his abject fear, is without illusion.

Malick reserves the most profound of the film's philosophical voice-over reflections for Train, a young man who, transfixed with apprehension, babbles incoherently to his Sergeant in the bowels of the troop ship on its way to the island where gruesome battle is expected. The film's character list is long; most characters make only fleeting appearance; only by incidental context are soldiers identified by name. We can identify the voice-overs on some occasions with the concurrent images, but other times not. As Lloyd Michaels has noted, the similarity of Southern accents for Bell, Witt, and Train has contributed to confusion in the critical commentary about the identities of the voice-over speakers (Ibid., pp. 61–62). Train's soliloquies are perhaps more easily attributable to Witt. Witt is attractive, admirable, courageous and one of the few characters who links multiple scenes. Train appears only briefly, at the beginning and end of the film; he is abundantly fearful and uncharismatic. Still, close attention will confirm that the four most essential voice-overs are in Train's voice.

Malick's choice of this character to deliver the core philosophical reflections of the film is importantly counterintuitive. Some commentators on the film resign themselves not being able to identify some of the voice-over speakers, particularly the first instance that opens the film. The confusion of Train's voice for Witt's is rampant in the literature on the film. Michaels identifies the final soliloquy, which quickly follows Train's second and last appearance and dialogue in the film, as Witt "from beyond the grave." (Ibid., pp. 73, 76, 77). Others attribute Train's earlier soliloquies to Witt (Kline, 2000, pp. 141–142; Morrison and Schur, 2003, p. 26; Silberman, 2003, p. 167; Bersani and Dutoit, 2004, p. 131; Chion, 2004, pp. 69–74, 81, 86; Dreyfus and Prince, 2009, pp. 40–42). Davies attributes Train's last voice-over to Welsh (2009b, pp. 48–60).

What makes Train's central placement as the surrogate author of the film's reflections upon violence crucial is that he is a man who is openly afraid, however much reception of the film will resist that association and attribute Train's messages to soldiers who show courage. We have, in fact, no more reason to believe that the man who is afraid is any more susceptible to illusion and less inclined to wisdom than is the courageous man, which is a crucial lesson to underscore with regard to the horrors of combat.

Train experiences unadulterated fear, and expresses that fear without any shred of illusion or coping. The soldiers of the story all construct reflections to place their experiences into a context that extends their perspective beyond their immediate experience. Train's reflections penetrate the present intensely and more profoundly still. His thoughts confront the nature of being. Malick chooses to open and close the film with this voice, and to use it at two crucial junctures where Train's voice overlays images of chaotic combat. Train's soliloquies confront an unidentifiable deity without anger and without fear, but with insistent, though challenging wonder. Do darkness and light, strife and love partake equally in the design of the world? Train petitions the deity to see through his eyes, to experience what he has. What answers would there be if these experiences formed the basis for answering those questions?

Unmistakably, Train's reflections echo significant themes in the extant fragments of the Pre-Socratic Greek thinker, Heraclitus: "One should see that war is common and justice is strife, and that everything is happening according to strife and necessity" (Heraclitus, 1995, p. 35). Pvt. Train's lines also echo closely lines from William Wordsworth's *Prelude* (Wordsworth, 1967, p. 335). The substitution of "strife and love" for "tumult and peace" and Wordsworth's subject of rain and wind instead of war invoke this well-known metaphysics of Heraclitus.

The noise of the chaos and horror of an American routing of a Japanese stronghold recedes from the soundtrack of *The Thin Red Line* with the gradual crescendo of Hans Zimmer's solemn, incessant dirge. An insistently protesting counterpoint intones the inevitability of the horror and the yearning for release from it at a slow tempo that undercuts the frenetic action. Then Zimmer's music segues into the opening section of Charles Ives' *The Unanswered Question* (1906). An eerie near-silence of a string ensemble's sustained, distant notes provides the background for a solo trumpet intoning a serene, querying melody.

Michael Chion delineates how the melodic query, at first unanswered, but then inspires futilely confuted responses by concise, confident woodwind refrains that become increasingly agitated (2004, pp. 9–13). Train's commentating voice-over intones fretfully, softly, and defiantly at this point against this great evil of war. He poses unanswerable questions—reminiscent of the trumpet's query—challenging meaning and purpose in life, redemption, and divinity. Where had this destruction come from? What had been its seed? Who was delivering death to some and horror, humiliation, spiritual poisoning, and ignominy to the survivors? Do war and strife lie in the heart of nature? Does nature vie with itself? Does the land battle with the sea? Does nature avenge? Are there two powers or one?

Malick's film does not offer answers to these queries; surely, any attempt to do so would be trite. The absence of facile closure in Malick's film, in contrast to the neatly composed thematic conclusion of Steven Spielberg's *Saving Private Ryan* (1998), demonstrates what makes Spielberg highly successful in mainstream cinema, and Malick an outlier, as Michaels points out (2009, pp. 59–60). To be successful in mainstream popular film requires trite messages.

The opening and closing images of *The Thin Red Line* embody Heraclitean oppositions. The crocodile slips from land into muddy water—an animal capable of sudden savage violence, at home and thriving in that muddy world of death and rebirth. Destruction always marks the possibility of rebirth. In the concluding image, a coconut lies at water's edge on the vast empty island beach. The woody nut has sprouted, and a short stem has grown out, its single leaf fluttering gently in the wind. This peaceful location, however, obviously will not sustain growth. The absurd isolation of the seed—where the sea will wash it away from its precarious placement on the shifting edge of land to become absorbed into the organic residue of the sea—reflects this same ubiquitous conflict of strife and love. Rebirth is always subject to the sudden intrusion of destruction.

Critical commentary on Malick's films regularly notes that he studied philosophy, with focus on the writings of Heidegger, having translated one Heidegger text. We can understand Train's meditation in terms that Martin Heidegger elaborates regarding an important fragment of Heraclitus' sayings. Heidegger's influence is evident in *The Thin Red Line* (Heidegger, 1975, pp. 59–78). The filmmaker, however, has not explicitly elaborated the connection between his cinema and his philosophical background. Attempts to make that connection on his behalf have mostly gotten no further than broad generalities about Heidegger's writings and Malick's films. Morrison and Schur (2003, pp. 68–69, 97–100), along with Marc Furstenau and Leslie MacAvoy (2003, pp. 173–185), delve in vague association of Heideggerian thought with the film. In contrast to this vague association with Heidegger's thought, Hubert Dreyfus and Camilo Salazar Prince are able to construct useful insights into *The Thin Red Line* with just one point of departure from Heidegger and another from the Nineteenth Century Danish existentialist philosopher, Søren Kierkegaard (Dreyfus and Prince, 2009, pp. 30–43).

Train's meditation is out of time and out of place—not just casual musings transposed into voice-over. Train's questions sequester what life gathers from the experience of the most imaginably fiery storm of being—combat. Fateful experience lays bare for soldiers what the hard core of existence has laid upon mortals. "War," Heraclitus says: "is the father of all, the king of all, and he has shown some as gods, others as human beings; he has made some slaves, others free" (1995, p. 23). Witt sought the divine, the soldiers were all mortal, and all were enslaved. Train's soliloquies speak for all of them—they would be able to find deliverance only in the *thoughtfully questioning* confrontation with existence.

The soldiers' philosophical musings shield them against debilitating terror. Heidegger says that not opening up to or forgetting the essence of this fiery being obscures being. From the outset, the history of Western philosophy and the civilization it reflects, beginning with the ancient Greeks, abstained from the meditation on being. In its forgetfulness, this civilization has unleashed overwhelming force from its probing of being-as-it-finds-it in the

structures of the natural world, grasping it only scientifically and technologi-
cally. This has provided monumental danger without redemption (Heidegger,
1975, p. 76).

3. Conclusion

Within the genre of American war films runs a countercurrent of anti-war war
films that shows war for what it is and for what it means to soldiers. The employment of anti-war messages will entail resistance to conventional structures
of character development, narrative, and message that the film industry has
found successful in marketing its product, particularly pandering to the easy
reactions of celebrating courageous vindication against despicable enemies.

Amy Coplan's fine essay on the cinematic textures of *The Thin Red Line*
establishes how Malick employs the potential of the medium to diverge from
standard narrative and cognitive regimen of mainstream cinema (2009, pp.
65–86). Perception of these elements contrary to mainstream genre definition
tends to be lost in the study of these films that aim to place their content within a perceived spectrum of political-ideological positions. Focus upon genre
or social-historical circumstances of the production of these films obscures
perception of these elements. There are numerous examples of this sort of
misreading of the clear intention of Malick's film. (McCormick, 1999, pp.
46–49; Rambuss, 1999, pp. 97–125; Suid, 2002, pp. 523–529, 637–638; Donald, 2005, pp. 20–28; Polan, 2005, pp. 53–61; Westwell, 2006, p. 109).

The broad-scope sort of film studies approach tends to define a salient
attribute in the simplest fashion to facilitate compiling lists of examples that
share that trait, while missing important particularities of how some of those
examples may generate depth and complexity in that regard while others do
not. Jeanine Basinger, along with other film studies scholars, has developed
articulations of the war film genre (Kane 1982, pp. 13–23; Basinger, 1986,
pp. 15–82). Thus, a film is as easily labeled "anti-war" as being "a film about
infantry" or "a film about air battles." Genre generalizations invariably gloss
over just *how* a film composes a message regarding war. Determining whether
that message emerges intelligently or tritely, however, comes from examining
in some depth the *how* of the construction.

The thirteen traits delineated above are not so much a set of criteria that
defines a form or a genre as a beginning set of an expandable list of inventive
compositional strategies. Careful reading of a film reveals indelible anti-war
content wherein the direct portrayal of the experience of horror undermines
the warrior cult. Importantly, these strategies are not simple negations of traditionally recognized traits of the war film genre. These traits will also help to
identify how some war films fail as anti-war films, in spite of intention, and
how some anti-war elements can occur in films that may otherwise fail to
register as anything other than part of the war film genre that vaguely glorifies

war. In either case, such readings will contradict much of the continuing assumptions and commentary on war films.

A good example of a failed anti-war war film is Dalton Trumbo's *Johnny Got His Gun* (1971). Trumbo's film does not engage any of the strategies listed in any more than a fleeting fashion. The focus of the story is the stream of consciousness of a horribly mutilated soldier allowed to live under the supposition of being brain dead and hence worthy of preservation for the sake of medical science. His predicament, however, bears no necessary relationship with injury from combat. Neither does the story explore the experiences of being a soldier in combat.

The crux of the story would be the same had the hapless protagonist been a victim of disease or an industrial accident. The sole intimation of anti-war sentiment lies in the concluding titles on black screen listing the millions of individuals maimed or dead from warfare during the twentieth century. From the standpoint of the story, though, the culprit in the horrible prolongation of his life is the military physician who allowed it on the false supposition of the victim being brain dead. The message that the film may impart regarding war is to be wary of being eager to volunteer to serve in a war lest such a horrible fate happen to you. This amounts to no more than an extraordinary example of scare tactics.

Though having enjoyed a long, successful career writing screenplays in Hollywood Trumbo's one directorial effort demonstrates that experience writing screenplays alone is not sufficient to guarantee the filmmaker's mastery of the medium. Clarity of meaning relies upon mastery of the art that makes more intelligently penetrating cinema possible.

Critical and scholarly commentary of popular film has tended to assume a low level of intelligence being necessary to its creation and its broad comprehension by audiences. However much the film industry may encourage that assessment, the medium and its culture are far from absolutely devoid of exceptional cinema. Critical commentary that fails to perceive the difference between appeal to the lowest level of comprehension and exceptional cinema will contribute to the further hegemony of the dominant forces in film culture that promulgate the glorification of war because it sells well. The antidote for scholarly treatment is to persevere *all the way through to the end* of a completed comprehension, which means not pulling up short, not being satisfied with comprehending anything less than the full depths of meaning (Cavell, 1981, p. 37).

The easiest way to pull up short in the reading of a film is to declare an interest in the philosophical content only, which will focus upon literal content and tend to restrict attention to isolated instances of dialogue and plot. That sort of fixation readily misses the fusion of language, action, and drama with the potential for visual poetry that masters of the medium employ as essential to the composition of meaning and message. With the flood of philosophical explorations of films looking for their philosophical content, it is reassuring to see emerging criticism of philosophers' associations that happen to come to mind while sitting in a movie theatre (Mullarkey, 2009, pp. 15–28).

Similarly, the pronouncement to take film seriously as philosophy invariably relies upon the rhetorical content being understandable as rich enough to supply illustration of philosophical concepts and the more sophisticated argumentative strategy of thought experiments (Shaw 2009, pp. 5–6; Wartenberg, 2009, pp. 3–4). This guarantees that the proclamation to take film seriously *as philosophy* means anything but taking the *art* of cinema seriously. Fixation upon films that obliterate the continuity of human existence— typically through heavy reliance upon montage or special effects—may emulate the philosophical technique of the thought experiment. However, they do so only by virtue of creating a locus for drama alienated from the exigencies of human existence by creating enormous metaphysical fissures within the depicted continuity of human experience, which has garnered attention from philosophers eager to contemplate metaphysically variant existence (Grau, 2005). Enlisting this sort of film to provide an introduction for collegiate youth to the relevance of contemporary philosophical discourse does not show the ancient discipline in a flattering light.

Since the cinematic narrative is composed of images and rhythms, visual metaphor, narrative structure, character development, and drama, the predisposition to see only the explicit clues of philosophical-political stance will paradoxically ensure missing the philosophical challenges embedded in the substance of cinema. Telltale signs of this shortcoming are the inability to construe subtlety, irony, and the critical fixation upon concluding events in a film as insufficiently optimistic or pessimistic.

The standard philosophical analytical tool of clarifying the underlying general principle logically subsumed by a line of dialogue abets shallow interpretation of characterizations. Characterizations in cinema, literature, and drama, however, are ordinarily complex enough to include the capability of human beings to encompass full-fledged contradictory thoughts, inclinations, and actions. Similarly, relying upon the popular reception of a film reneges on the promise of philosophy to settle on the truth. What amounts to reifying the least intelligent reaction imaginable insists upon the reading of a film that will miss all but its blunt impact, which serves too easily as an excuse for being satisfied with blunt reactions in place of thoughtful study of the meaning of a film.

Exceptional cinema delivers substantial meaning even if not all who view it will be able to comprehend it completely. This is especially true in an era when reactionary politics rely upon manipulation of resentment for those with sophisticated intellect, and delivering messages bluntly for the sake of the non-edified reactionary forces of the culture. The non-edified forces will always align most easily with reactionary political forces.

The rejection of the glorification of war and violence, on the contrary, requires elevating the medium beyond conditioned responses that hold sway through repetition of blunt affects. As long as the war-film genre prevails in the depiction of war by conditioning its audience to expect and crave the emotional triggers for glorification of war, resorting to pacifist conditioning of different responses will necessarily fail. The films with enduring impact are those with the greatest depth. Hence, what we see in interesting anti-war war films are not systematic, repeatable conditioning of a contrary inclination, but an open-ended set of inventive, thoughtful strategies.

As with the *1812 Overture*, the glorification of war does not arise automatically with the simple depiction of war. Glorification arises from intentional construction according to reliable formulae, with the expectation of aligning audience sympathies. Kenneth Rose explores the discrepancy between the experience of combat in World War II and its depiction in mainstream Hollywood movies (Rose, 2008, pp. 164–174). Similarly, the anti-war war film agenda will not be able to rely upon sure-fire methods and images. More so than the established genre formulae for the glorification of war, strategies for the anti-war message need to be inventive and to elicit intelligent—instead of a predictably emotive—audience reaction. Anti-war war films strive to reverse the momentum of the conditioned reception of the war film genre. The examples identified above of strategies employed in war films to deliver anti-war messages provide evidence for the cogency of an elevated encounter with an audience of thoughtful viewers instead of passive receptacles for programmed responses.

We may witness a predilection among veterans of war to endorse subsequent wars. Nevertheless, no greater or more profound argument can be made against war than that which derives from direct experience of war's temporal and enduring horrors—testimony that can also be found vehemently expressed by war veterans. There are those for whom the combat experience is transcendent, and who are unabashed, even philosophical, in their longing for it. By comparison, life at peace engenders anguished ennui for them. Horrendous loss and sacrifice for some will not cancel out the meaningful exhilaration of confronting one's own trial of heroism and loyalty versus cowardice and betrayal under circumstances of absolute danger. J. Glenn Gray attributes this exhilaration to the nature of being human (1967).

We must wonder how this sort of trial could best occasion courage in any meaningful sense. Are there not better avenues to exercise this profound need other than the ones that entail violence and risk of death? Plato's discussion of courage first asserts that wisdom must inform courage for it to be different from foolhardiness. Further, military courage need not be the sole model of courage. Courage finds its best exemplifications where intelligence is the stronger defining element (Plato, 1963, pp. 134–141). Ralph Waldo Emerson perceived the ambivalent ideal of the impulsiveness necessary for a heroic military act (Emerson, 2000, p. 229). The cogent counterargument to the existential thrill of combat experience amounts to comparison with less than lofty resonance:

every time I have a tough day . . . or I get upset about something, I just ask myself . . . Am I being shot at? Is anyone going to be wounded as a result of what has gone wrong today? Is this life or death, or is it something that will [fade] in time? (Campbell, 2009b)

Given the dominant tendency among veterans to endorse militarism and war, the courage and integrity of those veterans who oppose future wars, based on their experiences, will be self-evident. Similarly, those filmmakers who explicitly undermine the war-glorifying strategies and reactions that the viewing audience expects war films to indulge, do so knowing that this will garner ire and misinterpretation.

Teaching anti-war war film will find the best models in what proves important in teaching film, literature, philosophy, art, and the humanities in general. For many, watching films is a passive experience. Instructors are often tempted use a film to instill an attitude or point of view in the manner of administrating a treatment or a drug. Using a different approach, instructors sometimes show students a film, and then wait for reactions, content with whatever they may be. Both approaches fail to achieve significant intellectual engagement and inspire only minimal comprehension. As with choice of literary texts, in choosing films for a course of instruction, one looks for films with sufficient depth, eloquence, profundity, complexity, and relevance to present a challenge for study and exploration. That engagement will be constructive as it builds supple skill in interpretation that relies upon careful mastery of the film, not just willfully prejudicial associations.

First and foremost, an instructor needs to master the structures of meaning in a film in order to be able to teach it, just as teaching a philosophical text requires mastering its discourse and arguments. Mastering cinema does not arise just from having studied philosophy. Having studied literature is a much better preparatory background for studying cinema, but also not sufficient in itself to grant facility with meaning in the visual narrative. Practice in the study of cinema is borne of careful encounters with the rich meaning that can occur in a film worth studying. Any text—or film—easily summarized in a single statement of meaning, by a simple interpretation, or by a single argument will not provide fruitful opportunity for study and growth.

Teaching arts and letters will always be a matter of promoting intelligence and learnedness. This is as important in teaching cinema as it is in teaching philosophy. The combination of the subjects bears a compound demand. Teaching peace likewise will rely upon promoting intelligence—and how could we expect it to be otherwise?

Exceptional anti-war war films will be those that promote intelligence about human experience with violence by posing intelligent challenges for their comprehension. These will be films whose authorial voice lays waiting for discovery in the intricacies of the expressive cinematic art. Teaching these films will rely on how well an instructor can command their complex structures of meaning, understand the filmmakers' strategies, and then put students in a position to embark upon making these same discoveries. The learning outcomes will depend much more on how well an instructor can meet the challenge than on which films an instructor chooses to explore.

Instilling in students an appreciation for careful, detailed observation and insight into the cinematic text creates practice in film-going experience that encourages not capitulating immediately to beliefs and feelings that are willingly and easily manipulated. That outcome will also be conducive to teaching peace.

Ten

THE POWER OF SONG FOR NONVIOLENT TRANSFORMATIVE ACTION

Colleen Kattau

The song is not a product. The song exists as a way to get to the singing. And the singing is not a product. The singing exists to form the community.
Bernice Johnson Reagan, *Sojourners Magazine*, 2004

These songs bind us together, give us courage together, help us to march together.
Dr. Martin Luther King, Jr., *Why We Can't Wait*, 1963

Politics can be strengthened by music, but music has a potency that defies politics.
Nelson Mandela, *Long Walk to Freedom*, 1995

1. Introduction

Popular music has been integral to social justice actions in the Americas (Fairley, 1989; Lieberman, 1989; Peddie, 2006). Songs of social commitment, as other art genres dedicated to justice, are vital to achieve transformative action that underlies nonviolent change. This chapter discusses the purpose and function of song regarding earlier social justice movements of Labor and Civil Rights and the more recent United States Army School of the Americas (SOA) Watch effort to close Western Hemisphere Institute for Security Cooperation (WHINSEC, formerly United States Army School of the Americas). It also examines what is generally termed *nueva canción* or new song, a flourishing of socially conscious music that was concurrent with the liberation struggles in Central and South America during the latter half of the twentieth century and which continues in contemporary cultural production in the Americas.

2. Theoretical Considerations

Many writers have studied the utility and meaning of music within social movements and how singing and group struggle have gone hand-in-hand for centuries (Bird, 1985; Eyerman, 1998; Reagon, 2001; Peddie, 2006; Reebee, 2006). Songs have always been an integral component of consolidating collective power and chronicling events in social change activism. Ron Eyerman and Andrew Jamison argue that song is an essential element of social transformation because it serves a ritualistic purpose (1988, p. 34). Ritual, in turn, is a principal way to rebel against and resist imposed ideas and to conceive alternatives to such imposition.

As part of its ritualistic nature, song operates mnemonically in that it rallies collective identity by resonating with popular sentiment, providing a means to mobilize shared traditions even after the political context that gave rise to the song has changed. It also links past and present events and struggles. In its ritualistic function, song serves as a conduit through which emotion and feeling can be expressed linguistically and non-linguistically. It provides a space for fleshing out and dealing with difficult issues and incidents.

While this chapter is concerned primarily with the music and lyrics of what are generally termed folk songs, examples of this creative capacity abound in other music genres as well. In its mobilizing capability, Eyerman and Jamison argue that song is an extension of Jean-Françoise Lyotard's notion of narrative knowledge that both documents a remembered past, also transforms it and infuses it with different meanings. To take Lyotard's idea one step further, song also functions as narrative knowledge within a remembered *present*, since the immediacy of song in specific sociopolitical contexts helps create and solidify resistance to experienced crises "in the moment" as well.

I argue, in the examples to follow, that the capacity of song to document lived experience, both individually and collectively, is crucial to social movement mobilization. Like other cultural practices such as visual art, poetry, theater, and film, song offers a space for collective identification and expression of commonly held values and attitudes.

Like other cultural practices, song plays a significant role in shaping beliefs and ideas. In this sense, Murray Edelman's assertion that visual art "creates realities and worlds" also holds true for music (1995, p. 8). More than merely reflect common realities, songs help shape and define them by describing and naming experience in an open-ended, non-determinant way and by tapping into and expanding rational and emotional aspects of human existence.

Linguistic and non-verbal elements unite in song to make for a multifaceted sensory experience by providing informational content on a conscious level through lyric and also tapping into non-verbal areas of subjectivity through melody, rhythm, instrumentation, and the interaction of all these with lyric. Those of us who participate in the process of listening to or partaking in song attest to the physicality and emotionality of the experience, which connects us to others in often profound and fundamental ways.

If this is the case within any genre of music, then it is equally if not more true in the case of lyric-based music within social movements where we find an advocacy of and adhesion to similarly held goals and ideas. A song collectively sung for instance, offers a unique moment in which people virtually sing with one voice. There is power in that communal recitation of shared knowledge.

The power of song also derives in part from lyric and melody allowing for multiple interpretations by listeners and participants. Their interpretation is further broadened and altered over time as new contexts and situations arise. In his essay, "*La Paquita del Barrio*," on the music of Mexican singer, Francisca Viveros Barradas, David William Foster, whose research interests focus on urban culture in Latin America, emphasizes what many music movement theorists affirm: "the enormously complex ways in which cultural production takes place and the multiple levels of interpretation it sets into motion" (2000, p. 4). This complexity cannot be underestimated or dismissed.

Paradoxically, these manifold meanings also have the effect of uniting people in a dialectic interchange between individual understanding and shared recognition. Songs can be interpreted in more than one way largely because of their primordial quality as a basic form of human expression. Like language itself, further amplified through non-linguistic aspects of melody and rhythm, songs have an expansive quality that opens us up to possibility. For social change movements then, whose very nature is to challenge and change the given order of things, music is useful for inspiring creativity and vision.

We can also view song as an aspect of what earth-centered author and activist Starhawk calls "imaginative action" in that, like other art forms, music parallels what nonviolent direct action within social movement accomplishes (2002–2009). Her list of what direct action does includes creating awareness, making injustice more visible, de-legitimizing unjust power (as it did for instance during the United States labor and Civil Rights movements), building solidarity and collective action, educating and fortifying opposition to injustice, legitimizing alternative voices, and demanding more transparency within hidden structures and institutions of power.

Song reinforces the goals of nonviolent direct action, which denounces injustice and inequality while simultaneously advocating for what ought to be by proffering a collective medium of expression that engenders hope and that declares that a better world is possible. Imaginative action has been essential to many social change efforts in the Americas such as work stoppages organized by the Industrial Workers of the World (IWW, aka Wobblies), Civil Rights sit-ins, women's peace encampments, vast mobilizations against violence and war, and "crossing the line" at SOA Watch vigils in Fort Benning, Georgia. These are just a few examples of peaceful civil disobedience practices that have been accompanied by songs, mainly collectively sung. Regardless of success, no social change movement has happened without music, since artistic creation is arguably as essential as any other basic human need.

3. Song in the United States Civil Rights Movement

An overview of music within social movements in the United States shows how song helps to sustain them and adds to their success, and how it influences individual and collective self-determination and identity. Enslaved Africans used coded songs and drumbeats to provoke rebellion and offer hope for freedom. The songs that emerged from conditions of slavery were often based on biblical tales of bondage and escape. As W. E. B. DuBois indicates in his decisive essay, "Of the Sorrow Songs," these heritage songs were both African (melody) and European (lyric) in origin (1953; 2003). That slave melodies are "far more ancient than the words," holds the essence of their power and resonance in expressing unspeakable brutality and indignities. That expression restores dignity and humanity by providing a space for memory and hope for the future (2003, p. xiii). The conditions of bondage within which those sorrow songs were created and sung is why, according to DuBois, music "remains as the singular spiritual heritage of the nation and the greatest gift of the Negro people" (2003, p. 253). That these songs are one of the first hybrid cultural forms in the United States—a distinct combining of both African and European cultural elements—underscores their importance within that spiritual and cultural heritage.

"Follow the Drinking Gourd," one of many African American slave songs, is emblematic of how many songs endure over time precisely because they effectively fulfill a mnemonic and ritualistic function. Songs such as "Follow the Drinking Gourd" link past and present struggles and remind us of the incomplete nature of freedom and justice. The song advises the listener to follow the Big Dipper north to "heaven," code for Canada:

> When the sun comes up and the first quail calls,
> Follow the drinking gourd
> For the old man is waiting for to carry you to freedom,
> Follow the drinking gourd

The "old man" in the song refers to abolitionist Harriet Tubman disguised to protect her identity in her work of liberation. The song provides useful information for the traveler, what path to follow, what river to ford, and other information crucial to the journey north. Its instructional narrative preserves the memory of slavery and offers the possibility of liberation. The last word before the refrain (normally a place of privilege in poetry and song), is "freedom." The achievement of freedom here requires both individual responsibility (to follow instruction and the signs of nature), and trust that "the old man," like the North Star, is unwavering and will be there at the end of the journey.

"Follow the Drinking Gourd" is illustrative of the broad reach of songs created within a specific social milieu that are so powerful that they maintain great meaning for audiences far removed from their original context. While the words of this song refer to a specific goal, other "sorrow song" lyrics are more general. Their content is metaphoric and allows them to be recalled and modified in later social movements. This process, identified by Eyerman and Jamison as the "mobilization of tradition," is best illustrated in the Civil Rights movement of the 1950s and 1960s in the United States, which, "for a brief moment made it possible for black music to bring a new kind of truth into American society, a redemptive, visionary, even emancipatory truth" (1998, p.

44). These modified songs provided a significant bridge for remembering the horrors of slavery and anticipating the possibility of just and moral change.

As the Civil Rights Movement flourished during the late 1950s and 1960s, so too did the songs that were crucial to the movement. Bernice Johnson Reagon, singer and founder of the music group Sweet Honey in the Rock, emphasizes the power of singing to ease tensions and create unity among disparate groups working together within the struggle for civil rights. As essential parts of a continuous oral tradition, songs of the Civil Rights era were a way to motivate, unify, and allay apprehension. Music created a sense of community and offered comfort from the fear of knowing that one could be beaten, jailed, or killed in doing the work of nonviolent direct action (Reagon, 2001). The title of Reagon's *If You Don't Go, Don't Hinder Me*, is taken from an African American spiritual sung during enslaved times. It starts with the verse (2001):

> I'm on my way to Canaan land
> I'm on my way to Canaan land
> I'm on my way to Canaan land
> I'm on my way, great God, I'm on my way

No longer needing to sing in code, the word "freedom" eventually replaced "Canaan" during the Civil Rights period. The song also reflected the importance of individual incentive for collective struggle and underscored the personal risk involved in opting to join the movement. The song's title and lyrics emphasize that someone who commits to social justice struggle is a role model for others to follow. It also expresses that this significant decision shifts the committed person in a permanent sense. In its new context of Civil Rights, leaving one place for another as the song suggests became a metaphor for the challenge of direct action:

> You did not leave town geographically, but rather stayed and moved yourself through new behaviors and challenges, throwing your life up against a system and demanding that it fall so that something different could take its place. (Reagon, 2001, p. 5)

The haunting melody of the best-known anthem of the Civil Rights movement, "We Shall Overcome," also originates in slave times. It originates in the pre-Civil War song, "No More Auction Block for Me." Decades later, this melody was used in a gospel song with the lyrics "I will overcome some day." From its gospel origins, the song found its way to become an anthem of labor struggles of the 1930s. Then, at the Highlander Folk School, where labor and civil rights activists came together in a unique bond to train and strategize for social change, the song was once more altered, becoming "We shall overcome." This song, perhaps more than any other, can be considered a bridge song—this time between labor and civil rights. The melody—a sorrow song—born of slavery provides its enduring quality and deep resonance.

Versions of this hymn being altered over time illustrates what folk legend Pete Seeger calls "the folk process" (MacDonald, 2005). The songs change to accommodate and define new circumstances, yet continue to reference the past (either reverently or irreverently). Songs modified by the folk process often have no definitive author or editor since the process itself usually means that a collective effort (conscious or otherwise) led to the song's alteration.

4. Songs in the United States Labor Movement

Labor struggles of the late nineteenth and early twentieth century in the United States are well documented in song. Music played a vital role within the most potent early labor movements. In 1908, the IWW published a little red book called *Songs to Fan the Flames of Discontent* that included labor anthems still sung today, such as, "The Internationale," "There is Power in a Union," "Solidarity Forever," and "The Rebel Girl." Songs such as these make plain the connection between militarism and capitalist exploitation of working people. They directly ridicule institutions such as industry, church, and police.

While many Wobblies songs are oppositional, they argue for solidarity and collective struggle to create a better world through participatory organization and overcoming differences. They describe the violence perpetrated on working people who try to organize for fair wages and decent working conditions, yet they do not advocate violence in response. Instead, they promote tough direct action tactics (strikes, work stoppage, sabotaging the factory line, organizing unions) that require unity in numbers.

"The Wobblies were a singing movement without peer in American labor history" (Bird, Georgakas, and Shaffer, 1985, p. 21). Like the songs of the Civil Rights movement, Wobblies songs were meant to be sung by crowds instead of individuals which encouraged group participation and strengthened collective resolve. One of the most famous Wobbly songs for group singing, "The Preacher and the Slave," was written by Joe Hill, the IWW's most well-known lyricist. Born Joseph Hillstrom in Sweden, Hill came to the United States to organize workers. He used song to rally people to join the union. "The Preacher and the Slave," a parody of "In the Sweet By and By," satirizes the Salvation Army, which promised a better life in heaven while ignoring the wretched conditions for working people on earth:

> Long-haired preachers come out every night
> Try to tell you what's wrong and what's right

But when you ask them for something to eat
They will answer in voices so sweet

You will eat by and by
In that glorious land beyond the sky (way up high)
Work and pray, live on hay
You'll get pie in the sky when you die (that's a lie).

In satirizing cultural imposition, this song, as with many produced by Hill and the other Wobbly songwriters, takes on the dominant discourses. In this case, the song transforms the discourse of religious proselytizing to expose its hypocrisy and contradiction.

Hill affirmed that the mobilizing power of song as an organizing strategy is stronger than brochures and broadsides because of its ability to be readily memorized and repeated. In a December 1914 issue of *Solidarity* he says:

If a person can put a few cold common sense facts in a song, and dress them up in a cloak of humor to take the dryness off of them he will succeed in reaching a great number of workers who are too unintelligent or too indifferent to read a pamphlet or an editorial on economic science. (Eyerman, 1998, p. 59)

Songs communicate directly and articulate the experience of exploitation in ways with which poorly educated people can access and identify.

In 1915, Joe Hill was framed for murder and executed by a firing squad in Utah. His life is commemorated in the song, "Joe Hill" (Alfred Hayes/Earl Robinson, 1936). This song's first person narrative describes meeting Joe in a dream where Joe assures the singer, "what they can never kill went on to organize. . . . In every mine and mill, where working folks defend their rights it's there you'll find Joe Hill." As in other tribute songs, the leader's death is mourned, honored, and made to serve as an impetus for continuing the struggle for justice. In this way, Joe Hill the individual actor is summoned as a symbol of all collective action and a reminder to the working class that its duty is to continue the struggles of others that came before. This song then, as with many labor songs, stresses continuity in struggle, links past successes and injustices to present realities, and relies on memory to create a sense of community and shared goals.

5. The "Singin'est Movement": The SOA Watch Vigil and Protest

The songs of the Civil Rights and Labor movements continue to be sung and transformed within contemporary social contexts. Song, puppetry, and visual arts play a central role in the ongoing movement to close the SOA, a military training school for Latin American soldiers. (The school was formerly called

The U.S. Army School of the Americas, but was renamed Western Hemisphere Institute for Security Cooperation [WHINSEC] in 2002).

Graduates of WHINSEC have been implicated in major human rights violations, including the assassination of Salvadoran Archbishop Oscar Romero and the massacre at El Mozote in El Salvador in the 1980s. More recently (2005), they were accused of the massacre that occurred in the San Jose de Apartado Peace Community in Colombia.

In 1990, Fr. Roy Bourgeois founded SOA Watch, a national organization based in Washington, D.C.; its purpose was to demand closure of WHINSEC. Each November since 1990, SOA Watch organizes a protest and vigil at the gates of Fort Benning, Georgia, where WHINSEC is currently located. The vigil symbolically commemorates the assassination of six Jesuit priests, their housekeeper, and her daughter, who were also victims of SOA graduates. The vigil also mourns the tens of thousands of other Latin Americans who have suffered at the hands of men trained at the school.

Since 1990, when only a handful of people protested at the gates, the movement has grown to become the largest continuous nonviolent action movement since the Civil Rights era. With 20,000 protesters each year, it has become a vast organizational and strategizing meeting place for dozens of progressive religious, labor, Latin American, and peace organizations.

Pete Seeger terms the SOA Watch vigil "the singin'ist movement in the Americas." Music is everywhere at the gathering as a formally structured part of planned events and as an informal part of the weekend, with many participants singing and playing instruments. At the Saturday rally, music is interspersed with a vast array of diverse speakers. Some performances are individual and some participatory.

While the main stage musician's collective provides most of the songs and invites listeners to sing along, collective participation is most apparent in the "Puppetista" parade that involves hundreds of volunteers who make instruments and puppets out of cardboard, wood, and paint. The street theater, which begins in the back of the gathered crowd and ends in a huge circle at the front, involves drumming and chanting of a creatively rendered story of good over evil in which people, birds, animals, and plants are the protagonists of their own liberation.

From 2006–2009, Colombian psychologist and theater director Hector Aristizabal, a torture survivor living in exile in the United States, has facilitated the pageant. Aristizabal uses methods developed by Agosto Boal's Theater of the Oppressed, which incorporates storytelling, dance, drumming and puppetry to promote healing and empowerment among the participants and the audience. Using these techniques, the puppetistas can involve masses of people in a grassroots display of the power of transformative action. Theater, like music, frees individuals to go farther in their commitment to nonviolent social change because its safe setting allows experimentation and challenges established boundaries of behavior.

I became aware of the social movement to close SOA when direct action activists in the Syracuse, New York area gave presentations and workshops to raise awareness of the school's covert existence. Inspired by this activism, in 1998, singer/songwriter Jolie Rickman and I recorded *Sing it Down: Songs to Close the School of the Americas*. For this recording, we used T-Bone Slim's "The Popular Wobbly" (a parody of the vaudeville song, "They Go Wild, Simply Wild over Me"), and altered the words to pay tribute to "prisoners of conscience" serving jail time for either crossing the line at Fort Benning or for altering signage at the entrance of the base to signal that torture techniques were advocated by the school:

> Well the SOA went wild over me.
> They say that I destroyed their property
> They say I wrecked their sign
> But to me it looked just fine
> And they went wild, simply wild over me.

The album included songs in the *nueva canción* tradition and was a mix of both satirical and somber songs. In "Romero," Jolie Rickman translated to English the words of Archbishop Oscar Romero's final sermon to create a poignant ballad that has become an emblematic song of the movement. This 1980 sermon was Romero's last before he was assassinated on the orders of Roberto D'Aubuisson, one of the most notorious graduates of the SOA. His homily is a powerful prayer for nonviolence in which he directly appealed to Salvadoran soldiers, who had been trained to kill their own compatriots, to lay down their arms:

> My brothers I assure you, you are not obliged
> To obey one who tells you to kill your people
> Now reclaim your conscience, now reclaim your people
> Even you a soldier can
> In the name of God listen to the cries of the suffering
> Rise up to the heavens
> Why? I beseech you, order you, beg you
> *Cese a la represión.* (Stop the repression).

Together with activists Ann Tiffany and Ed Kinane, who are based in Syracuse, New York, Rickman and I developed a presentation about militarism and the SOA using music, video, and discussion. We spoke to numerous religious and academic groups along the East Coast and in California. This experience provided more evidence of the importance of music and cultural expression in social change movements. As people heard about the SOA issue through song, film, and discussion, they were inspired to become part of the call for the school's closure. Many people also ventured to the Georgia protest vigil because of those presentations and started local groups to further aware-ness in their communities.

The 2008 puppetista theme for the SOA vigil was "Winds of the People." The phrase is the translated title of the epic song "*Vientos del pueb-lo*" by renowned Chilean singer and actor Victor Jara, who was tortured and murdered during the early days of the CIA backed coup d'état against demo-cratically elected Salvador Allende's Popular Unity government. It has recent-ly come to light that Jara's killer was also trained at the SOA.

Jara's name is one of the hundreds called out during the annual vigil at the gates of Fort Benning. In Latin America, it is customary to recall those who have passed on by saying, "*presente*," to declare that they are "still here." As protesters solemnly approach the gate holding crosses and Stars of David and carrying the names of the disappeared, names of the victims are stated and all respond by singing the single word "*presente*." This ritual also pro-vides the setting for those who have prepared to enter the base and risk arrest. For the last four years of the sustained protest, all those who now enter the base are arrested and serve six months or more of jail time.

The SOA Watch has successfully made music a vital part of its organi-zational strategy. Collective song's elemental quality that touches our hu-manity and lets us feel we are not alone is important in the context of the vigil because it offers a source of comfort and strength to hear the testimonies of violence and brutality that so many have experienced, and it also inspires hope to carry on the work of nonviolent activism.

6. *Nueva Canción* Movement in Latin America

"Winds of the People" is a signature song within the Latin American *nueva canción* movement, which had its roots in the sociopolitical upheavals in Lat-in America during the latter half of the twentieth century. In Chile, and in reaction to what Victor Jara called "cultural colonialism," proponents of this music sought to reclaim indigenous cultural production while decrying issues of injustice, poverty, inequality, imperialism, and militarized violence that pla-gued Latin America during this time. Jara's compositions sought to unearth the experience of "every man" and thus create an expression more in keeping with a people's popular culture. The song's final lyrics are a prayerful call to indi-vidual action that can only be realized by the power of the people:

> Winds of the people call me,
> Winds of the people carry me
> They open my heart and give breath to my voice.
> Thus the poet will sing when death takes me
> To ride on the winds of the people
> Now and forever.

The unrelenting power of hope expressed within "Winds of the People" and the dialectical exchange between the individual and the collective conveyed here is characteristic of nearly all *nueva canción* lyrics. Contrary to some claims that this genre tended to express militancy and divisiveness (Mattern, 1998), it is much more accurate to understand that *nueva canción* is an extension of a culture of resistance that already existed for centuries in Latin America. It has a great thematic complexity of lyric that in no way can be reduced to solely political pamphleteering. What distinguishes these songs is, "a common passion for, and commitment to, the fate of the individual, of their country and of their continent" (Fairley, 1989, p. 90).

Another key characteristic of the *nueva canción* movement is its ability to mobilize tradition and to create collective consciousness and solidarity within individual countries and across the continents alike. Artists such as Mercedes Sosa, Leon Gieco, and Atahualpa Yupanqui of Argentina, Victor Jara, Violeta Parra, Quilapayun, and Inti Illimani of Chile, Silvio Rodríguez and Pablo Milanes of Cuba, and Amparo Ochoa of Mexico, to name only a few, were able to capture the sentiments of youth and progressive activists. Their concerts (which many times included artists from all over Latin America) gathered people together in song in a unique and profound unity of audience and performer that spoke to the urgency of the moment and possibility for a better world amidst unspeakable violence and repression. These songs and their performance became a way to empower and vitalize thousands of people and to confirm common experience and attitudes.

Victor Jara, for example, played a significant cultural and educational role within the Allende government of Chile (1970–1973), giving concerts and workshops to thousands of students, unionists, and working class audiences. "*Plegaria a un Labrador*" ("Prayer to a Laborer"), "*Te recuerdo Amanda*," ("I Remember You Amanda"), and "*El arado*," ("The Plow"), are a just a few of the hundreds of compositions that named and validated ordinary people's lives. They called on poor people to act and organize from their personal experience.

One of Jara's best internationally known songs, "*Las casitas del barrio alto*" ("The Little Houses of the Upper Crust"), is actually a parody of United States' folk performer Malvina Reynolds's "Little Boxes." It is an example of how songs of the *nueva canción* movement translate across borders and are shared throughout the Americas. Jara was arrested during the first few days of the 1973 coup. He was rounded up with thousands of others and placed in the Chile Stadium (renamed Victor Jara Stadium in 2003), where he was singled out because of his celebrity. He was tortured and killed.

Jara has become a symbol of music's power to promote social change. His songs continue in popularity and dozens of artists throughout the world have memorialized him in song.

What musician Patricio Manns observes about the renowned Cuban musician Silvio Rodríguez is illustrative of the effectiveness and mobilizing capacity of *nueva canción*:

When Silvio Rodriguez makes thousands of people sigh and cry with only one line of verse in which he declares beautifully that "I live in a free country"—in three seconds he does away with thirty years of infamy and horror . . . . (Manns, Boyle, and Gonzalez, 1987, p. 194, author's translation)

Rodríguez's song is typical of how the genre unites performer and audience in close relation. They experience the song's power in the immediacy of the moment in the context of performance, in its referential aspect through the expansive quality of poetic lyric, and in its ability to "sum up" universal sentiment. Later, it is itself referenced as a source of mutual understanding or as a cultural unifier.

Similarly, when Argentine singer Mercedes Sosa, a founding voice of the genre, sang Chilean Violeta Parra's composition "*Volver a los diecisiete*" (Return to Age Seventeen) in the context of Argentina's "Dirty War," Parra's anthem to love became reinterpreted. Its meaning as a love song transformed to unite the audience in memory and loss, evoking the reality of thousands of mostly young people who were disappeared and imprisoned during the Argentine dictatorship. The song, which sings of the redemptive power of love, united the audience in hope for liberation:

Love is a whirlwind of original purity
Even the fierce animal has its sweet trill
It gives rest to the pilgrim
It liberates the prisoner
And with its work makes the old a child again

The promise of love to "free the prisoner" became a rallying cry to remember and demand justice for all those wrongfully imprisoned by the military junta. Like Rodríguez's simple phrase, "I live in a free country," Parra's line also took on an overdetermined meaning. The simplicity of the lyrics ironically created a space for the expression and comprehension of complex realities of the moment.

This chapter began with quotes from larger-than-life public figures and activists, all of whom have committed their lives to struggle for a more just and peaceful society. They say in few words what this chapter only begins to elaborate: that song is essential to create communities that challenge and resist forces of violence and repression. It can connect disparate groups, reinforce solidarity within common struggles, educate and empower the disenfranchised, and give courage in the face of danger and injustice. As such, song is vital and necessary for social change activism.

Eleven

WOMAN, MOTHER, AND
NONVIOLENT ACTIVISM

Danielle Poe

1. Introduction

The significance of mothering in Western society has been the subject of countless narratives, short stories, and poetry. The dominant theme of most of these accounts is that a woman's identity becomes subordinate to her children wherein she loses her independence. For some, becoming a mother is the fulfillment of childhood dreams and social expectations. For others, becoming a mother is suffocating and deprives them of their previous identity. In some contexts, though, mothering can be a continuation of a woman's previous identity instead of a new identity.

Michele Naar-Obed is a woman whose transformation into a mother connected her more deeply to her community and to the world. Because of her perceived connection with other mothers and their children, she left her twenty-three-month-old daughter in the care of her community while she, along with three other anti-war activists (a group self-named as Jubilee Plowshares East) disarmed a fast attack nuclear submarine at Newport News, Virginia, Shipbuilding on 7 August 1995.

In addition to disarming a particular nuclear vessel, the activists also wanted to convey a larger message that all nuclear proliferation ought to stop. The activists knew that their act was felonious and would result in a prison sentence, possibly a lengthy prison sentence. As a mother, Naar-Obed faced the conflict between participating in a non-violent felony action and staying with her daughter. She wanted to participate in the action to stay faithful to her interpretation of her Christian beliefs, but acting on these beliefs would separate her from her daughter and deprive her of the day-to-day activities of mothering. For her, the resolution to this conflict was to redefine mothering as an act that takes place with a community, rather than as a solitary act.

I will discuss Naar-Obed's narrative about maternity and nonviolence because she is an exception to many of our society's common beliefs. She gave up a lucrative job to live simply in community. She and her partner chose to have a child as part of that community rather than to become a separate nuclear family. Also she chose to break the law and serve time in prison to emphasize her interdependence with other mothers and their children.

I will use Luce Irigaray's discussions of cultivating intersubjectivity and maternity (1996; 2001; 2002) to argue that Naar-Obed's mothering offers a prophetic alternative to viewing motherhood and womanhood in conflict, and treating motherhood as inferior to womanhood. Naar-Obed resolves this conflict by being part of a community that actively participates in raising her child. Naar-Obed's resolution provides a concrete example of the kind of feminism proposed in Irigaray's work.

2. Isolated Mothering

In "Oi Mother, Keep Ye' Hair On! Impossible Transformations of Maternal Subjectivity," Lisa Baraitser contrasts woman prior to maternity as an "earlier independent, solitary, unitary self" with woman as mother who is "something messy, interdependent, and altogether more blurred" (2006, p. 218). She notes that in many popular accounts of motherhood, women look back with longing at whom they once were—women in control of their lives and projects. As mothers, they feel the weight of failure, being forced to choose between their former selves and their children (ibid., p. 220). Baraitser's description of becoming a mother reveals a grief that overwhelms her:

> Motherhood is the pitilessness of the present tense . . . . In this immediacy, I am brought face-to-face with the patched over, broken bits of myself, the cracks in relations with mother, lover, siblings, friends. Everything is challenged, like in analysis, painfully peeled back . . . in the grip of a mute and helpless grief . . . . I know that everything has changed. I am unsteady, dizzy, like I'm relearning to walk after a long illness. I imagine a war has taken place while I've been away. . . . Severed from myself, like the cut end of a worm, I am disorganized, stunned. (Ibid., p. 228)

Baraitser and other feminists have compared the woman-mother dyad to the masculine-feminine dyad. The masculine-feminine dyad is one in which masculine denotes characteristics that are active, understandable, and rational. Feminine characteristics are passive, unknowable, and emotional. The masculine-feminine dyad is then applied to actual men and women such that it becomes a prescription that men ought to be active and rational, while women ought to be passive and emotional. The characteristics of the feminine are prescribed for mothers especially, since mothering is treated as the ultimate expression of femininity. Baraitser's grief, regret, and longing lead her to reject the notion that becoming a mother is transformative in a positive way. She turns to the work of Irigaray to provide a basis for appropriating some characteristics of mothering in such a way as to promote a way for women to maintain their identities as women when they become mothers (ibid., pp. 235–237).

What strikes me about Baraitser's experience of motherhood, both hers and the others she cites, is that these women are quite solitary in their maternal experiences. The narratives that she provides indicate that many women may experience profound loss when they become mothers, seeing motherhood as a transition to interdependence, which is traumatic since it marks the end of a solitary self who is free (ibid., p. 227). The problem with Baraitser's analysis is that she accepts a masculine subjectivity as the ideal. The ideal subject that she describes is free from others, free from obligations to others and expectations from others. In this analysis, woman becomes more like the masculine of a traditional masculine-feminine binary.

Rather than trying to find a way for women to maintain a strong individualism when they become mothers, another strategy would be to criticize the ideal of individualism. If a woman's identity consists of being part of reciprocal relationships of obligations, then becoming a mother has a context that can be less disruptive to her identity. If a woman already has relationships in which she depends on others and others depend on her, those relationships can inform her work and identity when she becomes a mother.

According to Irigaray, women can also experience a positive transformation if they have cultivated an interdependent subjectivity. She believes that the stress on independence "is a denial, an annulment of these intersubjective relationships which, from infancy, have marked [the body]" (2001, p. 32). Naar-Obed's experience of mothering fits this alternative scenario, in which a woman's transition to motherhood is not experienced as an isolated event, but as an entry into transformed interdependence in her community.

No one begins as an isolated being in the world. Irigarary says, "in my present body I am already intention toward the other, intention between myself and the other, beginning in genealogy" (ibid., p. 32). We are inextricably interconnected with generations before us and with our offspring regardless of the quality of those relationships. This reality makes every person intersubjective regardless whether we admit to it or recognize it.

Intersubjectivity, however, does not mean that women have to naively or submissively accept an inferior position in relation to men. For Irigaray, cultivating the relationship of intersubjectivity means creating a horizontal relationship in which difference is emphasized without hierarchy. Cultivating subjectivity can lead to building communities that support each member and larger projects that contribute to making a society more just.

3. Intersubjectivity

Prior to discussing the role of maternity in Irigaray, we must first turn to her description of women's subjectivity developed through their relationships with others. While many philosophical theories of subjectivity treat the subject as an isolated individual, Irigaray begins with the observation that the subject is always already in relationships with other people. Subjectivity, holds Irigaray, should not be the sort of individual endeavor that Baraitser describes. Instead, subjectivity develops through vertical and horizontal relationships with other women and with men.

Any individual woman's subjectivity is irreducible to any other woman's subjectivity. Instead, her subjectivity is intertwined with that of others and is always intersubjective. The intersubjectivity that Irigaray prescribes allows for space between individuals and a return to the self, both of which provide protection against hierarchical and submissive relationships.

One of the first forms of relationship that individuals will experience is a vertical one, namely, parent-child. Vertical relationships take three forms according to Irigaray: persons in relation to the divine, persons in relation to their genealogy, and persons in relation to their teacher or student(s). Although a vertical relationship appears to indicate a hierarchy between subjects, verticality is better understood as a temporal relationship in which wisdom is transmitted.

Irigaray views the ideal relationship student-teacher relationship as opening up oneself to welcome the Other. Teachers, in this perspective, teach according to their own knowledge and their knowledge of the student. This perspective emphasizes the relationship between knowledge and the subjects instead of positing teaching as the transmission of purely objective material.

Teachers who try to transmit purely objective material fail to recognize that the personalities, learning styles, and knowledge that students already bring to the subject matter influences the learning and teaching relationship.

By comparison, Irigaray's conception of teaching emphasizes that every teacher and student relationship is unique and that the teacher should facilitate learning by taking that relationship into account. The relationship between student and teacher nurtures the unique development of the student instead of trying to make the student a replica of the teacher. This emphasis on a unique relationship will be evident in the relationship between Naar-Obed and the divine, and of that between Naar-Obed and her daughter. In each of these relationships, one party (teacher, divinity, and mother) guides and leads the other within the context of their relationship.

Irigaray also emphasizes the importance of horizontal relationships—the relationships of people of the same sex amongst themselves and the relationships between the sexes. Individuals may engage in vertical and horizontal relationships simultaneously with the same Other. For example, a woman has a vertical relationship with her mother by virtue of their genealogy and at the same time, she has a horizontal relationship her mother by virtue of their gender. The emphasis in the horizontal relationship is on difference, equality, and reciprocity. Even in the horizontal relationship of one gender—female for example—difference is still important because women are not reducible to a single, static definition. Instead, gender is continually defined by those who are of that gender. The definition of being a woman is therefore fluid and dynamic.

4. Non-Violent Direct Action

Examining Naar-Obed's vertical and horizontal relationships will allow us to understand why she chose to participate in a nonviolent direct action against the United States nuclear build-up even though her action put her at risk for an extended absence from her daughter.

The vertical relationships that influence Naar-Obed are her relationships with God and with her daughter. I will discuss the relationship with her daughter in the following section. Here, I will describe Naar-Obed's account of her nonviolent direct action in which she emphasized her relationship with God. That relationship allows her to discern a moral path and to create relationships with other people that help her to pursue that path. Naar-Obed does not believe that God requires us to strive for the religious conversion of others but that we work to secure human flourishing, to fight against forces that undermine human dignity.

Since 1991, Naar-Obed had been participating in minor nonviolent direct actions that resulted in at most a five-day jail sentence. In 1992, though, she was considering a direct action classified as a felony in the judicial system. She knew that this action would be severely disruptive to the doctor, the other staff, and the patients where she was working at the time and that without her job, she would have no way to support herself.

Consequently, she decided to join Jonah House, a community that intentionally lives according to its understanding of God's prescriptions (ibid., 1998, pp. 21–22). Jonah House lives according to a Bible passage that prescribes turning away from war to peaceful endeavor:

> And he shall judge among the nations, and shall rebuke many people: and they shall beat their swords into plowshares, and their spears into pruninghooks: nation shall not lift up sword against nation, neither shall they learn war any more. (Isaiah 2:4, King James Version)

Members of Jonah House established the "plowshare witness," which involves acts meant to reveal the destructive power of nuclear weapons and citizens' ability to refuse complicity with those weapons. The act of witness involves trespassing on property where these weapons are created or stored, symbolically or actually destroying the weapon, and, finally, a symbolic representation of the death that such weapons cause. Witnesses often pour their own blood on the weapons or on blueprints. Within the United States, these acts are felony offenses and witnesses accept imprisonment as a consequence of their actions (ibid., p. 15). Of these efforts Naar-Obed writes, "the plowshare witness is an attempt to bring Isaiah's vision to life. It envisions a time when all of God's people come together to live on the Holy Mountain to live as sisters and brothers" (ibid., p. 8).

Within Jonah House, residents view nuclear weapons as the greatest threat to people living together in peace. They also believe that God intends the Kingdom of Heaven to be lived in this world. They share an interpretation of Christianity that emphasizes interconnection among people and living peacefully together.

While Naar-Obed grants that multiple interpretations of the Bible are possible, she does not grant that any interpretation would be correct. She believes some interpretations can be wrong. For instance, an interpretation may be wrong because it misunderstands or mistranslates passages. The vertical relationship between Naar-Obed and the divine is particular to her and her community, but she does not define the interpretation. The interpretation is transmitted from outside of her. The community receives the Bible as God's teaching, and they interpret that teaching according to their particular context.

The vertical relationship between Naar-Obed and the divine is directly related to the horizontal relationships in her life. The relationships that contextualize Naar-Obed's nonviolent, direct action are her relationships with Jonah house, with her husband, and with the world community. Jonah House, as mentioned above, is a community that lives together to pursue their common Judeo-Christian values. Naar-Obed writes:

> The Sermon on the Mount seems to be most clear about what it means to be Christian. We are told not only to love our neighbor, but our enemy as well. We are told vengeance is no longer acceptable. No more eye for eye and no longer do we fight violence with violence. These instructions make it difficult to remain silent while living in the most militarized nation in the world. (Ibid., pp. 22–23)

The Jonah House community allows members to speak out against United States militarism. They support one another when members participate in nonviolent direct action whether through a demonstration condoned by public officials or a symbolic disarming of a nuclear submarine, a felony. The community supports itself by raising much of its food and earns money by painting houses. If some members are away for an action or to serve a prison sentence because of an action, the other members fill the absent members' roles. All of the actions that Jonah House members undertake are planned in advance by the community through prayer and discussion.

After joining Jonah House, Naar-Obed met and fell in love with Greg Boertje-Obed, who was a longtime member of the community. She writes:

> We felt that our union should serve to strengthen each other in our commitment as peacemakers. Our vows to live in voluntary simplicity and to support and love each other during periods of absence due to incarceration for acts of nonviolent resistance were incorporated into our marriage vows. (Ibid., p. 26)

For Naar-Obed and Boertje, marriage deepened their commitment to the Jonah House community and to the world community. From the beginning of their marriage, they challenged the view that romantic love inaugurates an isolated, nuclear family. Instead, they integrated their marriage into their previous commitment to community engagement.

Naar-Obed and Boertje's marriage demonstrates the kind of relationship that Irigaray recommends to welcome a child. The partners are equals. Each gives to the other, and each returns to the self. Their relationship can create the conditions of welcome for a child who is desired by the couple, but a child is not necessary to legitimate their relationship. Irigaray describes the path from the horizontal relationship between lovers that can lead them to welcome a child in *Between East and West*:

> Such a loving journey will also lead the man and the woman to acquire a possible parental identity. The horizontal coexistence between the sexes, the most necessary coexistence between the sexes, the most necessary coexistence, the most desirable but also the most difficult to realize, leads naturally and spiritually to the respect of ancestors and to hospitality toward future generations. (2002, p. 119)

The relationship between the sexes should not be predicated on the production of children. A physical relationship between the sexes should focus on the coexistence between two people. The couple's horizontal relationship maintains the difference between them. They are distinct, respected, and nurtured; any hierarchy inherent in their difference disappears. Only after their coexistence becomes fully horizontal can there be a *possibility* of a parental identity.

5. Intersubjective Maternity

The relationship between a mother and her child—a vertical relationship—ought to be founded on horizontal relationships. When Naar-Obed describes their decision to have a child, the relationships between her, Boertje, and Jonah House are all central. "We began talking with each other and with our community about our desire for a child with each other and with our community" (1998, p. 27). Naar-Obed uses "we" and "our" throughout the description of the process to indicate that she and Boertje together wanted a child. Their decision was also part of the relationship that they shared with others in the community. Just as their marriage was one in which they provided support for each other to participate in their community and in society, their decision to have a child was part of their commitment to the world beyond their personal relationship with each other.

Whereas Baraitser emphasizes the difficulties of the mother-child relationship in Western society, Naar-Obed's narrative offers a scenario in which those challenges are a result of sociopolitical context rather than necessarily arising from the mother-child relationship per se.

To better understand the significance of considering the mother-child relationship in a sociopolitical context, I will consider Amber Jacobs' critique of Irigaray. In "The Potential of Theory: Melanie Klein, Luce Irigaray, and the Mother-Daughter Relationship," Jacobs explores Irigaray's analysis of the mother-daughter relationship (2007, pp. 175–193). Jacobs admires Irigaray's criticism of traditional psychoanalytic theory in that it views the mother-daughter relationship as pathological, but she highlights that Irigaray's use of myth to create a new mother-daughter symbolic order falls prey to patriarchy:

> Irigaray, too, cannot seem to avoid reacting to and reproducing the projection onto the maternal that she so forcefully wants to undercut by offering up its opposite: the utopian benign mother who can give her daughter protection from the operations of the father's law that otherwise render her derelict. (Ibid., p. 185)

Jacobs concludes that theorizing about the mother-daughter relationship should start by rejecting some abstract law against which mothers and daughters react. She argues that mothers and daughters can construct better relationship by rejecting abstract and idealized relationships and by rejecting the idea that pathology is constitutive of the mother-daughter relationship (ibid., p. 191).

Jacobs performs a close textual reading of Irigaray's suggestion to display beautiful art in public places that depicts the mother-daughter relationship (ibid., pp. 180–181; cf. Irigaray, 2004, p. 189). She is critical of Irigaray's persistently positive language in describing the mother-daughter relationship because over-idealization misses much of the tension and difficulty in the relationship. I am particularly interested in the final lines from the quote that Jacobs cites:

> This cultural restoration will begin to heal a loss of individual and collective identity for women. It will heal many of women's ills—not just distress but competitiveness and destructive aggressiveness. It will help women move out of the private into the public sphere, out of the family and into the society where they live. (Jacobs, 2007, p. 180)

This passage allows us to see how Naar-Obed's relationship with her daughter—a vertical relationship founded in Naar-Obed's horizontal relationships with her partner and community—achieves Irigaray's goal of bringing the mother and daughter into society, and avoids over-idealization of the mother-daughter relationship.

First, we can explore what Irigaray means when she writes that the mother-daughter couple has a "very special relationship to nature and culture." In "How to Ensure the Connection between Natural and Civil Coexistence," Irigaray writes, "the natural survival of the human species has, for centuries, been entrusted above all, to the family: it produces or reproduces life, shelters it, maintains it" (2004, p. 225). She uses the "natural" to signify life, the production of life, and the safeguarding of life. She emphasizes that, for human beings, the natural always happens in a sociopolitical context.

Irigaray contends that the current sociopolitical context is pathological in that it tends to reduce women and children to their roles in the family instead of seeing the family as a place of return, from which each member goes out to the public. The natural is in relationship to the civil. Irigaray further explains that the natural, within the context of the family:

> represents the place of the return to the state of nature, not only through reproduction and the raising of children but also through bodily and carnal relationships, emotional life, physical rest and regeneration. (Ibid., p. 225)

For Irigaray, the natural refers to the material world, but she always recognizes that for human beings nature and culture intertwine and are not easily distinguished from each other. With respect to the family, biological reproduction is natural, but how human beings interpret reproduction happens within a cultural context. The natural can and does entail having children and raising children, but that happens within a context of physical relationships among other members of the family—especially the physical relationship between parents. The natural also includes our emotions and resting.

Irigaray's description of the natural understands that the family's ability to carry out their natural tasks is largely dependent on how the natural coexists with the civil, which is Irigaray's term for culture. She uses the term civil to indicate that human beings should consciously evaluate and produce cultural relationships that are peaceful. Relationships in which mothers are cut off from the civil and reduced to the natural tasks of mothering can lead to a profound sense of loss when a woman becomes a mother, as Baraitser describes.

Irigaray describes another possibility, wherein the natural and the civil coexist and people can find happiness. This happens when people pay attention to patterns in themselves and in nature, and evaluate those patterns to understand and create relationships that allow human beings and nature to minimize violence and conflict (ibid., p. 232). Civil society should be founded on human flourishing instead of on economic development.

In *Between East and West*, Irigaray describes the family as "a cultivation of the union between man and woman in the respect for their differences, which implies that nature becomes consciousness" (2002, p. 118). Her use of the cultivation as a metaphor is significant because she indicates a process by which human effort helps plants to grow and thrive. When she applies this metaphor to human beings, she wants the reader to think about the ways in which human effort can help human beings to be happier and more at peace.

Cultivation begins with a reflection on the material; in this case, it begins by noticing bodies and nature. Bodies and nature are then evaluated and cared for by adopting practices that take care of the body's health and nature's health. For human beings to be happy, their minds must also have care. Irigaray's discussions of cultivation frequently refer to her yoga practice, which can deepen our understanding of what she means by cultivation (ibid., pp. 56–57). While other ways are possible to care for the body and mind, yoga is an ideal example because the poses have helped Irigaray care for her body at the same time that the meditation allows her to care for her mind. She also uses yoga as an example because it emphasizes the importance of the practitioner's autonomy and the relationship between student and teacher. According to Irigaray, yoga's focus on breathing indicates the importance of autonomy.

At birth, breathing is our first autonomous gesture (ibid., p. 73). Throughout life, focusing on respiration and how it can increase the body's energy is an opportunity to will autonomy (ibid., p. 74). While autonomy is significant for people, relationships are also important, and Irigaray also emphasizes the role of the relationship between student and teacher in creating the conditions for happiness (ibid., p. 58).

The mother who wants to nourish the possibility of happiness in her relationship with her child should begin by cultivating her own happiness. In the case of Naar-Obed, her happiness relates to her autonomy, her relationship to her husband, and her relationship to the Jonah House community. She is neither reducible to, nor subservient to her partner or to her community. Her relationship with her husband and her community opens a way for her to be a mother who is very different from the mothers that Baraister describes as typical in the United States. The mothers she describes are isolated from each other, themselves, and their partners. Naar-Obed's experience is unique because she understands that militarism threatens the happiness of herself, her child, and her community. Many people in the United States question the need for military superiority.

Naar-Obed succeeds in discovering her purpose in life, finding a community that will nourish her purpose and be nourished by her, developing a horizontal relationship with her partner, and understanding her choice to become a mother as a further opening of her Other relationships as opposed to closing possibilities. Still, she becomes a mother in the United States where money that could be spent on human flourishing (housing, health care, education, childcare, art) is diverted to weapons and prisons. When she becomes a mother, she is well aware of the tension between her values and those of the nation. She is committed to a path that challenges what she perceives as the United States' culture of death. During her pregnancy, she becomes increasingly aware of the connection between her own mother-daughter relationship and other mother-child relationships:

Sometime during my pregnancy, I received a set of pictures of the Hiro-shima-Nagaski bombing. Mostly, they were pictures of the children. One in particular, a burnt and bloodied infant nursing at its mother's burnt and bloody breast, haunted me. After Rachel was born, and especially while I was nursing her, I would visualize that infant in my arms. For a moment, I would become that mother, and the pain I felt was excruciating. More and more, I was drawn to participate in the plowshare witness. I could not let their deaths be in vain. I would do it for them, for the children that are currently under threat, and for Rachel. (1998, p. 29)

When she became a mother, Naar-Obed experienced new empathy with other mothers, their children, and their suffering. Moreover, she believed that their suffering was largely caused by her nation and was preventable. Her maternity inspired her to participate in the plowshare witness, nonviolent civil disobedience. To fulfill her witness, Naar-Obed would almost certainly have to leave her daughter who inspired her to act.

6. Activism toward Social Transformation

When we think about mothers who intentionally commit felonious acts as a form of social protest, the most challenging question we can ask is whether such symbolic acts can justify the personal sacrifice necessary to engage in them. We must consider that these felonious acts are unlikely to create any change in social policy. They may result in limited change in public opinion or even turn some against them. We can posit, however, that the mother's relationship with their children will quite likely be harmed. Naar-Obed's action, therefore, disrupts the calculus that most of us would use to determine whether to act in this way is justified.

While most of us cannot understand why anyone would risk a long prison sentence for something unlikely to produce the desired change, Daniel Berrigan, S.J. offers a cogent model of the motivation that inspires many activists. In the film, *Investigation of a Flame*, Berrigan describes the process of deciding to participate in burning draft files with homemade napalm, and he says that he could not "not participate" (Sachs, 2003).

Normally, this sort of double negative would make little sense to a listener, but in this case, it describes why Berrigan chose to do something that he did not want to do. His response emphasizes his commitment to the act despite his reluctance—he concluded that he had to participate.

Many of our actions are determined by what we want to do: for example, we want to go for a walk on a nice day; we want to eat our favorite foods; we want to spend time with our friends. Other actions are determined by the result we want to get from the action: we want to lose weight by going for a walk or giving up our favorite foods; we want knee replacement surgery to walk without pain. Berrigan, however, knew that burning draft files would not end the Vietnam War. He also knew that he would go to prison for being a part of the act. Nevertheless, he chose to participate in the protest and to accept consequences that would not be pleasurable.

Berrigan was not physically forced to participate in this act. We will have to seek another explanation for why he "could not" not participate. Many years after the action that I have described above, I heard Berrigan give a public lecture at Fordham University, after which he answered questions. One student asked Berrigan why he participates in these kinds of protests when he does not expect them to produce changes in policy. Berrigan responded that he did not engage in that sort of cost-benefit analysis. Instead, he decides whether the act is the right thing to do. If it is right, he acts. For Berrigan, an act is right when it upholds the dignity of the person, is nonviolent, and announces a new possibility. He decided to burn the draft files because it was the right thing to do regardless of the results or consequences.

Naar-Obed and Berrigan have similar motives for their actions. Both look at the militarism in United States' society and feel compelled to act. Berrigan participated in using homemade napalm to burn the draft files of hundreds of men during the Vietnam War. His act was unmistakable in its purpose and meaning: it conveyed that the Vietnam War was wrong and the United States ought not to use napalm bombs against people; the United States government was wrong to draft men to participate in this unethical war; and burning the draft files impedes the government's ability to do so.

Naar-Obed's ethical message is equally clear: the United States government is wrong to stockpile nuclear weapons. Berrigan and Naar-Obed both affirm the dignity of every person by destroying—physically, for Berrigan, symbolically, for Naar-Obed—things that would destroy people. Both use nonviolent methods since their methods would not injure people or any property that sustains people.

While some would argue that these protestors destroy property—draft files, for example—Berrigan and Naar-Obed rationalize that only things "proper" to human flourishing are property. They argue that nuclear weapons and draft files are part of a culture of death and are therefore not property according to their perspective.

The final motive for these sorts of acts is to announce a new possibility: the possibility of international relations built on cooperation instead of force and violence.

The comparison between Berrigan and Naar-Obed that finds them so alike becomes strained when we consider that Berrigan is a Jesuit priest and Naar-Obed is a mother. When Berrigan chose to participate in a nonviolent protest that would lead to a felony conviction, he had to consider the cost of this action to himself and to his Order. While his sentence would put a strain on the community, others in the community could compensate for his absence. He also knew that serving time in a federal prison would be an incredibly unpleasant experience, but he was willing to choose that suffering for the sake of those in Vietnam who had no choice about being there.

Naar-Obed, on the other hand, had to consider her community, her husband, and her young daughter. The concerns that we might have about the effects of Naar-Obed's actions on her community and her husband are relatively easy to dispense with since both encouraged her and fully supported her decision to symbolically disarm a nuclear submarine. Her daughter, however, was much too young to appreciate what her mother was doing, what the effects would be, and to consent. All of these considerations are true for any parent of a very young child.

For example, at twenty-three months, my son Asher would bite people. When he did this, we imposed a time out. He had no idea why biting resulted in a time out, and he was unable to consent to a time out. From his perspective, biting was effective: he bit another child and the child gave him the toy he wanted. What I wanted him to learn was that biting people is inappropriate, even if someone has done something we dislike and even if it gets us what we want. At that tender age, I was trying to instill in my son values that he would understand later. Likewise, Naar-Obed's separation from her daughter was intended to instill values and provide an example that her daughter would understand later.

Naar-Obed knew that her daughter would be well loved and cared for during her absence. She also knew that her absence would be less disruptive for her daughter than it would be in a nuclear family. Her daughter had always been parented by many of the adults in the community, not just her biological parents. Naar-Obed had the opportunity to model alternatives to the value placed on violence in United States society. Her act would not actually disarm a nuclear submarine, but it would state that the violence and destruction built into this weapon is wrong, and that United States citizens do not have to be passive when something is wrong regardless of whether our particular acts will immediately produce the changes we desire. Naar-Obed introduced her daughter to the idea that a person can act based on an analysis of right and wrong instead of calculating costs against benefits.

Ultimately, Naar-Obed's act is not that different from the decisions that mothers make every day. We set up the conditions that we believe will make our children's flourishing possible. We fight against conditions that interfere with their flourishing. We hope that sacrifices we make and discipline we enforce will make sense to our children as they grow. We hope that our children will choose to pursue what is right even when others give up, when it is difficult, and when they may not receive immediate compensation for doing the right thing.

7. Conclusion

Those who believe that Naar-Obed's choice to participate in a plowshares witness constituted neglect of her daughter might criticize her actions. This criticism, though, mistakenly assumes that mothering is an activity that only happens within the relationship between a mother and a child. Naar-Obed's mother-child relationship is intersubjective—it arises from her commitment to her partner and to her community. She writes, "Rachel thrived during my absence. She was given much love, and she in turn enriched the lives of those around her" (1998, p. 23).

Certainly, Naar-Obed missed her daughter and missed the daily, corporeal tasks of mothering, but she entrusted those tasks to the community and her partner. Her act also allowed her to cultivate an awareness of the connection between all people with her daughter. She demonstrates that maternity can be joyful, hopeful, and a continuation of the mother's projects instead of abandonment of them.

Further, Naar-Obed offers an example of the mother-child relationship that does not depend on an impossible idealization of the world. Instead, she faces that which is destructive in United States culture and uses her opposition to that culture to cultivate new ways of living with her child, her partner, her community, and her society.

Twelve

THE BLUE GUITAR, BLUE FROG, AND THE BLUES

Katina Sayers-Walker

1. Introduction

I advocate for and am committed to social justice. In my life, this mean pay-
ing conscious attention and making sincere efforts to reveal inequities and
inequalities in the public sphere that too many have falsely accepted as the
status quo. In my college classroom, this means that I regularly rely on teaching methods associated with critical pedagogy. I believe some have not done
enough to reveal the hidden curriculum regarding these inequities in public
schools and universities, and I believe that the hidden curriculum has far more
impact on students than many choose to believe. For this reason, I begin each
semester by thinking about ways to lift my students out of the false consciousness of their lives—the limited awareness of the situations and conditions that have resulted in inequalities and injustices in society—and delve
into cultural beliefs and understandings that have led to unquestioning acceptance of inequities and inequalities.

In this chapter, I describe a teaching project based on a mini-film series.
The goal was to increase awareness of social justice issues, with special emphasis on combating oppression and marginalization of historically under-
represented groups. Following each film, participants engaged in a group discussion to analyze the film plot using a critical lens. The discussion questions
centered on issues of power and privilege. While I document the details of the
film-series and group discussions here, the main focus of this chapter is the
unexpected emotional response of the participants and my concerns over their
responses. I provide a brief review of the literature to support critical pedagogy supplemented by the use of images. This is followed by the details of the
mini-film series, the participants' emotional response, and my analysis of
their response. At the conclusion, I offer readers curricular recommendations
for teaching about and toward social justice.

Incorporating movies into critical pedagogy is especially effective in engaging students in dialogue. The combination of critical pedagogy and movies
also brought about a powerful emotional response. Whether the emotions
were useful in achieving the goal of the film series is difficult to judge at this
juncture, but feeling something should not be discounted as insignificant in
the process of seeking social justice and, ultimately, peace.

2. The Arts and Imagination

Wallace Stevens' penned "The Man with the Blue Guitar" (1982) upon gaz-
ing at Pablo Picasso's *The Old Guitarist*, which he painted in 1903. Here,
Wallace renders the blue guitar as a metaphor for the imagination. The guitar,
an instrument for expression, permits the player to escape conventional approaches to his music as he can invent and reinvent melodies, sometimes, to
the initial discomfort of his listeners:

> The man bent over his guitar,
> A shearsman of sorts. The day was green.
> They said, "You have a blue guitar,
> You do not play things as they are."
> The man replied, "Things as they are
> Are changed upon the blue guitar."
> And they said then, "But play, you must,
> A tune beyond us, yet ourselves
> A tune upon the blue guitar
> Of things exactly as they are.

As philosopher Maxine Greene so eloquently explains, "to play upon the
blue guitar is to play upon the imagination" (1995, p. 19). For me, the arts hold
the key to opening the imagination and should be recognized as a key component when teaching about and for social justice. The arts provide the medium
to imagine alternatives and without alternatives, we have only paralysis of attitudes and habits.
    The arts have historically held a special place in societies. Likewise, art-
ists have been universally revered for their ability to render imagination into
dream-like art forms. These art forms are the compromise between the real
and the surreal, the inner and outer vision. What has always intrigued me is
the interesting transaction of how mental renderings turn into something tang-
ible for others to appreciate and how we attach meaning to art forms.
    In the field of education, inclusion of the arts into the curriculum can be
positively recommended, especially for its ability to release the imagination
and create new mental images. Greene, in a series of lectures given at the Lincoln Center Institute for the Arts in Education and now compiled into the
pages of *Variations on a Blue Guitar* (2001), asks readers to delve into a new
sort of education—one that releases the imagination and relies heavily upon
the arts to do so.
    What is the value of such an education? With aesthetics as the core of
the curriculum, Greene believes the arts, for example, film, literature, or print
media, can bring social change because of its ability to act as a launch pad to
create new cognitive images and alternative ways of being alive. According to
Greene, the arts open the imagination by asking students to consider "as if"

(1995; 2001). I prefer the alternative to this by asking my students, "what could be?"

Can the arts move us to want to restore some kind of order, to repair, to heal society? Can the arts be a component in a teacher's curriculum devoted to social justice? I believe the arts can complement methods of critical pedagogy by engaging students in dialogue. Through this dialogue, they are able to reshape and understand the conditions and concerns of others and through this a new future can be forged.

Greene, remarkably well versed in many fields of literature, often refers to the ideas of John Dewey. In *Art as Experience* (1934), Dewey speaks of the many experiences held by the artist and receiver of art. As the title of the book suggests, art *is* an experience for both parties. Experience is always rooted in transaction. For Dewey, experience can be best described as an active epistemology in which a series of "to and fro" adjustments occur between the subject and object—simultaneous thinking, feeling, doing—that does away with dualities and demonstrates the interrelatedness of self and society, mind and body, idea and act. An important aspect of experience is the projection of meaning into the transaction—a transfer of values, emotional attachment, sensations, purpose, intrinsic connections, and associations. Common to all of these is the psychological component. The meaning we attach is a psychological intersection of the past and present meet. It is the cumulative effect of cultural attitudes and beliefs meeting with ideological manifestations.

For educators devoted to social justice and interested in improving the conditions of society, the arts have significant power to close the gap between ourselves and the Other through participation in a process that we could not know unless the imagination was aroused, unless we intentionally choose to play upon the blue guitar.

3. The Arts and Image-Based Research

As a graduate student, I was introduced to qualitative research methods, and then variations upon the methods. I strayed from the typical quantitative methods, unlike most of my peers, as it did not philosophically fit with my conceptions of knowledge, reality, and values. As much as I enjoyed qualitative research methods, even they became ordinary. Then one day in my advanced qualitative research methods course, my professor discussed a study, which she and a group of researchers performed in the inner city of Philadelphia.

Members of the community were asked to comment on their surroundings and school system based upon what they saw in a photo exposé presented to them. As a fan of photographer Ansel Adams, I was thrilled with the prospect of pursuing this form of qualitative research. This one event provided the foundation for my future research projects, including my dissertation.

Henceforth, I will refer to this form of research as image-based research (IBR), which relies on "moving images in the form of film, and video, or still

images, such as photographs, cartoons, and drawings." IBR is highly phenomenological due to its ability to draw out and trigger the consciousness
(Prosser, 2003). In general, IBR utilizes forms of art as an interpretative de-
vice to study the human experience.

Unlike the hard sciences—which attempt to rely on objective reality for
validity—image-based researchers in the social sciences recognize images as
interpretative devices. Images communicate messages to the viewer. These
messages are usually expressed or associated with feelings, thoughts, memo-
ries, awareness, and perceptions. Roland Barthes explains, "all we can say is
that the object speaks; it induces us, vaguely, to think" (1981, p. 138).

IBR is an ideal method to introduce the Other to our students. Below, I
will provide details of the mini-film series. My premise is that students and
teachers alike must be empathetic to the lives of others to be committed to
social justice. They must first be open to multiple lived realities, which means
they must reflect upon the conditions of their lives to understand that ways of
being alive in the world exist other than theirs. Then, they must cross the
physical or mental space to the Other through either direct or vicarious experiences. They are asked to use their imagination to appreciate the plight of
others and to learn to care about the suffering of the Other. They must feel as
if they have the power and ethical responsibility to take action to improve the
condition of the Other.

The arts provide the avenue to create new cognitive images and supply
the impetus to imagine "what could be." The imagination will be above all
that which enables us to feel empathetic to the lives of others.

4. The Arts, Imagination, and Emotion

In Greene's style of research, I wrote an application for a small, college-
funded grant to host a mini-film series. Based on my IBR experiences, I believed that the film series would be informative and provide the launch pad to
engage attendees in dialogue about social justice issues. More importantly, the
event would provide an opportunity for participants to meet the Other. The
larger purpose was to focus on combating oppression and marginalization of
historically under-represented groups.

The two movies chosen were *Rabbit Proof Fence*, directed by Phillip
Noyce (2002) and *Pumpkin*, directed by Anthony Abrams and Adam Larson
Broder (2002). Previously, I had taught a course entitled, "Culturally Relevant
Teaching," in which a movie night played a large part of the curriculum. The
two films I used then had generated discussions that I hoped to replicate during this project. For readers unfamiliar with these films, I will provide a short
summary of the plots:

Rabbit Proof Fence (PG rating). Set in 1931, this documentary relates
the true story of a young Aborigine girl, Molly Craig. Molly, her sister,

and cousin are removed from their family by the Australian government and sent to live in a government-created camp. The camp trains children to be domestic workers with the intention of reintroducing them into society later. Molly will lead her family members to escape. Their route home is 1,500 miles across Australia's barren outback. They will follow the rabbit proof fence that bisects the continent to guide them home. Today, children from these camps are known as the Stolen Generation.

Pumpkin (R Rating). A fictional tale, Carolyn is a college student involved in a sorority. Her sorority wants to win the coveted sorority of the year award and takes on the responsibility of coaching individuals with mental and physical challenges. Carolyn has never had experience with this group of individuals. At first, she is terrified at the prospect at coming in contact with her athlete, Pumpkin. Later she will have a change of heart. To the dismay of her family and friends, she falls in love with Pumpkin. Consequently, she becomes an outcast. Carolyn will go through a transformation as she begins to question the realities of her perfect life.

The attendees included college students, many of whom were my students enrolled in the teacher-education program, some of my faculty peers, and local community members. Informal observation indicated that attendees were mostly White, European-Americans. These demographics constituted a significant factor in analyzing responses to the movie. I will return to this point later.

The movies were shown at the Blue Frog, a charming, eclectic, coffee shop located only a few blocks from the college and centrally located in the larger community. The purpose of such a location was to enable attendees to escape the formality of academia and to improve the image of the college to the larger community. Approximately twenty to thirty people attended each film showing. Each film was shown to one group.

At the conclusion of each movie, the audience was separated into groups using no particular method. Graduate students and I then led them through a series of discussion questions. In addition to graduate students helping to ensure small groups, their participation also demonstrated my belief that student-to-student dialogue is as important as student-to-teacher dialogue in the learning process. After small group discussions, a large group discussion ensued, followed by a final summation where audience members were invited to further discuss their concerns. Facilitators were also given the option to establish ground rules for discussion to ensure people would feel safer and more secure while discussing these sometimes sensitive issues.

Critical pedagogy involves the use of teaching methods designed to reveal issues of power and privilege that students previously accepted without question as the status quo. The arts are one medium to address such issues. Dialogue and discussion are other routes. Therefore, the discussion questions for each movie were focused on getting attendees to think about power and privilege in relation to the film's story line.

To compensate for my concern that students might view the films more as entertainment than as an educational endeavor, I developed a set of discussion questions for both movies, documentary and fiction, with the same level of seriousness. Below are the discussion questions for each film:

Discussion questions for *Rabbit Proof Fence*:

(1) How were the Aborigine people portrayed? List characteristics and traits.

(2) How were the government officials portrayed? List characteristics and traits.

(3) What were the government's goals? Was the government successful in their efforts to convert Aborigine people into Western culture? Why or why not?

(4) Who was in a position of power in this movie? What does it mean to have power? How was this illustrated in the movie?

(5) What does it mean to lack power in society? How was this illustrated in the movie?

(6) In our society today, what group(s) maintain or lack power?

Discussion questions for *Pumpkin*:

(1) In the first half of the movie, what stereotypical assumptions does Carolyn hold toward people with disabilities?

(2) Discuss how these stereotypes are supported or debunked by the end of movie?

(3) Describe Carolyn and Pumpkin's relationship at the beginning of the story and at the end? Who saved whom?

(4) What has been your experience of working with people with disabilities? Describe your initial thoughts and behaviors?

(5) In the media, are people with disabilities under or overrepresented? In a positive or negative light? In subordinate or dominant roles? How do we explain this?

After each group reported out, the other groups offered feedback and additional thoughts. Finally, participants were invited to provide personal commentary, which may not have been included earlier in the discussion. At the end, I summarized all the ideas shared by the groups and provided some additional commentary.

The following text is from a set of personal notes that I used as a guide for the commentary portion of the evening after viewing *Rabbit Proof Fence*. Providing readers with my "uncooked" notes offers a glimpse of my relationship to social justice issues. In qualitative research, the voice of the authors is necessary as they are a part of (not apart from) the research process:

The film accurately portrays the Australian Government's policy toward Aboriginal children; from 1910–1970, approximately 100,000 children were taken from parents under state and federal laws; known as the Stolen Generation; viewed as a humane alternative

Native Americans (American Indians) were viewed as domestic foreigners or the "White man's burden." similar situation around the same time in the United States—the Bureau of India Affairs (BIA) set up off-reservation boarding schools. Most famous was the Carlisle Boarding School in Carlisle, Pennsylvania. Patterned after the Hampton Institute for African-American children; taught skills for low-paying jobs.

Carlisle Indian School motto was, "Kill the Indian, Save the man." (show cover of book—inquire about the "before" and "after" pictures?)

From the day that the children arrive, the deculturalization process began. Discuss deculturalization (destroy a culture). Clothing was taken from them, hair cut (a sign of mourning), native language prohibited (sign language until they could speak English) convert to Christianity, etc. Many were physically and sexually abused).

Long term consequences: alcoholism, poverty, unemployment, poor health, low academic achievement; psychological damage; generation of lost languages; culture suffered and people continue to suffer.

For educators: as teachers, how do we allow children of any race/culture/ethnicity to develop their identity in a way that is affirming and positive? How do we teach about other cultures without imposing values of the dominant culture? how do we honor other cultures and stop believing that some cultures are deficient or need changed?

For the community: Is social justice a matter of community concerns? Is it a moral issue? Ethical? Spiritual? A matter of human rights?
Who carries the responsibility to promote social justice? Is it a global responsibility? Do you have the courage to do what's right?

The end of my commentary was met with complete silence. All I could hear was the hum of the audiovisual equipment. It was awkward. I saw most of these students three times a week in class where they always had something to say, and now there was nothing. I intuitively believed that I was witnessing were transformative moments. I figuratively call these moments as the chewing and digesting of information. Finally, someone asked if the Australian government had ever issued an apology to the Aboriginal peoples. I was able to relate that the Australian government had issued a formal apology only a few weeks earlier (Tim Johnston, "Rudd Apologizes to Australia's Aborigines." *New York Times, February* 2008).

At the end of the evening, I conversed with my loved ones, who had assisted me that evening, during the car ride home regarding the events of the evening. My family members continued to ask questions about the movie and ensuing discussion. At one point I asked my mother-in-law about her son. "Nancy, could you imagine if someone came and took Jeff from you when he was a toddler? Could you imagine what it would be like to live your life with no knowledge of a child that is yours? Could you imagine the government telling you that you must give up your child and they will pursue you until you do?" Tears came to Nancy's eyes and she let out a choking sound.

At that moment I realized that to restore justice, we need to put ourselves in another's place. We need to imagine ourselves as the Other so that we can feel the plight and suffering of the Other.

Often, when people hear of the suffering of others, they immediately respond, "I can't imagine what that must be like." For this reason—that information alone cannot create empathy—teaching for social justice must also include the ability to imagine the reality of another. Moreover, Julian Beck advises us that teaching toward social justice must also attempt to induce an emotional response:

> If we could really feel, the pain would be so great that we would stop all the suffering . . . . If we could really feel it in the bowels, the groin, in the throat, in the breast, we would go into the streets and stop the war, stop slavery, stop the prisons, stop the killings, stop destruction . . . . When we feel, we will feel the emergency; when we feel the emergency, we will act; when we act, we will change the world. (Bucciarelli, 2004, p. 136)

5. The Blues

Nancy's reaction during that car ride home should have prepared me for what was coming, but it did not. I believed that once they had assimilated the new information, participants would become empowered, wanting to go forth and make a change in the world—not in the sense that they become political activists or incite riots, but in the sense that they would become advocates for social justice and peace. As White, European-Americans, now possessing knowledge *and* holding power to improve the conditions of others, I believed that they would feel confident to position themselves to take up the concerns and struggles of schools, and larger society.

Instead, as I continued to return and revisit the issues from the movies in my classes, students expressed a wide range of emotions—guilt, sadness, anger, frustration, immobility, powerlessness, paralysis, despair, disgust, confusion—which I term "the blues." These emotions appeared to be anything but empowering. As I listened, I replied to their questions with more questions for their consideration.

The most interesting exchange of ideas and thoughts came from a graduate student via an e-mail following *Rabbit Proof Fence*. I will share some of this correspondence along with my immediate thoughts and actual response.

Student E-mail: Good movie, even better discussion. Since I had two cups of coffee and can't get to sleep anyway, I thought I would send you some more thoughts that your movie has inspired. I wonder sometimes if the United States is suffering from collective guilt (forgive me, I'm about to go off the politically correct road, it may get bumpy). Of course we all know that there have been atrocities committed against other cultures by the dominant white culture and that we should never make light of them or repeat them.

The Native American population has suffered incredible destruction at the hands of an invading White population, just as thousands of other races and cultures have suffered under a dominant invader throughout history. The Native Americans committed atrocities against one another before the white man came. This cannot be undone. Feeling guilty or saying sorry won't make it better. All we can do is learn from our forefathers' mistakes and refuse to repeat history. But what can we do for the Native Americans now that their culture has been destroyed? What can we do if the Native American rejects the dominant culture? The casinos won't restore their culture. I don't know the answer to this one but feeling guilty helps none.

If I moved to China for work (as many Latinos have moved here), would I be in my right mind to demand the Chinese people to respect my culture, set up schools in my language and learn English to accommodate me? Or would it be reasonable for me to learn to adapt to the culture I'm in, to respect their way of doing things, and to learn their language? Wouldn't I find I had more success there if I conformed to the dominant culture? That wouldn't mean I would forget who I was or what my culture was, it just means I know what I need to do to succeed in the culture I am in. The truth is that the Latino population chose to leave their culture behind to come here, why must we change our culture for them?

I am not some sort of White supremacist. My best friend in middle school was Native American (the last I heard he was in jail), the mother of my oldest son is half African-American and half Jamaican, and I worked in South Carolina as a foreman to an all Latino construction crew. Twelve men that became my good friends, even though half of them never learned English.

Ironically, as a male elementary teacher, I still have an unfair advantage—as a minority! So the question you asked us to answer in the groups tonight comes back again, "who really has the power?" I hope you won't hold this against me :)

My Thoughts in planning my reply: *I'm not familiar with the phrase "collective guilt." Does the collective represent the dominant culture, White, European-Americans? If so, shouldn't we call it White guilt? Is White guilt a form of suffering?*

Well, we can now understand the conditions that have led the Native American culture to hold hostility and mistrust toward White, European-Americans. We can live our lives with more tact and sensitivity. We can support the rights of Native Americans.

As for the casinos, I would say it's a smart move on their part—they open casinos, build resorts and in doing so, the "White man" comes to spend money. The Native Americans use that money to buy back land which was unjustly stolen from them.

Most individuals who do immigrate to the United States retain their culture, but the culture is mostly supported within the confines of the home. Publicly, these individuals do learn to adapt and many will assimilate/acculturate into the American-way of life all at varying degrees.

No need to justify/qualify your position here by declaring you have relationships with people of color . . . relationships with the "Other" can either serve to discount the dominant ideology or support it . . .

Do you feel oppressed? Do you feel that you have an unfair advantage in the job market? If so, that's funny because most men whom I talk with in the field of education think they have an advantage in the interview process purely based upon their gender. Most claim they represent a strong male role model where there is typically none available . . .

As educators, we need these types of reflective moments to learn compassion toward our students and to understand that all people suffer—some privately, some publicly—even people who are part of the dominant culture. What surprised me the most about my students' reactions was that contrary to my expectation that my pedagogy being one of inspiration, hope, and freedom, it became one of guilt.

My Actual E-mail Response: Thanks for taking time to write and more importantly, a willingness to want to further discuss these issues. While I doubt whether I can adequately respond to all of your concerns, there's one thing I want to say: You should not feel personally responsible, nor should you feel guilty. What has happened is systemic and institutional in our American way of life woven throughout all that we do; much of it is invisible.

What has always amazed me is how the oppression and marginalization of people still continues in light of this knowledge. That is, once the dominant culture recognizes it, how do we morally and ethically allow it to continue and why don't the people who have been oppressed rebel to make the situation better. For an explanation, look into the sociological literature and more specifically, into the topic of hegemony. This gives insights into the pervasive injustices and the lack of activism to improve one's living conditions.

Guilt and despair are counter-productive when working toward social justice. I refuse to believe that critical pedagogy is merely a theory that has no practicality in the public classroom. Critical pedagogy is not empty talk and teaching without theory demonstrates a mindless approach to teaching. I believe that the emotional response signifies that my students must have in mind another state of affairs in which things would be better, or else they would not recognize the harshness of the situation and for this reason, I believe that the blues can be transformative.

6. Understanding the Blues

Are the blues a necessary step in the process of becoming an advocate for social justice? If so, what will it take to move individuals toward a productive state of being? After some consideration, I realized that the answer lies in my own life path. As I reflect upon my experiences from where I am today, I see that my exposure to social justice issues did not come about until graduate school—a similar place, developmentally, to where my students find themselves.

As a young child growing up in West Virginia, I did not resist the "isms" (such as racism and sexism) because I did not question the authority of my teachers. I accepted the teachers' word. So when I received messages from my teachers, parents, clergy, and friends about what it meant to be female, it translated as, "Katina, good little girls carry pocketbooks" or "Katina, good little girls don't get dirty and don't fight. They stay clean." There were also universally accepted historical stories, such as "Columbus sailed the ocean blue in 1492," and to this day his discovery of indigenous people—the Tainos—who *already* existed shapes my White, European-American experience.

Graduate school was an intellectual exercise that brought me into contact with concepts that were new to me and new ways of looking at the world.
For example, for the first time I was asked to consider whether our traditional
educational system might perpetuate social class distinctions. Of my assigned
readings, Johnathan Kozol's, *Amazing Grace* (1996) stands out firmly in my
memory. It transformed my way of thinking about education and social issues. I became convinced that a child's environment, race, class, and gender
impact their cultural capital. To this day, it is an important piece of literature
that continues to influence how I teach.

As I began to examine my education and the ideology that shaped my
existence, I felt deceived, mis-educated, guilty, embarrassed, foolish, and ignorant. I questioned my entire educational experience and, more importantly,
the curriculum: *Where is the story of the Tainos? Where is the history of Afri-
can-Americans, women, individuals with disabilities, children, Latinos,
Asians, Native Americans? There must be more Black people in history besides W. E. B. Dubois and George Washington Carver. Was Rachel Carson
the only female scientist?*

Critical pedagogy is inextricably linked to critical theory as it questions
and analyzes the link between historically privileged and oppressed groups,
and social institutions (such as public education) that shape knowledge construction. Critical theorists put forth the doctrine of "do not let yourselves be
deceived" by uncovering invisible social structures and hidden agenda of
school and society, in which color dominates ideologies. The starting point of
lifting the veil of deception and experiencing transformation by introduction
to the Other usually requires us to feel uncomfortable, uneasy, and eventually
guilty and sad because it confronts our ingrained social concepts.

My introduction to the Other was through literature. But regardless of
the path, when we come to realize the influence of the hidden curriculum, we
are likely to adopt a more questioning attitude about the taken-for-granted
structures of school and society. In my teaching, I take action to encourage
students to question those hidden structures with the hope that they will do the
same in their future classrooms.

My teaching could best be expressed as creating possibilities for students to critically think and reflect upon the human condition. If they feel
guilty, sad, paralyzed, disgusted, or confused during the process, I contend
that these responses are a necessary step in the process of becoming an advocate for social justice. I do not advise my students to avoid these feelings, but
try to make them aware of the conditions and structures that led to oppression
and marginalization.

The blues also represent an intentional thoughtfulness or empathetic attitude to the circumstances of the Other, which in many ways signals that students understand that privileges and power have profound implications—that
being White has cultural implications. In *White Privilege: Unpacking the In-*

visible Knapsack, Peggy McIntosh writes of the daily effects and advantages to being White in the United States:

> I can go shopping alone most of the time, pretty well assured that I will not be followed or harassed.....when I am told about our national heritage or about civilization, I am shown that people of my color made it what it is....I can do well in a challenging situation without being called a credit to my race....I can choose blemish cover or bandages in flesh color that more or less match my skin....I can easily buy posters, postcards, picture books, greeting cards, dolls, toys, and children's magazines featuring people of my race. (1990, pp. 31–36)

When I share McIntosh's statements with my students, I ask them to think about what it means to them in their lives. It is important to remind readers that the majority of students in teacher-education programs are White, European-Americans. Pre-service teachers enrolled in teacher-education programs closely resemble the racial and ethnic makeup of the current in-service teacher workforce in the United States. Although I do not volunteer students of color to be the spokesperson for their entire race, inevitably, some student of color will speak up, carefully saying, "This has happened to me." The reality of the situation then becomes more apparent to the White, European-American students, and, again, the students fall silent.

I also disclose at this point in the discussion that my step-brother is African-American who married a woman originally from Mexico. They have children who have a skin tone that is a beautiful cinnamon shade. When I need to buy my niece and nephew birthday cards, I cannot find cards that have children that look similar to them. I ask my students, "why not?" In my mind, no reason can be found except that the existence of people of color has for too long been denied.

Further analysis of the blues also led me to research the racial identity development of White people. A full discussion of racial identity is beyond the scope of this paper, but according to Janet Helms, racial identity refers to "a sense of group and collective identity based on one's perception that he or she shares a common heritage with a particular racial group" (1993, p. 3). In Helms research on racial identity (which was performed primarily with adults), she identified six stages of development. Listed from lowest to highest development, these are contact, disintegration, reintegration, pseudo-integration, immersion/emersion, and autonomy. As I further thought about my students' blues and "White guilt," I concluded that they fell into the second level, disintegration. According to Helms:

> People may develop a close working relationship with a person of color or taking a course or reading a book that challenges old comfortable assumptions. . . . People often feel uncomfortable and guilty about their

privilege. They begin to become aware of the racism that prevails in the media, recognize it in interactions with friends and families, and may try to confront other Whites. (Ibid., p. 73)

I concluded that the blues and the guilt expressed by my students place them, in general, in a developmentally low-level stage of racial identity, which can be attributed to their experiences (or lack of experiences) in school and society.

In "Whiteness and Critical Pedagogy" Ricky Lee Allen's discussion of White guilt is informed by the ideas of Paulo Freire Freire in *Pedagogy of the Oppressed* (2005), a seminal work in understanding the purpose of critical pedagogy. Allen contextualizes White guilt through Freire's oppressor-oppressed relationship. In Allen's opinion, guilt signifies that individuals view themselves as oppressors, which is a difficult realization to make as it is always psychologically easier to view ourselves as the oppressed.

According to Allen, in the oppressor-oppressed relationship, the oppressor's dysfunctional state of mind justifies its dehumanizing and immoral acts toward the Other. Yet, when individuals work against the dominant ideology of the White community, says Allen, the media portrays them as "opting out of Whiteness" or "traitors to the White community." Allen believes this predicament brings about psychological anguish because these individuals are rarely regarded as having loyalty to humanity. To compound the problem, Allen claims, "White guilt is rarely dealt with in transformative ways that emphasize cross-racial solidarity against White supremacy" in public schools (2005, pp. 59–60).

For instance, in history lessons, the curriculum seldom, if ever, reveals that there are "bad Whites." The contributions of "good Whites" and "working-class Whites" are mentioned, but little room is left in the curriculum for students to study "Whites as oppressors" (Leonard, 2005). Add to this, the color-blind approach adopted by most teachers that minimizes racial differences between students. The color-blind approach fails to recognize that people by the very nature of their skin color have different experiences, cultures, and histories. When teachers take a color-blind approach, they inadvertently support the status quo as the curriculum is one that is already built around whiteness—whiteness is the norm. Teachers must work to reveal the injustices and inequalities in society because race does matter.

7. The Blues and Working toward Social Justice in the Curriculum

The dilemma remains as to how the emotion of the blues and guilt can provide the inertia to move students from non-active states to active states and cross-race solidarity (Allen, 2005). How does a teacher use the blues as a starting point for strengthening the racial identity of White students? How does a critical pedagogue undo a lifetime of learning about White privilege, White subjectivity, White ideology, and White behavior when it has become apparent that a critique of Whiteness serves to minimize the voice of students?

I have witnessed and recorded on numerous occasions the silence that befalls my students when I attempt to de-center Whiteness in the curriculum. But, beyond the silence, there inevitably comes the questions from students about my personal agenda and why I am inclined, as a non-person of color, to address these issues. More often than not, I am met with a resistant attitude rather than a open-minded attitude that would be ideal in this situation. They resist because they are uncomfortable; much of their discomfort could be due to their guilt.

Freud, on the issue of guilt, explains that guilt is a motivator for moral action, such as stopping harmful action, repairing damage from a misdeed, and engaging in future pro-social behavior (Berk, 2008, p. 387). If Freud is correct, the blues can be the motivator for us to pursue social justice and avoid doing further harm.

Having used critical pedagogy and IBR methods over the last eight years, and repeatedly seeing responses similar to those produced in this informal study, I believe these are beneficial methods. But colleges cannot assume the responsibility to do so alone. Public schools are the first line of social defense against the breakdown of democracy and a deteriorating moral compass. Public schools should incorporate critical theory, critical pedagogy, and the use of the arts as a means to prepare the consciousness to recognize alternative ways of being alive in the world. Until more is done in the public schools to de-center Whiteness as the favored epistemological stance, we can experience only limited progress toward social justice.

Schools have historically favored the values associated with capitalism over those values that allow for improving the psychological and emotional well-being of students. Undoubtedly, life in the United States revolves around the capitalistic system, but it does not mean that the schools should buy into the same values.

Imagine an alternative—what if schools taught to the whole student? Everyday would be dedicated to experiences that develop students holistically—physically, mentally, socially, emotionally, and spiritually—and children would be allowed to feel successful and good about themselves. Likewise, imagine an economic system that might share the same set of values as schools, where students are more than a test score or a widget passed along an assembly line from one year to the next. Public school curricula have the power to encourage students to be more fully human by placing freedom, hope, love, and humanization at its core. However, according to Allen, this may not be realistic until schools relinquish practices that serve the status quo.

Public schools contribute to this dilemma in that they function to silence and separate people of color by not identifying inter-ethnic racism as an obstacle to democracy. This lack of attention allows Whites to maintain the status quo as people of color continue to push each other further down. Critical pedagogy must deal with inter-ethnic racism if it is to have any chance of playing a role in uniting people of color against White supremacy. It must work to facilitate the desires of people of color to name those groups who have more power and privilege and describe how members of those groups perpetuate White privilege vis-à-vis inter-ethnic racism. (2005, p. 61)

What prevents educators from implementing teaching methods associated with critical pedagogy? In *Finding Freedom in the Classroom: A Practical Approach to Critical Theory*, Patricia H. Hinchey, agrees with the ideas set forth by Freire, criticizes those who claim that such implementation is impractical in the classroom (1998). She agrees with Peter McLaren, who describes the prevailing cultural mindset as:

normalized greed, the right to be racist, the logic of self-interest, a desire for private gain, and a hatred for conscientious dissent...where hope is held hostage, where justice is lashed to the altar of capital accumulation, and where the good works of our collective citizenry have been effaced by despair. (Hinchey, 1998, p. 140)

With Hinchey, I also wonder what the alternative might be. Should I accept the status quo, or do I work for change and for a better society? As readers stop to reflect upon this question, I ask that you consider want you would like to see in your child's classroom: a teacher who supports the unjust structures of society (racism, sexism, homophobia), or a teacher who works for positive social change?

Hinchey discusses the misconception that critical pedagogy is a political act. However, when one studies the history of the educational system, education has *always* been political in our country. There has always been a struggle to decide who will be educated, what will be taught, and how it will be taught. Much of the same continues today in light of the No Child Left Behind Act (NCLB).

That there is room in the curriculum for teaching methods associated with critical pedagogy is irrefutable despite the pending criticisms and the guilt students might feel. For this reason, I now offer my curricular recommendations for teachers who are advocates for and committed to social justice. I start with one based on Helms' work as cited by Ricky Lee Allen (2005, p. 65), and list the recommendations that I have formulated based on my research:

(1) Help students develop a healthy, positive White identity (non-racist) by creating an environment of dissonance that brings White students to a point of identity crisis.

(2) De-center Whiteness as the favored epistemological stance.

(3) Engage students in cross-racial dialogue using multiple forms of text; meet the Other.

(4) Implement problem-based teaching models (ideally project-based) for students to deal with the unresolved past.

(5) Use the arts to throw students' cognitive schemas into chaos and follow-up with "what if" discussions.

(6) Encourage conversation, not silence.

(7) Humanize your students.

(8) Create a safe place in the classroom for these discussions.

(9) Avoid trivial classroom activities that perpetuate stereotypes.

(10) Encourage students to be a part of their community through service-learning projects.

(11) Resist banality and mindlessness in the curriculum.

As we devote ourselves to supporting and engaging in social change, the imagination should be put into action. It will be the imagination above all else that allows us to envision new beginnings, new possibilities, and new patterns for being in the world.

Wallace Stevens' closes his "The Man with the Blue Guitar" with:

You as you are? You are yourself.
The blue guitar surprises you. (1982)

I encourage teachers to allow their teaching to surprise you, and in doing so it will make you a better teacher and encourage your students more empathetic toward others.

WORKS CITED

Chapter One: Richard Werner

Adler, J. (2002) *Beliefs Own Ethics*. Cambridge, Mass.: The MIT Press.

Blackburn, Simon. (2005) *Truth*. Oxford: Oxford University Press.

Bush, George W. (2001) Address to a joint session of Congress (20 September 20). CNN.com. http://archives.cnn.com/2001/US/09/20/gen.bush.transcript/ (accessed 17 November 2009).

Cady, Duane. (1990) *From Warism to Pacifism*. Philadelphia, Pa.: Temple University Press.

Camus, Albert. (1951/1992) *The Rebel: An Essay On Man In Revolt*. New York: Vantage Press.

Center for Defense Information. (1996) US Military Spending, 1945–1996. Prepared by Martin Calhoun. http://www.cdi.org/Issues/milspend.html (accessed 23 October 2009).

Clifford, William Kingdon (1999) "The Ethics of Belief," p. 77. In *Ethics of Belief and Other Essays* (Amherst, N.Y.: Prometheus Books).

Dewey, John. (1896) "The Reflex Arc Concept in Psychology," *Psychological Review*, 3, pp. 357–370.

Diamond, J. (2004) *Collapse*. New York: Viking Publishers.

Domasio, Antonio R. (1994) *Descartes' Error: Emotion, Reason, and the Human Brain*. New York: Avon Books.

Feldman, R. (2000) "The Ethics of Belief," *Philosophy and Phenomenological Research*, 6:1, pp. 667–695.

Gladwell, M. (2002) *The Tipping Point: How Little Things Can Make a Big Difference*. New York: Back Bay Books.

Groopman, J. (2003) *The Anatomy of Hope*. New York: Random House.

Havel, Vaclav. (2009) *The Power of the Powerless*. Cambridge: Routledge.

Klein, N. (2008) *The Shock Doctrine: The Rise of Disaster Capitalism*. New York: Picador.

Marcuse, Herbert. (1964/1991) *One-Dimensional Man: Studies in the Ideology of Advanced Industrial Society*. Boston: Beacon Press.

McDermott, J. J. (1977) *The Writings of William James: A Comprehensive Edition*. Chicago: University of Chicago Press.

Mckibben, B. (2008) *Deep Economy: The Wealth of Communities and the Durable Future*. New York: Holt Paperbacks.

Painter, N. I. (2008) *Standing at Armageddon*. New York: W. W. Norton.

Phillips, K. (2002) *Wealth and Democracy*. New York: Broadway Books.

Power, S. (2002) *The Problem from Hell*. New York: Basic Books.

Rice, Condoleezza. (2008) Rice Keynote Address at World Economic Forum Meeting. http://www.america.gov/st/texttrans-english/2008/20080123183031bpuh0.4350092.html (accessed 23 October 2009).

Silentio, Johannes. (2006) *Fear and Trembling*. Edited by Sylvia Walsh and C. Stephen Evans. Cambridge: Cambridge University Press, 2006.

SIPRI Military Expenditure Database. (2008) http://www.sipri.org/databases/milex (accessed 23 October 2009).

Speth, J. G. (2008) *The Bridge at the Edge of the World*. New Haven: Yale University Press.
Stiglitz, J. E., and L. J. Bilmes. (2008) *The Three Trillion Dollar War*. New York: W. W. Norton & Company.

Chapter Two: Robert L. Muhlnickel

Feinberg, J. (1984) *Harm to Others: The Moral Limits of the Criminal Law*. New York: Oxford University Press.
Gilligan, C. (1982) *In a Different Voice: Psychological Theory and Women's Development*. Cambridge: Harvard University Press.
Hoffmaster, B. (2006) "What Does Vulnerability Mean?" *Hastings Center Report*, 36:2, pp. 38–45.
Kidder, R. (2005) *Moral Courage*. New York: William Morrow.
Levering, R. (1986)"Martin Luther King, Jr.: The Challenge of Inclusive Peacemaking," pp. 198–226. In *Peace Heroes in Twentieth Century America*. Edited by C. DeBenedetti. Bloomington: Indiana University Press.
MacIntyre, Alasdair. (1999) *Dependent Rational Animals*. Chicago, Ill.: Open Court.
Martin, J. (1999) *This Our Exile: A Spiritual Journey with the Refugees of East Africa*. Maryknoll: Orbis Books.
Merton, T. (1980) *The Nonviolent Alternative*. New York: Farrar, Strauss, and Giroux.
Noddings, Nell. (1984) *Care: A Feminine Approach to Ethics and Moral Education*. Berkeley: University of California Press.
Rorty, Amelie O. (1986) "The Two Faces of Courage," *Philosophy*, 61, pp. 51–71.
Slote, M. (2007) *The Ethics of Care and Empathy*. New York: Routledge.
Swanton, C. (2004) *Virtue Ethics: A Pluralistic View*. New York: Oxford University Press.

Chapter Three: Sanjay Lal

Ansboro, J. J. (1982) *The Making of a Mind*. New York: Orbis.
Arendt, Hannah. (1963) *Eichmann in Jerusalem*. New York: Penguin
Gandhi, Mahatma K. (1948) *The Collected Works of Mahatma Gandhi*. Volume 48. New Delhi: Indian Government.
———. (1955) *Truth is God*. Ahemedabad: Navajivan Truth.
———. (1971) *The Story of My Experiments with Truth*. Boston, Mass.: Beacon.
Homer, J. A., Ed. (1956) *The Gandhi Reader*. Bloomington: Indiana University Press.
Iyer, R., Ed. (1986) The Moral and Political Writings of Mahatma Gandhi. Volume 1. New Delhi: Claredon Press.

Chapter Four: William C. Gay

Ackerman, P., and J. DuVall. (2000) *A Force More Powerful: A Century of Nonviolent Conflict*. New York: St. Martin's Press.
Adams, David, S. A. Barnett, N. P. Bechtereva, et al. (1990) "The Seville Statement on Violence," pp. 221–223. In *A Reader in Peace Studies*. Edited by P. Smoker. Oxford: Pergamon.

Bondurant, J. V. (1988) *Conquest of Violence: The Gandhian Philosophy of Conflict.* Princeton, N.J.: Princeton University Press.

Cady, Duane. (1989) *From Warism to Pacifism: A Moral Continuum.* Philadelphia, Pa.: Temple University Press.

Childress, J. (1972) "Nonviolent Resistance and Direct Action," *Journal of Religion,* 52:4, pp. 376–396.

Dreyfus, Hubert L. (1990) *Being-in-the-World: A Commentary on Heidegger's* Being and Time. Boston, Mass.: The MIT Press.

Gay, William C. (1980) "Analogy And Metaphor: Two Models of Linguistic Creativity," *Philosophy and Social Criticism,* 7:3–4, pp. 299–317.

———. (1998) "The Practice of Linguistic Nonviolence," *Peace Review,* 10:4, pp. 545–547.

———. (1999a) "The Language of War and Peace," pp. 303–312. In *Encyclopedia of Violence, Peace, and Conflict.* Volume 2. Edited by L. Kurtz. San Diego, Calif.: Academic Press.

———. (1999b) "Linguistic Violence," pp. 13–35. In *Institutional Violence.* Edited by R. Litke and D. Curtin. Amsterdam: Rodopi.

———. (2004) "Public Policy Discourse on Peace," pp. 5–17). In *Putting Peace into Practice: Evaluating Policy on Local and Global Levels.* Edited by N. Potter. Amsterdam: Rodopi.

Gilligan, C. (1982) *In a Different Voice: Psychological Theory and Women's Development.* Cambridge: Harvard University Press.

Gorsevski, E. W. (2004) *Peaceful Persuasion: The Geopolitics of Nonviolent Rhetoric.* Albany: State University of New York Press.

Hamington, M. (2004) *Embodied Care: Jane Addams, Maurice Merleau-Ponty, and Feminist Ethics.* Champaign: University of Illinois Press.

Heidegger, Martin. (1962) *Being and Time.* Translated by J. Macquarrie and E. Robinson. New York: Harper.

Jafari, S. (2007) "Local Religious Peacemakers: An Untapped Resource in U.S. Foreign Policy," *Journal of International Affairs,* 61:1, pp. 111–130.

King, Martin Luther, Jr. (1964) *Letter from a Birmingham Jail.* New York: Harper and Row.

Mandela, N. Nelson (1994) Mandela's Address to the People of Cape Town, Grand Parade, on the Occasion of His Inauguration as State President. (9 May) http://www.anc.org.za/ancdocs/history/mandela/1994/inaugct.html (accessed 17 November 2009).

Tanenbaum Center for Interreligious Understanding. (2007) *Peacemakers in Action: Profiles of Religion in Conflict Resolution.* Edited by David Little. Cambridge, UK: Cambridge University Press.

Thonssen, Lester. (1964) Representative American Speeches: 1963–1964. New York: H. W. Wilson.

Mortenson, G., and D. O. Relin. (2006) *Three Cups of Tea: One Man's Mission to Promote Peace One School at a Time.* New York: Penguin Books.

Rosenberg, M. B. (2005) *Nonviolent Communication: A Language of Life.* Encinitas, Calif.: Puddle Dancer Press.

Sharp, G. (1992) "The Techniques Of Nonviolent Action," pp. 223–229. In *A Peace Reader: Essential Readings on War, Justice, Nonviolence and World Order.* Edited by J. J. Fahey and R. Armstron. Mahweh, N.J.: Paulist Press.

Chapter Five: Joseph Betz

Kymlicka, Will. (2007) *Multicultural Odysseys: Negotiating the New International Politics of Diversity*. Oxford, Oxford University Press.

Chapter Six: Anna Lübbe

Bar On, Dan. (2008) *The "Others" Within Us: Constructing Jewish-Israeli Identity*. New York: Cambridge University Press.

Davies, J., and E. Kaufman, Eds. *Second Track/Citizens' Diplomacy: Concepts and Techniques for Conflict Transformation*. Lanham, Md.: Rowman & Littlefield.

Francis, Diana. (2004) "Culture, Power Asymmetries, and Gender in Conflict Transformation," pp. 91–107. In *Transforming Ethnopolitical Conflict: The Berghof Handbook*. Edited by A. Austin, M. Fischer, and N. Ropers. Wiesbaden, Germany: VS Verlag für Sozialwissenschaften.

Fisher, Ronald. (2002) "Historical Mapping of the Field of Interactive Conflict Resolution," pp. 61–78. In Davies and Kaufman. *Second Track/Citizens' Diplomacy*.

Franke, Ursula. (2004) *Systemische Familienaufstellung* (*Systemic Family Constellation*). München/Wien, Germany: Profil Verlag.

Hellinger, Bert. (2005) *Der Große Konflikt. Die Antwort*. (*The Large Conflict: The Answer*). München, Germany: Wilhelm Goldmann Verlag.

———, and Hunter Beaumont. (2007) *Healing Love: A Teaching Seminar on Love's Hidden Symmetry*. DVD 3. Berchtesgaden, Germany: Video Verlag Bert Hellinger International.

Höppner, G. (2001) *Heilt Demut, wo Schicksal wirkt? Eine Studie zu Effekten des Familien-Stellens nach Bert Hellinger* (*Does Humility Heal where Fate Operates? A Study on the Effects of Family Constellations according to Bert Hellinger*). München, Germany: Profil Verlag.

Kaufman, Stuart. (2001) *Modern Hatreds: The Symbolic Politics of Ethnic War*. Ithaca, N.Y.: Cornell University Press.

———. (2006) "Escaping the Symbolic Politics Trap: Reconciliation Initiatives and Conflict Resolution in Ethnic Wars," *Journal of Peace Research*, 43:2, pp. 201–218.

Kelman, Herbert. (2002) "Interactive Problem Solving as a Tool For Second Track Diplomacy," pp. 81–105. In Davies and Kaufman. *Second Track/Citizens' Diplomacy*.

König, Eckard, and Gerda Vollmer. (1999) *Systemische Organisationsberatung. Grundlagen und Methoden* (*Systemic Organizational Consulting: Principles and Methods*). Weinheim, Germany: Deutscher Studien Verlag.

Kohlhauser, Martin, and Friedrich Assländer. (2005) *Organisationsaufstellungen evaluiert* (*Organizational Constellations Evaluated*). Heidelberg, Germany: Carl-Auer-Systeme Verlag.

Kühner, Angela. (2003) *Kollektive Traumata. Annahmen, Argumente, Konzepte. Eine Bestandsaufnahme nach dem 11. September* (*Collective Trauma: Assumptions, Arguments, Concepts. A Review after 9/11*). Berlin, Germany: Berghof Forschungszentrum für konstruktive Konfliktbearbeitung.

Lübbe, Anna. (2007) *"Ethnopolitische Konflikte: Das Potenzial Der Systemaufstellungsmethode"* ("Ethnopolitical Conflict: The Potential of Systemic Constellations"), *Zeitschrift für Konfliktmanagement*, 1, pp. 12–16.

———. (2009) "Us versus Them: Splitting Dynamics and Turning Points in Ethnopolitical Conflict," *Journal of Peace, Conflict, and Development*, 13. http://www.peace studiesjournal.org.uk/dl/Issue%2013%20Article%2016%20final%20version%20 pdf.pdf (accessed 30 October 2009)

Mraz, Rudolf. (2006) "*Nachgeprüft. Ergebnisse einer 10-Jahres-Katamnese aus über 850 Aufstellungen*" ("Reconsidered. Results of a Ten Year Catamnesis from over 850 Constellations"), *Praxis für Systemaufstellungen*, 2, pp. 94–101.

Münkler, Herfried. (2002) *Die Neuen Kriege* (*New Wars*). Reinbek bei Hamburg, Germany: Rowohlt Verlag.

Ruppert, Franz. (2007) "*Wie zuverlässig ist die Aufstellungsmethode?*" ("How reliable is the Constellation Method?"), *Praxis für Systemaufstellungen*, 2, pp. 76–92.

Sen, Amartya. (2006) *Identity and Violence: The Illusion of Destiny*. New York: W. W. Norton.

Simon, F. (2004) *Patterns of War: Systemic Aspects of Deadly Conflicts*. Heidelberg, Germany: Carl-Auer Verlag.

Smith, Dan. (2004) "Trends and Causes of Armed Conflict," pp. 111–127. In *Transforming Ethnopolitical Conflict: The Berghof Handbook*. Edited by A. Austin, M. Fischer, and N. Ropers. Wiesbaden, Germany: VS Verlag für Sozialwissenschaften.

Volkan, Vamik. (1999) *Das Versagen der Diplomatie: Zur Psychoanalyse Nationaler, Ethnischer und Religiöser Konflikte* (*The Failure of Diplomacy: On the Psychoanalysis of National, Ethnic, and Religious Conflict*). Gießen, Germany: Psychosozial Verlag.

———. (2004) "*Das Baum-Modell*" ("The Tree Model "), pp. 69–96. In *Mediation—Theorie und Praxis. Neue Beiträge Zur Konfliktregelung* (*Mediation—Theory and Practice: New Contributions to Conflict Resolution*). Edited by P. Geißler. Gießen, Germany: Psychosozial-Verlag.

———. (2007) *Killing in the Name of Identity: A Study of Bloody Conflicts*. Charlottesville, Va.: Pitchstone Publishing.

von Schlippe, Arist, and Jochen Schweitzer. (2000) *Lehrbuch der Systemischen Therapie und Beratung* (*Textbook on Systemic Therapy and Consulting*). Göttingen, Germany: Vandenhoeck & Ruprecht.

Wendt, Alexander. (1999) *Social Theory of International Politics*. Cambridge, Mass.: Cambridge University Press.

Chapter Seven: Joseph Rayle

Au, W., B. Bigelow, and S. Karp. (2007) *Rethinking Our Classrooms*. Milwaukee, Wis.: Rethinking Schools.

Bain, K. (2004) *What the Best College Teachers Do*. Cambridge, Mass.: Harvard University Press.

Berliner, D., and B. Biddle. (1995) *The Manufactured Crisis: Myths, Fraud, and the Attack on America's Public Schools*. Reading, Mass.: Addison-Wesley.

Bertalanffy, Ludwig von. (1968) *General System Theory: Foundations, Development, Applications*. New York: G. Braziller.

Bowers, C. A. (1997) *The Culture of Denial: Why the Environmental Movement Needs a Strategy for Reforming Universities and Public Schools*. Albany: State University of New York Press.

Capra, Fritjof. (1983) *The Turning Point: Science, Society, and the Rising Culture*. New York: Bantam Books.

————. (1994) "From the Parts to the Whole: Systems Thinking in Ecology and Education," *Elmwood Quarterly*, Fall-Summer, pp. 35–41.

————. (1997) *The Hidden Connections: A Science for Sustainable Living*. London: Flamingo.

Counts, George S. (1978) *Dare the School Build a New Social Order?* Carbondale, Ill.: Southern Illinois University Press.

Cremin, L. (1990) *Popular Education and Its Discontents*. New York: Harper & Row.

De Assis, Sebastian (2003) *Revolution in Education*. Landham, Md.: Scarecrow Press.

deMarrais, K., and M. LeCompte. (1999) *The Way Schools Work: A Sociological Analysis of Education*. New York: Longman.

Gatto, John Taylor. (2006) *The Underground History of American Education: A Schoolteacher's Intimate Investigation into the Prison of Modern Schooling*. New York: Oxford Village Press.

————. (2008) *Weapons of Mass Instruction: A Schoolteacher's Journey through the Dark World of Compulsory Schooling*. Philadelphia, Pa.: New Society Publishers.

Giroux, Henry A. (2003) *The Abandoned Generation: Democracy beyond the Culture of Fear*. New York: Palgrave Macmillan.

Glassner, B. (1999) *The Culture of Fear: Why Americans are Afraid of the Wrong Things*. New York: Basic Books.

Keegan, J. (1993) *A History of Warfare*. New York: Alfred A. Knopf.

Kohn, A. (1999) *The Schools Our Children Deserve: Moving beyond Traditional Classrooms and "Tougher Standards."* Boston, Mass.: Houghton Mifflin.

Kozol, Jonathan. (2005) *The Shame of the Nation: The Restoration of Apartheid Schooling in America*. New York: Crown Publishers.

Linton, R. (1936) *The Study of Man: An Introduction*. New York: D. Appleton-Century Co.

Loewen, J. (2005) *Sundown Towns: A Hidden Dimension Of American Racism.* New York: New Press.

Loewen, J. W. (2007) *Lies My Teacher Told Me: Everything Your American History Textbook Got Wrong*. New York: Simon & Schuster.

McCaw, D. S. (2007) "Dangerous Intersection Ahead," *School Administrator*, 64:2, pp. 32–40.

Palmer, P. J. (1998) *The Courage to Teach: Exploring the Inner Landscape of a Teacher's Life*. San Francisco, Calif.: Jossey-Bass.

Peters, L. H., E. J. O'Connor, A. Pooyan, and J. C. Quick. (1984) "The Relationship between Time Pressure and Performance: A Field Test of Parkinson's Law," *Journal of Occupational Behaviour*, 5:4, pp. 293–299.

Ravitch, D. (1983) *The Troubled Crusade: American Education, 1945–1980*. New York: Basic Books.

————. (2000) *Left Back: A Century of Failed School Reforms*. New York: Simon & Schuster.

Rayle, J. (2007) *Educational Ecology: A New Perspective on Educational Problems*. Presentation at the Annual Conference for the National Network for Educational Renewal. October. Charleston, WV.

————. (2008) *What's at Stake for You: Connecting White Students Education with Social Justice*. Presentation at the Annual Equity Social Justice Conference. April. The Richard Stockton College.

Rochester, J. M. (2002) *Class Warfare: Besieged Schools, Bewildered Parents, Betrayed Kids, and the Attack on Excellence*. San Francisco, Calif.: Encounter Books.

Sandlin, J. A., and J. L. Milam. (2008) "Mixing Pop (Culture) and Politics: Cultural Resistance, Culture Jamming, and Anti-Consumption Activism as Critical Public Pedagogy," *Curriculum Inquiry*, 38:3, pp. 323-350.

Schell, J. (2003) *The Unconquerable World: Power, Non-Violence, and the Will of the People*. New York: Metropolitan Books.

Spring, J. (2005) *The American School: 1642–2004*. Boston, Mass.: McGraw-Hill.

Tozer, S., G. Senese, and P. Violas. (2007) *School And Society: Historical and Contemporary Perspectives*. New York: McGraw-Hill.

Tyak, D., L. Cuban. (1995) *Tinkering toward Utopia: A Century of Public School Reform*. Cambridge, Mass.: Harvard University Press.

Vygotsky, L. S. (1978) *Mind in Society: The Development of Higher Psychological Processes*. Cambridge, Mass.: Harvard University Press.

Chapter Eight: Paul J. Parks

Birenberg, Yoav. (2006) Barenboim's Coexistence Orchestra. *Ynetnews.com*. http://www.ynetnews.com/articles/0,7340,L-3343876,00.html (accessed 23 October 2009).

Campbell, J. (1974) *The Mythic Image*. Bollingen Series. Princeton, N.J.: Princeton University Press

Hague Convention for the Protection of Cultural Property in the Event of Armed Conflict. (1954) Preamble. The Netherlands, The Hague.

Holladay, J. (2007) "Eyes on the Prize," *Teaching Tolerance*, (Fall), 32. Montgomery, Ala.: Southern Poverty Law Center.

Josten, K. (1994–2007) *Project Description: Global Art Project for Peace*. http://www.globalartproject.org/about/projectdescription.html (accessed 23 October 2009).

Kilman, C. (2007) "One Nation, Many Gods," *Teaching Tolerance* (Fall), 32. Montgomery, Ala.: Southern Poverty Law Center.

Lyon, C. (2009) My Moksha: Solo Thesis Exhibition Statement (May). Cortland: State University of New York at Cortland.

Rank, C. (2008) Promoting Peace through the Arts: The Role of Anti-War and Peace Art in Building Cultures of Peace. Paper presented at the 2008 IPRA Conference: Art and Peace Commission. Leuven, Belgium.

Read, H. (1969) "Art and Society." In *The Arts and Man: A World View of the Role and Function of the Arts in Society*. Paris: UNESCO.

Chapter Nine: Dennis Rothermel

Aldrich, R., Dir. (1956), *Attack*. United Artists.

Basinger, J. (1986) *The World War II Combat Film: Anatomy of a Genre*. New York: Columbia University Press.

Bersani, L., and U. Dutoit (2004) *Forms of Being: Cinema, Aesthetics, Subjectivity.* London: British Film Institute.

Britten, Benjamin. (1963) *War Requiem.* Op. 66. Decca. (First performance 1962.)

Campbell, D. (2009a) *Joker One: A Marine Platoon's Story of Courage, Leadership, and Brotherhood.* New York: Random House.

Campbell, D. (2009b) Interview with T. Gross. *Fresh Air.* National Public Radio. 5 March.

Castle, R. (1998) "Kubrick's Ulterior War," *Film Comment,* 34:5 (September/October), pp. 25–29.

Cavell, S. (1981) *Pursuits of Happiness: The Hollywood Comedy of Remarriage.* Cambridge: Harvard University Press.

Chion, M. (2004) *The Thin Red Line.* Translated by T. Selous. London: British Film Institute.

Coplan, A. (2009) "Form and Feeling in Terrence Malick's The Thin Red Line." In Davies. *The Thin Red Line.*

Coppola, Francis Ford, Dir. (1979) A*pocalypse Now!* Zoetrope Studios.

Critchley, S. (2009) "Calm—On Terrence Malick's The Thin Red Line." In Davies. *The Thin Red Line.*

Davies, D., Ed. (2009a) *The Thin Red Line.* London and New York: Routledge.

———. (2009b) "Vision, Touch, and Embodiment in The Thin Red Line." In *The Thin Red Line.*

Dombrowski, L. (2008) *The Films of Samuel Fuller: If You Die, I'll Kill You.* Middletown, Conn.: Wesleyan University Press.

Donald, R. R. (2005) "From 'Knockout Punch' to 'Home Run': Masculinity's 'Dirty Dozen' Sports Metaphors in American Combat Films," *Film and History,* 35:1 (May), pp. 20–28.

Dreyfus, H., and C. S. Prince (2009) "The Thin Red Line: Dying without Demise, Demise without Dying," In Davies. *The Thin Red Line.*

Eastwood, Clint, Dir. (2006) *Letters from Iwo Jima.* Malpaso Productions.

Eberwein, R., Ed. (2005) *The War Movie.* New Brunswick: Rutgers University Press.

Emerson, R. W. (2000) *The Essential Writings of Ralph Waldo Emerson.* Edited by B. Atkinson. New York: The Modern Library.

Endfield, C., Dir. (1964) *Zulu.* Diamond Films.

Ford, J., Dir. (1939) Drums Along the Mohawk. Twentieth Century-Fox Film Corporation.

Ford, J., Dir. (1945) *They Were Expendable.* Metro-Goldwyn-Mayer.

Fuller, S., Dir. (1980) *The Big Red One.* Lorimar Productions.

Furstenau, M., and L. MacAvoy (2003) "Terrence Malick's Heideggerian Cinema: War and the Question of Being in The Thin Red Line." In Patterson. *The Cinema of Terrence Malick.*

Goulding, E. (1938) *The Dawn Patrol.* Warner Bros. Pictures.

Grau, C., Ed. (2005) *Philosophers Explore The Matrix.* Oxford: Oxford University Press.

Gray, J. G. (1967) *The Warriors: Reflections on Men in Battle.* 2nd edition. New York: Harper and Row.

———. (1970) *On Understanding Violence Philosophically and Other Essays.* New York: Harper and Row.

Grossman, D. (1995) *On Killing: The Psychological Learning to Kill in War and Society*. New York: Back Bay Books.

Gruben, P. (2005) "Practical Joker: The Invention of a Protagonist in Full Metal Jacket," *Literature Film Quarterly*, 33:4, pp. 270–279.

Hawks, H., Dir. (1930) *The Dawn Patrol*. First National Pictures.

Heidegger, M. (1975) "Logos (Heraclitus, Fragment B 50)." In *Early Greek Thinking: The Dawn of Western Philosophy*. Translated by D. F. Krell and F. A. Capuzzi. San Francisco: Harper.

Heraclitus (1995) *Heraclitus: Translation and Analysis*. Edited and translated by D. Sweet. Lanham, Md: University Press of America.

Hickox, R., Conductor. *War Requiem, Sinfonia da Requiem, Ballad of Heroes*. Libretto, by B. Britten. Translated by Eric Roseberry. London Symphony Orchestra and Chorus. Chandos Compact Disc Recording.

Hüppauf, B. (1995) "The Photographic Representation of War." In *Fields of Vision: Essays in Film Studies, Visual Anthropology, and Photography*. Edited by L. Devereau and R. Millman. Berkeley: University of California Press.

Imhoof, D. (2008) "Culture Wars and the Local Screen: The Reception of Westfront 1918 and All Quiet on the Western Front in One German City." In *Why We Fought: America's Wars in Film and History*. Edited by P. C. Rollins and J. E. O'Connor. Lexington: The University Press of Kentucky.

Ives, Charles. (1906) *The Unanswered Question*. (New York: Southern Music Publishing Co., 1953, Plate 246-5.)

Jagger, M., and K. Richards. (1966) "Paint It Black." London: 45-LON.901 (US).

Kane, K. (1982) *Visions of War: Hollywood Combat Films of World War II*. 2nd Edition. An Arbor, Mich.: UMI Research Press.

Kelly, A. (2005) "The Greatness and Continuing Significance of *All Quiet on the Western Front*." In Eberwein. *The War Movie*.

Kline, M. (2000) "Guadalcanal as Mental State: Narrative Strategy in Terrence Malick's *The Thin Red Line*." West Virginia University Philological Papers (September), pp. 137–144.

Kubrick, Stanley, Dir. (1957) *Paths of Glory*. Bryna Productions.

———, Dir. (1964) *Dr. Strangelove Or: How I learned to Stop Worrying and Love the Bomb*. Columbia Pictures Corporation.

———, Dir. (1987) Full-Metal Jacket. Warner Brothers Productions.

———. (2001) *Stanley Kubrick Interviews*. Edited by G. D. Phillips. Jackson: University of Mississippi Press.

Lean, D., Dir., (1957) *The Bridge on the River Kwai*. Horizon Pictures.

———, Dir. (1962) *Lawrence of Arabia*. Columbia Pictures.

McCormick, P. (1999) "War is a Hell of a Movie," *U.S. Catholic*, 64:5 (May), pp. 46–49.

Malick, T., Dir. (1998) *The Thin Red Line*. Fox 2000 Pictures.

Michaels, Lloyd. (2009) *Terrence Malick*. Urbana and Chicago: University of Illinois Press.

Milestone, L., Dir. (1930) *All Quiet on the Western Front*. Universal Pictures.

———., Dir. (1945) *A Walk in the Sun*. Twentieth Century-Fox.

———., Dir. (1959) *Pork Chop Hill*. United Artists.

Misek, R. (2008) "Exploding Binaries: Point-of-View and Combat in *The Thin Red Line*," *Quarterly Review of Film and Video*, 25:2, pp. 116–123.

Morrison, J., and T. Schur (2003) *The Films of Terrence Malick*. London: Praeger.

Mullarkey, J. (2009) *Refractions of Reality: Philosophy and the Moving Image*. New York: Palgrave Macmillan.

Naremore, J. (2007) *On Kubrick*. London: British Film Institute.

Nelson, T. A. (2000) *Kubrick: Inside a Film Artist's Maze*. Bloomington: Indiana University Press.

Paris, M., Ed. (2000) *The First World War and Popular Cinema: 1914 to the Present*. New Brunswick, Rutgers University Press.

Patterson, H., Ed. (2003) *The Cinema of Terrence Malick: Poetic Visions of America*. London: Wallflower Press.

Perkins, V. F. (1972) *Film As Film*. New York: Penguin Books.

Plato (1963) *The Collected Dialogues of Plato*. Edited by E. Hamilton and H. Cairns. Princeton: Princeton University Press.

Polan, D. (2005) "Auteurism and War-teurism: Terrence Malick's War Movie." In Eberwein. *The War Movie*.

Power, S. P. (2003) "The Other World of War: Terrence Malick's Adaptation of The Thin Red Line." In Patterson. *The Cinema of Terrence Malick*.

Rambuss, R. (1999) "Machinehead," *Camera Obscura*, 14:42 (September), pp. 97–125.

Renoir, J., Dir. (1937) *The Grand Illusion. Réalisations d'Art Cinématographique*.

Renoir, J. (1974) *My Life and My Films*. New York: Atheneum.

Rose, K. D. (2008) *Myth and the Greatest Generation: A Social History of Americans in World War II*. New York: Routledge.

Sanchez, R. (2008a) *Wiser in Battle: A Soldier's Story*. New York: Harper.

————. (2008b) Interview with Terri Gross. *Fresh Air*. National Public Radio. (7 May).

Shaw, D. (2009) "Film and Philosophy: Taking Movies Seriously," *American Society for Aesthetics Newsletter*, 28:33 (Winter), pp. 5–6.

Siegel, D., Dir. (1962) *Hell Is for Heroes*. Paramount Pictures.

Silberman, R. (2003) "Terrence Malick, Landscape and 'This War At the Heart of Nature.'" In Patterson. *The Cinema of Terrence Malick*.

Stone, O., Dir. (1986) *Platoon*. Hemdale Films.

Suid, L. H. (2002) *Guts and Glory: The Making of the American Military Image in Film*. Revised and expanded edition. Lexington: The University Press of Kentucky Press.

Swofford, A. (2003) *Jarhead: A Marine's Chronicle of the Gulf War and Other Battles*. New York: Scribner's.

Tanovic, D., Dir. (2001) *No Man's Land*. Noé Productions.

Tchaikovsky, P. I.. (1882) *1812 Overture. (The Year 1812, Festival* Overture in E flat major, Op. 49). Earliest orchestral recording Royal Albert Hall Orchestra. Conducted by Landon Ronald. HMV (1916).

Trumbo, D., Dir. (1971) *Johnny Got His Gun*. World Entertainment.

Virillio, P. (1989) *War and Cinema: The Logistics of Perception*. Translated by P. Camiller. London: Verso.

Walsh, S. (2005) "Friendly Fire: Epistolary Voice-Over in Terrence Malick's *The Thin Red Line*," *Literature Film Quarterly*, 33:4, pp. 306–312.

Wartenberg, T. E. (2009) "Teaching Thinking on Screen," *American Society for Aesthetics Newsletter*, 28:3 (Winter), pp. 3–4.

Weir, P., Dir., (1981) *Gallipoli*. The Australian Film Commission.

Wellman, W., Dir. (1945) *Story of G. I. Joe*. United Artists.

Westwell, G. (2006) *War Cinema: Hollywood on the Front Line*. London: Wallflower Press.

Wordsworth, W. (1967) *Poetry and Prose*. Cambridge: Harvard University Press.

Chapter Ten: Colleen Kattau

Bird, S., D. Georgakas, and D. Shaffer. (1985) *Solidarity Forever: An Oral History of the IWW*. Chicago, Ill.: Lake View Press.

Blackburn, Inés Dolz, and M. Agosín. (1992) *Violeta Parra O La Expresión Inefable: Un Análisis Crítico De Su Poesía, Prosa Y Pintura* (*The Ineffable Expression of Violeta Parra: A Critical Analysis of Her Poetry*). Santiago, Chile: Planeta.

Du Bois, W. E. B. (2003. "Of the Sorrow Songs," pp. 252–257. In *The Souls of Black Folk*. New York: The Modern Library.

Edelman, M. (1995) *From Art to Politics: How Artistic Creations Shape Political Conceptions*. Chicago, Ill.: University of Chicago Press.

Eyerman, R., and A. Jamison. (1988) *Music and Social Movements: Mobilizing Traditions in the Twentieth Century*. Cambridge, Mass.: Cambridge University Press.

Fairly, Jan. (2001) "The Local and the Global in Popular Music," pp. 272–289. In *The Cambridge Companion to Pop and Rock*. Edited by Simon Frith. Cambridge: Cambridge University Press.

———. (1989) "New Song: Music and Politics In Latin America," pp. 88–97. In *Rhythms of the World*. Edited by F. May and T. Hanly. New York: BBC Books.

Ferrari, Carol. (2006) "Please Remember Music," *The Dominion*, 3:1 (January 10) http://www.soaw.org/newswire_detail.php?id=1010 (accessed 23 October 2009).

Foster, David William. (2000) "Paquita La Del Barrio: Singing Feminine Rage." (January) http://www.lehman.cuny.edu/ciberletras/v01n02/Foster.htm (accessed 23 October 2009).

Garofalo, R., Ed. (1992) *Rocking the Boat: Mass Music and Mass Movements*. Boston, Mass.: South End Press.

Johnson Reagon, Bernice. (2001) *If You Don't Go, Don't Hinder Me*. Lincoln: University of Nebraska Press.

Lieberman, R. (1989) *My Song Is My Weapon*. Urbana: University of Illinois Press.

MacDonald, Katherine. (2005) Reflections of the Modern Folk Process. Master's thesis, Bryn Mawr College, Bryn Mawr, Pa. http://www.ssf.net/people/thyme/main.htp (accessed 23 October 2009).

Manns, P., C. Boyle, and M. Gonzalez. (1987) "The Problems of the Text in Nueva Canción," *Popular Music*, 6:2, pp. 191–195.

Mattern, M. (1998) *Acting in Concert: Music, Community, and Political Action*. New Brunswick, N.J.: Rutgers University Press.

Peddie, I. (2006) *The Resisting Muse: Music and Social Protest*. Burlington, Vt.: Ashgate.

Rodnitsky, Jerry. (2006) "The Decline and Rebirth of Folk-Protest Music," pp. 17–29. In *The Resisting Muse*. Edited by I. Peddie. Burlington, VT: Ashgate.

Rivera, Anny, and Rodrigo Torres. (1981) *Encuentro de Canto Poblacional* (*Meetings on Popular Song*). Santiago, Chile: CENECA.

Shepard, John. (1991) *Music as Social Text*. Cambridge, Mass.: Polity Press.

Small, Christopher. (1987) *Music of the Common Tongue: Survival and Celebration in African-American Music*. New York: River Run Press.

Starhawk. (2002–2009) What a Direct Action Campaign Can Do. http://www.star
    hawk.org/activism/trainer-resources/directaction-campaigns.html (accessed 23
    October 2009).
Williams, Raymond. (1977) *Marxism and Literature*. Oxford: Oxford University Press.

Chapter Eleven: Danielle Poe

Baraitser, L. (2006) "Oi Mother, Keep Ye' Hair On! Impossible Transformations of
    Maternal Subjectivity," *Studies in Gender and Sexuality*, 7:3, pp. 217–238.
Irigaray, Luce. (2001) *To Be Two*. New York: Routledge.
———. (2002) *Between East and West: From Singularity to Community*. New York:
    Columbia University Press.
———. (2004) *Key Writings*. New York: Continuum.
Jacobs, A. (2007) "The Potential of Theory: Melanie Klein, Luce Irigaray, and the
    Mother-Daughter Relationship," *Hypatia*, 22:3, pp. 175–193.
Naar-Obed, M. (1998) *Maternal Convictions: A Mother Beats a Missile into a Plow-
    share*. Maple, Wis.: Laurentian Shield Resources for Nonviolence.
Sachs, L. (2003) *Investigation of a Flame*. Documentary Film. United States: First
    Run/Icarus Films.

Chapter Twelve: Katina Sayers-Walker

Allen, Ricky Lee. (2005) "Whiteness and Critical Pedagogy." In *Critical Pedagogy
    and Race*. Edited by Zeus Leonardo. Malden, Mass.: Blackwell.
Barthes, R. (1981) *Camera Lucida*. New York: Hill and Wang.
Berk, L. (2008) *Infants, Children, and Adolescents*. 6th Edition. Boston, Mass.: Pear-
    son.
Bucciarelli, D. (2004) "If We Could Really Feel: The Need for Emotions of Care
    within the Disciplines." In *Educating for a Culture of Peace*.
    Edited by R. Eisler and R. Miller. Portsmouth, N.H.: Heinemann.
Cooper, M. (1999) *Indian School: Teaching the White Man's Way*. New York: Clarion
    Books.
Dewey, John. (1934) *Art as Experience*. New York: Perigee Books.
Greene, Maxine. (1995) *Releasing the Imagination*. San Francisco, Calif.: Jossey-
    Bass.
Helms, Janet. (1993) Black and White Racial Identity: Theory, Practice, and Research.
    Westport, Conn.: Praeger.
Hinchey, Patricia H. (1998) *Finding Freedom in the Classroom: A Practical Introduc-
    tion to Critical Theory*. New York: Peter Lang.
———. (2001) *Variations on a Blue Guitar: The Lincoln Center Institute Lectures on
    Aesthetic Education*. New York: Teachers College Press.
Kozol, Jonathan. (1996) *Amazing Grace*. New York: Harper Collins.
Leonardo, Z. (2005) "The Color of Supremacy: Beyond the Discourse of 'White Privi-
    lege.'" In *Critical Pedagogy and Race*. Edited by Z. Leonard. Malden, Mass.:
    Blackwell.
McIntosh, P. (1990) "White Privilege: Unpacking the Invisible Knapsack," *Indepen-
    dent School* (Winter) 49:2, pp. 31–36.

Prosser, J (2000) "The Moral Maze of Image Ethics." In *Situated Ethics in Educational Research*. Edited by H. Simons and R. Usher. London: Routledge.

Ramsey, P. (2004) *Teaching and Learning in a Diverse World*. 3rd Edition. New York: Teachers College Press.

Stevens, Wallace. (1982) *The Collected Poems of Wallace Stevens*. New York: Knopf.

ABOUT THE AUTHORS

JOSEPH M. BETZ is Professor of Philosophy at Villanova University. Betz has been the editor of the *Journal of Social Philosophy*, and President of two scholarly societies: the Society for the Advancement of American Philosophy and the North American Society for Social Philosophy. For the past twenty-five years, he has focused on the ethics of war as applied to United States-sponsored or conducted wars in Central America, Iraq, and Afghanistan. This has resulted in numerous conference papers, book chapters, and articles.

ANDREW FITZ-GIBBON is Associate Professor of Philosophy and Director of the Center for Ethics, Peace, and Social Justice at the State University of New York College at Cortland. He earned his PhD from the University of Newcastle-upon-Tyne, UK. His academic interests include nonviolence, love, mysticism, and community. He is the author, editor, or co-author of six books and fourteen articles and book chapters in peer-reviewed volumes. He is working on a book, *Love as a Guide to Morals*. Fitz-Gibbon is an Associate Editor of VIBS, Rodopi, where he edits the Social Philosophy Series (two books published in 2009 and one forthcoming in 2010). He is a fellow of the American Philosophical Practitioners Association, certified in client counseling. He is abbot of the Lindisfarne Community, Ithaca New York, which is a small ecumenical religious order.

ARUN GANDHI is the fifth grandson of Mohandas K. "Mahatma" Gandhi. He learned from his parents and grandparents that justice does not mean revenge, it means transforming the opponent through love and suffering. His grandfather taught him to understand nonviolence through understanding violence.
He shares these lessons all around the world. For the past five years, he has participated in the Renaissance Weekend deliberations. He has spoken at the Women's Justice Center in Ann Arbor, Michigan and has delivered talks at the Young President's Organization in Mexico, the Trade Union Leaders' Meeting in Milan, Italy, and the Peace and Justice Center in St. Louis, Missouri. He has also spoken in Croatia, France, Ireland, Holland, Lithuania, Nicaragua, China, Scotland, and Japan. Gandhi is very involved in social programs and writing. He worked for thirty years as a journalist for *The Times of India*. He is the author of several books on poverty and politics in India and a compilation of M. K. Gandhi's wit and wisdom. He also edited *World without Violence: Can Gandhi's Vision Become Reality?* and authored *The Forgotten Woman: The Untold Story of Kastur, the Wife of Mahatma Gandhi*, jointly with his late wife Sunanda.

WILLIAM C. GAY is Professor of Philosophy at the University of North Carolina at Charlotte. He is past editor of *Concerned Philosophers for Peace Newsletter* (1987–2002) and, since 2002, Editor of CPP's Special Series on "Philosophy of Peace" (Rodopi, VIBS). He is past President and past Executive Director of Concerned Philosophers for Peace. With T. A. Alekseeva, he is coauthor of *Capitalism with a Human Face: The Quest for a Middle Road in Russian Politics* (1996); and coeditor of *On the Eve of the 21st Century: Perspectives of Russian and American Philosophers* (1994) and *Democracy and the Quest for Justice: Russian and American Perspectives* (2004). With Michael Pearson, he is coauthor of *The Nuclear Arms Race* (1987). With I. I. Mazour and A. N. Chumakov, he is coeditor of *Global Studies Encyclopedia* (2003). He has also published articles and book chapters on peace, justice, and nonviolence from the perspectives of philosophy of language and political philosophy.

COLLEEN KATTAU is Associate Professor of Spanish at the State University of New York College at Cortland. She researches arts activism in the Americas and has published articles on *Nueva Cancion* (New Song); and on the Small Farmers Movement of Cajibio, Colombia, and its sister community relationship with Central New York. She is also a social change musician.

SANJAY LAL is Professor of Philosophy at Minnesota State Community and Technical College in Moorhead, Minnesota. His published works also include "Gandhi's Universal Ethic and Feminism: Shared Starting Points but Divergent Ends," "Globalization through the Father's Eyes," and "Hume and Gandhi: A Comparative Ethical Analysis." Lal received his PhD in philosophy from the University of Tennessee Knoxville in 2006. His dissertation is entitled The Tension and Coherence of Love, Identification, and Detachment in Gandhi's Thought.

ANNA LÜBBE is Professor of Legal and Alternative Conflict Resolution at the University of Applied Sciences in Fulda, Germany. She is a mediator, systemic constellations facilitator, and supervisor of mediators. She is a political consultant in the field of post war dialogues. She has published in the fields of constitutional and administrative law, the history of law, and philosophy. The focus of her academic work in the peace and conflict field is on systemic conflict transformation. Her recent publications include *Us versus Them: Splitting Dynamics and Turning Points in Ethnopolitical Conflict*; *The Violence within Non-Violence*; and *Ethnopolitische Konflikte: Das Potential der Systemaufstellungsmethode*.

ROBERT L. MUHLNICKEL is Assistant Professor of Philosophy at Monroe Community College in Rochester, New York. He has recently published on conscientious objection in *The Review Journal of Political Philosophy* and has presented papers at the Society for Philosophy in the Contemporary World, Society for Ethics across the Curriculum, and the Wesleyan Philosophical Society.

PAUL J. PARKS is Adjunct Professor of Art History at State University of New York College at Cortland, specializing in the arts of Asia, Africa, and the Americas. He has taught a variety of courses in art history and aesthetics for Syracuse University, Tompkins Cortland Community College, The Network for Learning, and Christie's East. During his career in the arts and education, he has been Director of several galleries in New York, Curator of Photography for the Everson Museum, and an independent curator and lecturer. He has been active in the peace movement throughout his life as a staff member of the Vietnam Moratorium Committee, Quaker Projects for Peace, and Tompkins County Alliance for Peace in the Middle East.

DANIELLE POE is Associate Professor of Philosophy at the University of Dayton. Her research interests include contemporary issues of peace and the work of Luce Irigary. Her recent work includes "Mothers and Civil Disobedience," (2009); "Replacing Just War Theory with an Ethics of Sexual Difference" (2008); and "On U.S. Lynching: Remembrance, Apology, and Reconciliation" (2007). With Eddy Souffrant, Poe edited *Parceling the Globe: Philosophical Explorations in Globalization, Global Behavior, and Peace* (2008).

JOSEPH RAYLE is an Associate Professor of Foundations of Education in the Foundations and Social Advocacy Department at the State University of New York College at Cortland, where he is currently developing a Peace Education course. His research interests include complex systems theory, peace education, and teacher candidate dispositions. He serves on the Advisory Board of the Center for Ethics, Peace, and Social Justice.

DENNIS ROTHERMEL is Professor of Philosophy at California State University, Chico. His recent publications include an essay on *The Piano, Crouching Tiger, Hidden Dragon, The Pianist*, and *Hero* in the *Quarterly Review of Film and Video*; book chapters on *Mystic River* and *My Darling Clementine*, and "Slow Food, Slow Film," also in the *QRFV*. Forthcoming are contributions to separate collections: "Julie Taymor's Musicality," "Anti-War War Films," an essay on Bertrand Tavernier's *In the Electric Mist*, and an essay on *No Country for Old Men*.

KATINA SAYERS-WALKER is an Assistant Professor in the Childhood/Early Childhood Department at the State University of New York College at Cortland. Her research interests are in curriculum studies, critical theory, and foundations of education. She received her EdD at West Virginia University. She is a qualitative researcher who regularly relies on image-based research methods. This is her first publication.

RICHARD WERNER is the John Stewart Kennedy Professor of Philosophy at Hamilton College, Clinton, New York. He specializes in ethics, pragmatism, and social philosophy. He is the author of "Ethical Realism" (1983); "Ethical Realism Defended" (1985); "Abortion: The Ontological and Moral Status of the Unborn," in *Ethics: Theory and Practice* (1985); "Nuclear Deterrence and the Limits of Moral Theory" (1987); "South Africa: University Neutrality and Divestment," in *Neutrality and Academic Ethics* (1994); 'Reconceiving the Abortion Argumentz" (2002); "Pragmatism for Pacifists" (2007); and numerous other philosophical articles in journals, anthologies, and a dictionary. He is co-editor with Duane Cady of *Just War, Nonviolence, and Nuclear Deterrence* (1991).

INDEX

Abkhazia, 44, 45
Ackerman, Peter, 33
   A Force More Powerful, 33
acquiescence of the populace, 33
activism, 2, 107, 115, 118, 143
   nonviolent a., 116, 119–132
Adams, Ansel, 135
Address to the Joint Session of Congress
      (Bush), 7
Adler, Jonathan, 2
Afghanistan, 35, 36, 79
Africa, 41, 45
   A. cultural elements, 110
   east A. refugees, 16
African Americans, 43, 63, 64, 71, 139,
      142, 145, 146
   enslaved A. A., 109, 111
   A. A. slave/spiritual song, 110, 111
African National Congress (ANC), 6, 7
AIDS, 1
Aldrich, Robert, 76
   Attack, 76
alienation, 88, 90, 102
All Quiet on the Western Front (Miles-
      tone), 78–80, 82, 83, 86, 88
Allen, Ricky Lee, 146–148
Allende, Salvador, 116, 117
Allied countries, 26, 27, 41
Altman, Robert, 76
Amazing Grace (Kozol), 144
American society, 59, 110
American way of life7, 142, 143
Amish, 43
ancestors, 11, 53, 55, 125
anger, 84, 89, 92, 98
aniconism , 71
anti-war films, 75–105
anxiety, 5
apartheid, 7, 35
Apocalypse Now! (Coppola), 76, 94
Arabic calligraphy, 71
Aristizabal, Hector, 114
"Art beyond the West" (Parks), 73

Art as Experience (Dewey), 135
art history, 67–73
arts, 68–73, 75, 104, 113, 134–137, 147, 149
"Art and Society" (Read), 72
Asia, 40, 45, 70, 72, 144
   A. Minor, 71
assimilation, 43, 44, 50
atrocities, 50, 141
Attack (Aldrich), 76
attitudes, 17, 30, 52, 55, 57, 68, 104, 108,
      117, 134
   cultural a., 135
   empathetic a., 144
   non-dominence, a. of, 18
   patronizing a., 56
   postive, 4, 6
   questioning a., 144
   resistant vs. open-minded a., 147
   self-serving a., 63
   unconscious a., 56
audiences, 34, 68, 68, 75, 76, 78–80, 82,
      87, 90, 93, 101, 103, 104, 110,
      114, 117, 118, 137
Australia, 42, 43, 94, 137, 139, 140
authenticity, 7–9, 77
autonomy, 148
   minority a., 40, 42, 44, 45
   practitioner's a., 128
   territorial a., 39, 43, 47

Bar On, Dan, 54
   "To Reflect and Trust," 54
Baraitser, Lisa, 120–122, 125, 127
   "Oi Mother, Keep Ye' Hair On!" 120
Barenboim, Daniel, 68, 69
Barthes, Roland, 136
Bauman, Zygmunt, 60
Beaumont, Hunter, 53
behavioral modification, 92
Being-in-the-World (Dreyfus), 32
Belgium (Belgians), 43, 46
belief(s), 69, 73, 105, 108
   cultural b., 133

belief(s), *con't.*
  ethics of, 1–11
  ideological manifestations, b. meeting
    with, 135
  nonviolence, b. in, 24
  possibility of peace, b. in, 65
  religious b., 20, 96, 119
  threat, b. one is under, 15
Berrigan, Daniel, 129, 130
Bertalanffy, Ludwig von, 64, 65
Between East and West (Irigaray), 125, 127
Betz, Joseph M., 39
Bible, 123, 124
Bill of Rights, 8
biological processes, 13–15
Blackburn, Simon, 2
Blacks, 20–22
blame, 26, 28, 32, 60, 84, 85, 94
blue frog, 133–149
blue guitar, 133–149
Boal, Agosto, 114
bodily function, 15
Boertje-Obed, Greg, 124
Bondurant, Joan, 34
Böszörményi-Nagy, Ivan, 50
Bourgeois, Roy, 114
brain and body chemistry, 3, 4
The Bridge on the River Kwai (Lean), 79
Britten, Benjamin, 78, 93
  War Requiem, 78, 93
Buddhism, Chan, 71
Bureau of India Affairs (BIA), 139
Bush, George W., 5, 7, 84
bystanders, 27, 28
Byzantium, 71

Cady, Duane, 8, 33
Campbell, Donovan, 79, 84
Campbell, Joseph, 70
  The Mythic Image, 70
Camus, Albert, 1, 7
  The Rebel, 1
Canada, 39–43, 110, 22
car(e)(ing), 8, 13, 16, 18, 20–22, 34, 84,
    136
  c. ethics, 32, 33, 37

Gilligan's concep of c., 33
health c., 18, 128
medical c., 91, 128
mutual c., 76
not caring, 95
self-c., 21, 128
"The Care Structure" (Dreyfus), 32
Carson, Rachel, 144
Carver, George Washington, 144
catharsis, 78, 79
Central America, 107
chaos, 10, 94, 98, 149
chauvinism, 62
childcare, 16, 119, 128
China, 1, 71, 141
choice(s), 4–6, 10, 128, 130, 131
cholecystokinin (CCK), 4
church, 112
  c. bells, 77
  peace c., 43
  separation of state and c., 36
cinema. *See* anti-war films
civic engagement, 63
civil rights, 6, 7, 35, 107, 109–114
civilization, 99, 145
  ancient c., 72
  Western c., 75
claims, 6, 50, 117, 146
class, 62, 63
  aristocratic c., 79
  social c., 60, 144
  working c., 113, 117, 146
classroom management skills, 59
Clifford, William Kingdon, 2
  "The Ethics of Belief," 2
coexistence, 35, 73, 125
cognition, 3, 4, 15, 100, 134, 136, 149
collective, 51, 55, 148
  c. action/effort, 109, 112–114, 116
  c. bequeathal, 72
  c. consciousness, 117
  c. guilt, 141, 142
  c. hopes and fears, 50
  c. identity, 108, 109, 126, 145
  c. power, 107
  c. rights, 47

collective, *con't.*
  c. struggle, 111
  c. survival, 30
  c. trauma, 49, 50, 54, 56
coloni(alism)(zation), 46, 56
  British c. of India, 7, 35
  cultural c., 116
  decolonization, 43
  c. soldiers, 93
  post-c. Asia and Africa, 45, 46
combat(ants), 21, 72, 75, 76, 78–80, 83,
    84, 90, 93, 97–101, 103
commitment
  act, c. to, 129
  collective c. to join army, 86
  community engagement, c. to, 125
  fate of individuals, c. to, 117
  partner, c. to, 132
  jihad, c. to, 36
  nonviolent social change, c. to, 114
  phobia, 53
  social c., 107
communication, 84
  nonviolent, 31, 33
  political c., 33–35, 37
companionship, 18
compassion, 85, 142
compensation, 50, 131
complacency, 7
concatenation of problems, 1, 2, 7, 10
conflict(s), 55, 82, 99
  Bosnian c., 41
  cultural c., 67
  c. emotions, 78, 119, 120
  ethnopolitical c., 49, 50, 54
  Iraq c., 84
  Middle East c., 54
  minority c., 39–41, 45, 46
  national c., 42
  nonviolent c. resolution, 35–37, 54–59
  religious c., 35
  (non)violent c., 19, 30–34, 127
confrontation, 69, 77, 80, 83, 85, 91, 96, 99
Confucianism, 71
conscience, 23, 24, 26, 28, 30, 89, 115

consciousness, 25, 101, 117, 127, 133,
    136, 147
consequences, 1, 6, 30, 40, 75, 130, 139
consequentialist theory of moral right-
    ness, 13
consumer(ism)(s), 1, 7–10
consumption, 7, 9, 10, 64
cooperation, 21, 25–29, 33, 34, 55, 73, 130
Copenhagen Declaration, 46
Coplan, Amy, 100
Coppola, Francis Ford, 76, 94
  Apocalypse Now! 76, 94
corporate elite, 67
Counts, George S., 59, 60
courage, 13, 20–22, 80, 82, 84, 87, 91, 97,
    100, 103, 104, 107, 118, 139
critical fixation on concluding events in a
    film, 102
Croatia, 44
"Culturally Relevant Teaching" (Sayers-
    Walker), 136
culture, 34, 42, 46, 70, 73, 86, 90, 101, 107–
    109, 116–118, 126, 127, 139
  American/United States c., 5, 60, 62,
    75, 110, 128, 132
  c. attitudes/beliefs, 133, 137
  c. boundaries, 72
  c. (un)acceptable, 55
  c. capital, 144
  c. colonialism, 116
  c. conflict, 67, 68
  cooperative c. programs, 68
  cross-c. discourse, 72
  death, c. of, 130
  deculturization process, 139
  dominant c., 139–143, 148
  ethnoc. group, 40
  European c., 110
  c. expression, 115
  fear, c. of, 63
  c. health of a nation, 76
  homogenous c. group, 40
  indigenous c., 116
  c. innovation, 62
  Latin American urban c., 109
  militarism, c. of, 76

culture, *con't.*
    minority c. group, 43
    multiculturalism, 39–46, 59
    nonviolent/peaceful c., 35, 59, 61, 62,
        64, 65, 127
    c. property, 72
    reactionary forces of c., 102
    reductionist c. orientation, 60
    resistance, c. of, 117
    satirizing c., 113
    socio-c. context of schools, 64
    solutions, c. sensible, 49
    status quo, c. forces that maintain, 59
    violence, c. of, 60, 64
    Western c., 55, 75, 138
Culturally Relevant Teaching, 136
curriculum, 59–62, 65, 69, 133–136, 144,
    146–149
cynicism, 1, 6, 7, 11
Czechoslovakia (Czech Republic), 41, 45

D'Aubuisson, Roberto, 115
danger, 1, 3, 61, 79, 91, 94, 95, 100, 103,
    118
Danish resistance, 7
Dawn Patrol (Goulding/Hawks), 76
Dayton Agreement, 41
DeAssis, Sebastian, 59
Declaration of the Rights of Persons Belong-
    ing to National, Ethnic, Religious,
    and Linguistic Minorities, 42
defense, 9
    self-d., 39, 50, 85, 147
democracy, 8, 39, 42, 147, 148
Denmark, 43
Department of Homeland Security, 63
desires, 5, 19, 33, 49, 50, 51, 148
despair, 1–3, 18, 78, 96, 141, 143, 148
destabilization, 40, 50
destruction, 1, 25, 80, 96, 98, 99, 131,
    140, 141
developmental theorists, 63
Dewey, John, 5, 41, 135
dialectical exchange, 117
Diamond, Jared, 10

diegesis, 95
dignity, 28, 50, 63, 70, 110, 123, 130
Dirty War of Argentina, 118
disabilities, 138, 144
disappeared, the, 53, 54, 72, 116, 118
discouraged populace, 5
draft files, burning, 129, 130
Dr. Strangelove (Kubrick), 92
Dreyfus, Hubert L., 32
    Being-in-the-World, 32
    "The Care Structure," 32
Drums along the Mohawk (Ford), 93
DuBois, W. E. B., 109, 110, 144
    "Of the Sorrow Songs," 110
DuVall, Jack, 33
    A Force More Powerful, 33

Eastwood, Clint, 76
    Letters from Iwo Jima, 76
ecological framework, 62
ecological theory. See system(s) (ecolog-
    ical) theory
economic problems, 1
Endfield, Cy, 93
    Zulu, 93
Edelman, Murray, 108
education, 16, 18, 73, 128, 134, 138, 142,
    144, 148
    e. in Allende government, 117
    e. funding (funding)
    minority-language higher e., 47
    peace e., 59–65
    teacher-e. program, 137, 145
    tolerance e., 67
Educational Publishers, Assoc. of, 67
Egypt, 56, 68
Eichmann, Adolph, 27
1812 Overture (Tchaikovsky), 77, 78, 103
Einstein, Albert, 8
el-Sadat, Anwar, 56
Embodied Care (Hamington), 37
Emerson, Ralph Waldo, 103
emotion, 1, 4, 15, 18, 19, 32, 34, 51, 54, 77,
    78, 80, 87, 89, 90, 92, 93, 103, 108,
    120, 127, 133, 135, 136, 140, 141,
    143, 146, 147

empathy, 33, 34, 37, 76, 87, 93, 129, 136, 140, 144, 149
  imaginative e., 18–20
Endfield, Cy, 93
  Zulu, 93
enem(ies)(y), 9, 21, 46, 78, 79, 81–88, 94–96, 100, 124
enkephalins, 4
environmentalism, 59
Estonia, 44, 54
ethics
  e. of belief, 1–11
  e. of care, 13, 32, 33, 37
  e. of justice, 32
  Kantian e., 32
  e. of nonviolent rhetoric, 31, 36
"The Ethics of Belief" (Clifford), 2
ethnicity, 43, 45, 46, 49, 50, 70, 139, 145
  e. cleansing, 41, 44
  e. Germans outside Germany, 43
  e. majorities/minorities, 42, 44, 46
  racism, inter-e., 147, 148
ethnocultural group, 39, 40
Europe, 1, 9, 11, 29, 41, 43–46,
  art, non-E., 72
  cinema narrative, E. style, 87
  E. lyric, 110
  E. monastic artisans, 72
  White, E.-Americans, 137, 140, 142, 143, 145
European Union, 9, 43, 44
eviden(ce)(tialism), 1–3, 6, 7, 9, 13, 25, 28, 61, 70, 76, 80, 91, 96, 103, 115
evil, 23, 24, 26–30, 50, 78, 94, 98, 114
evolution, 14
Eyerman, Ron, 107, 108, 110

failure, 13–16, 20, 55, 84, 91, 120
fallibilist, pragmatic, 3
family sculptures, 50
family therapy, 50, 57
famine, 1, 7
Far East, 41
fear, 1, 5, 9, 20, 26, 49, 50, 69, 78, 80, 81, 89, 91, 94, 97, 98, 111
  minorities, f. of, 44, 63

White's f., 19
Fear and Trembling (Kierkegaard), 5
Feinberg, Joel, 14
Feldman, Richard, 2
film. *See* anti-war films. *See also* movies
Finding Freedom in the Classroom (Hinchey), 148
Finding Our Way (Kymlicka), 39
folk process, 112
"Follow the Drinking Gourd" (unknown), 110
force (*graha*), 23, 26, 64, 72, 81, 130
  cohesive f. among atoms, 25
  love/soul, f. of, 23, 25
  military f., 84, 85, 95, 99
  moral f., 24
A Force More Powerful (Ackerman and Duvall), 33
Ford, John, 76, 93
  Drums along the Mohawk, 93
  They Were Expendable, 76
Foreman, Carl, 79
forgiveness, 83
Foster, David William, 109
  "*La Paquita del Barrio*," 109
flourishing, 107, 123, 127, 128, 130, 131
France, 40, 41, 43
freedom, 7–9, 42, 44, 62, 63, 109–111, 142, 147, 148
Freire, Paola, 146, 148
  Pedagogy of the Oppressed, 146
Full Metal Jacket (Kubrick), 80, 81, 85–87, 90, 94
Fuller, Sam, 76
  The Big Red One, 76

Gandhi, Mohandas K., 5, 7, 10
  G. nonviolence, 23–30, 34, 35
Gatto, John Taylor, 63
Gay, William C., 31
gender, 37, 62, 122, 142, 144
genocide, 1, 7–9, 36, 49
geopolitics, 31–37, 67
Georgia, 44, 45, 109, 115
Germany, 26, 27, 43, 51, 52, 86
  East G., 35

Gieco, Leon, 117
Gligorov, Kiro, 34
Gilligan, Carol, 13, 32–34, 37
Giraffe language, 31–33. *See also* Wolf
    language
Giroux, Henry A., 60
Gligorov, Kiro, 34
Global Art Project for Peace (GAP), 69
global warming, 1, 7
goals, 59, 108, 109, 113, 138
God, 25, 111, 115, 123, 124
good, the, 13–17, 19–21, 27–30
    evil, g. over, 94, 114
goodness, 23–30
goods, 8, 9, 18, 71
good will, 19
Gorsevski, Ellen, 31, 33–35, 37
gospels, Christian, 72
Goulding, Edmund, 76
government officials, 35, 36, 67, 138
gratitude, 76
Greece, Hellenistic, 71
Greene, Maxine, 134–136
grief, 120
Groopman, Jerome, 3
guilt, 54, 140
    collective g., 141, 142
    White g., 142, 143, 145–148

Hamington, Maurice, 37
    Embodied Care, 37
harm, 14, 20, 21, 87, 147
harmony, 23, 44, 71
Havel, Vaclav, 7, 8
Hawks, Howard, 76
healing, 52, 55, 114
Heidegger, Martin, 32, 99
Hell is for Heroes (Siegel), 81
Hellinger, Bert, 51–53
Helms, Janet, 145, 148
Heraclitus, 98, 99
    H. oppositions, 99
heroism, 79, 78, 86, 90, 92, 93, 103
    h. bravery vs. pointless sacrifice, 81, 82
Hicks, Edward, 11
    The Peaceable Kingdom, 11

Highlander Folk School, 111
Hill, née Hillstrom, Joseph, 112
    "The Preacher and the Slave," 112
Hinchey, Patricia H., 148
    Finding Freedom in the Classroom, 148
history, 25, 27, 28, 30, 43, 62, 77
    American h., 61
    art h., 67–73
    Black h., 144
    cinema, h. of, 75
    invaders throughout h., 141
    education system, h. of, 146–148
    group's h., 49, 50
        h. underrepresented g., 136
    labor h., 112
    socio-h. circumstances of film, 100
    stories, h. accepted, 143
    war, h. context of, 94, 96
    Western philosophy, h. of, 99
Hitler, Adolf, 42, 43
Hobbes, Thomas, 9
Hoffmaster, Barry, 15
holistic approach, 55, 65, 147
Holladay, Jennifer, 67
homogenous national groups, 40, 45
hope(lessness), 1–11, 16–19, 39, 41, 45,
    50, 65, 69, 96, 109, 110, 116–
    118, 131, 132, 136, 142, 144,
    147, 148
"How to Ensure the Connection between
    Natural and Civil Coexistence"
    (Irigaray), 126
human rights, 34, 36, 42, 45, 46, 114, 139
    Kymlicka's h. r., 41
humanitarian intervention, 9
humanity, 1, 3, 23–26, 34, 54, 63, 73, 80,
    83, 85, 110, 116, 146

ideas, 9, 71, 73, 138, 141
    Dewey, i. of, 135
    Eastern i. through Western lens, 73
    Freire's i., 146, 148
    Gandhian i., 23, 30
    imposed i., 108
    peace in isolation from other i., 60, 61
    threatening i., 62, 63

identity
    collective i., 108–110, 145, 146, 149
    i. crisis, 149
    ethnic i., 49, 50, 139
    national i., 50
    parental i., 125
    racial i., 145
    women's i., 119, 121, 126
If You Don't Go, Don't Hinder Me (Reagon), 111
ignorance, 69
"I Have a Dream" (King), 35
ill will, 19, 28
Illimani, Inti, 117
image-based research (IBR), 135, 136, 147
images, 16, 71, 87, 133
    cognitive/mental i., 134
    film, i. in, 92, 94, 97–99, 102, 103, 135
imagination, 1, 6, 70, 134–136, 149
    imaginative action, 109
    imaginative empathy, 17–20
immigra(nts)(tion), 40, 142
    i. quota system, 43
    Muslim i. in Great Britain, 44
immune system, 3, 4, 6
indigenous peoples, 39, 40, 43, 72, 116, 143
Industrial Workers of the World (IWW, *aka* Wobblies), 109, 112
    Songs to Fan the Flames of Discontent, 112
industry, 112
inequalit(ies)(y), 60, 109, 116, 133, 146
inequities, 133
infrastructure, national, 8, 20
injustice, 33, 109, 113, 116, 118, 133, 143
inner cities, 8
innocence, 26, 28, 88
insight, 2, 6, 60, 73, 99, 105, 143, 146
instrumentation, 108
interdisciplinary connections in learning, 62, 64
International Covenant on Civil and Political Rights, 46
"The Internationale" (Pottier), 112

interpretation, 72, 73
    film, i. of, 82, 96, 102, 104
intersubjectivity, 120–122
intervention, 9, 46, 55, 56, 95
    Christianity, i. of, 119, 124
    humanitarian i., 9
    military i., 40, 41
    multiple i., 108, 109, 124
    peaceful i., 41
Inuit, 40
Investigation of a Flame (Sachs), 129
Iraq, 45, 72, 79
    I. insurgency, 84
    I. Wars, 8, 44
Irigaray, Luce, 120–122, 125–128
    Between East and West, 125, 127
    "How to Ensure the Connection between Natural and Civil Coexistence," 126
Iron Curtain, 35
irony, 92, 102
Irvin, Nell, 7, 8
    Painter, 7
Israel, 35, 56, 68
Italy, 43
Ives, Charles, 98
    The Unanswered Question, 98
IWW. *See* Industrial Workers of the World (IWW, *aka* Wobblies)

Jacobs, Amber, 126
    "The Potential of Theory," 126
Jafari, Sheherazade, 35, 36
    "Local Religious Peacemakers . . .," 35
James, William, 1, 2, 6, 7
    "The Sentiment of Rationality," 2
    "The Will to Believe," 2
Jamison, Andrew, 107, 108, 110
Japan, 26, 82, 94–96, 98
Jara, Victor, 116, 117
    "Vientos del pueblo," 116
Jews, 7, 35, 41, 52
"Joe Hill" (unknown), 113
Johnny Got His Gun (Trumbo), 101
Jonah House, 123–125, 128
Josten, Katherine, 69

Jubilee Plowshares East, 119
Judeo-Christian values, 124
Jungian duality, 87
justice, 1, 31–33, 41, 46, 56, 59, 61, 98,
    107, 109–111, 113, 116, 118,
    133–136, 139, 140, 143, 144,
    146–148

Kant, Immanuel, 32, 41
  K. ethics, 32
Kattau, Colleen, 107
  Sing it Down, 115
Kaufman, Stuart, 54
Kelman, Herbert, 54
Kidder, Rushworth, 21
Kierkegaard, Søren, 5, 99
  Fear and Trembling, 5
Kinane, Ed, 115
King, Martin Luther Jr., 5, 19, 20, 35, 99,
    107
  "I Have a Dream," 35
  "Letter from a Birmingham Jail," 35
knowledge, 1, 135, 140, 143, 144
  embodied k., 37
  narrative k., 108
  students, relationship between k. and,
    122
Knowledge is the Beginning (Smaczny),
    69
Kohlberg, Lawrence, 32
Kozol, Jonathan, 144
  Amazing Grace, 144
Kubrick, Stanley, 80, 82, 86, 87, 89–92
  Dr. Strangelove, 92
  Full Metal Jacket (Kubrick), 80, 81,
    85–87, 90, 94
  Paths of Glory, 80–84, 86, 89, 90, 92–
    94
Kyi, Aung San Suu, 34
Kymlicka, Will, 39–47
  Finding Our Way, 39
  Multicultural Odysseys, 39
Kyoto Treaty, 9

labor, 114
  forced l., 52

l. movements, 107, 109, 111, 112, 113
l. songs, 112, 113
Lal, Sanjay, 23
Latinos, 141, 144
Lawrence of Arabia (Lean), 76
laws, 42, 139
leader's trap, 54
leadership, 36, 54, 67, 84, 86, 94
Lean, David, 76, 79
  The Bridge on the River Kwai, 79
  Lawrence of Arabia, 76
learning outcomes, 61, 105
"Letter from a Birmingham Jail" (King),
    35
Letters from Iwo Jima (Eastwood), 76
Levering, Ralph B., 19
liberal theories, 14
liberation, 107, 110, 114, 118
Lies My Teacher Told Me (Loewen), 61
linguistic
  melody and rhythm, non-l. aspects of,
    109
  l. minorities, 42
  l. nonviolence, 31, 36, 37
  song, l. elements in, 108
literature, 68, 75, 104, 133–135, 143, 144
  l. of film, 97, 102
"Local Religious Peacemakers . . ." (Ja-
    fari), 35
Loewen, James, 61, 63
  Lies My Teacher Told Me, 61
loss, 52, 62, 73, 78–80, 82, 83, 86, 89,
    100, 103, 118, 121, 126, 127
love, 24, 24, 54, 88–90, 98, 99, 118, 147
  lovers, 120, 125
  interpersonal l., 16
  interracial l., 22
  marital l., 124
  maternal l., 131, 132
  neighbor and enemies, l. of, 124
  romantic l., 125
loyalty, 43, 44, 76, 80, 103, 146
Lübbe, Anna, 49
Lyon, Crystal, 73
  "My Moksha," 73
Lyotard, Jean-Françoise, 108

lyrics (lyric), 108, 110–112, 116, 118.
  See also melody; *nueva canción*;
  song
nueva canción 1., 117

Macedonia, 34, 35
MacIntyre, Alasdair, 15
Malick, Terrence, 80, 82, 95, 97–100
  The Thin Red Line, 80–83, 85, 86, 88,
    94, 95, 99, 100
mandala, 71
Mandela, Nelson, 5, 107
  N. M.'s Innaugural Address, 35
Manns, Patricio, 117
Marcuse, Herbert, 1, 7–9
marriage, 124, 125
Martin, James, 16, 17, 19
Marx, Karl, 10
  M. thinking, 60
maternity, 119–121,
  intersubjective m., 125, 129, 132
McCarthyism, 9
McLaren, Peter, 148
media, the, 52, 54, 61, 138, 146
  mass m. messages, 63
  print m., 134
  visual m., 70
melody, 89, 98, 108–112. *See also* lyrics;
  nueva canción; song
memory, 110, 113, 118
merit schemes, 59
Michaels, Lloyd, 97, 98
Middle East, 41, 45, 54
Milanes, Pablo, 117
Milestone, Lewis, 76, 78–83, 86, 88, 93
  All Quiet on the Western Front, 78–
    80, 82, 83, 86, 88
  Pork Chop Hill, 76
  A Walk in the Sun, 79
militarism, 76, 86, 104, 112, 115, 124,
  128, 130
military spending, 8, 9
minorities, 39, 41–47, 63
misfortune, 8
mobilizing power, 113

morality, 10, 13, 20, 32, 40, 41, 59, 61,
  78, 86, 87, 92–94, 96, 111, 123,
  139, 143, 146, 147
  Camus' m. ideal, 1
  m. conscience, 23–26, 28, 30
  m. courage, 21
  m. logic, 43
  nonviolence, m. method of, 23
  m. persuasion, 27
  m. philosoph(ers)(y), 20
  m. psychology, 14
  m. relativism, 42
  m. superiority, 29
  transformation, mass m., 27, 29
Morrison, James, 95, 97, 99
Mortenson, Greg, 36
  Three Cups of Tea, 36
mother(hood)(ing), 119–132
motives, 55, 130
movie(s), 76, 79, 102, 103
  pedagogy, incorporating movies into
    critical, 133–141
Muhlnickel, Robert L., 13
Multicultural Odysseys (Kymlicka), 39
multiculturalism, liberal, 39–46, 59
music(ians), 68, 69, 134. *See also* song
  film, m. in, 90, 94, 98
  m. irony, 92
  military m., 77, 78
  socially conscious m., 107–112, 114–
    117
Muslims, 35, 36, 40, 43, 44, 46
"My Moksha" (Lyon), 73
mythic forms, 70

Naar-Obed, Michele, 119–132
Narcissism, 8
narrative structure (of film), 102
national debt, 8
nation-state(s), 39–41, 43
Native Americans, 43, 139, 141, 142, 144
NATO, 41, 43–46
natural vs. civil dichotomy, 127
natural world, 100
Nazis(m), 7, 9, 27, 29, 41, 52, 86

needs, 28, 33, 54
    military n., 92, 97
    political n. of George W. Bush, 84
neo-imperialism problem, 55, 56
New Zealand, 42, 43
Newport News Shipbuilding, 119
Nietzsche, Friedrich, 9
1954 Hague Convention for the Protec-
    tion of Cultural Property in the
    Event of Armed Conflict, 72
nirvana, 73
No Child Left Behind Act (NCLB), 59,
    64, 148
No Man's Land (Tanovic), 82
Noddings, Nel, 13
non-verbal elements, 108
nonviolence, 20, 67, 69
    n. action, 7, 9, 20, 21, 107–132
    art, promote n. through, 69
    n. conflict resolution, 19, 35
    Gandhian n., 23–30
    n. rhetoric, 31–37
    n. resistance (passive), 64
Nonviolent Communication (Rosenberg),
    33
North American Society for Social Phi-
    losophy, 39
nuclear submarine, 119, 124, 131
nueva canción, 107, 115, 117
    n. c. movement, 116

Obama, Barrack H., 5
objectivity, 8, 26, 122, 136
Ochoa, Amparo, 117
"Of the Sorrow Songs" (DuBois), 110
"Oi Mother, Keep Ye' Hair On!" (Ba-
    raitser), 120
one-dimensional people, 7
opponents, 23, 24, 26, 30, 34
oppress(ed)(ors), 28–30, 33, 34, 43–46, 114,
    133, 136, 142–144, 146
Orchestra of Coexistence, 68
Organization for Security and
    Cooperation, 46
organizing strategy, 113

Other, the, 21, 28, 50, 54, 57, 64, 69, 80,
    97, 122, 128, 129, 135, 136, 140,
    142, 144, 146, 149
overpopulation, 1, 10

pacifism, 33, 75
pagoda, Chinese, 71
Paint It Black (Rolling Stones), 92
Painter (Irvin), 7
Pakistan(is), 36, 44
"*La Paquita del Barrio*" (Foster), 109
parables, India's ancient religious, 72
parental relationships, 53, 64, 122, 125,
    127, 131, 139, 143
Parks, Paul J., 67
    "Art beyond the West," 73
Parra, Violeta, 117, 118
    "*Volver a los diecisiete*," 118
past, 49, 50, 52, 56, 57, 60, 73, 110, 112,
    113
    present, where p. meets, 135
    remembered p., 108
    unresolved p., 54–57, 149
pathology, 126
Paths of Glory (Kubrick), 80–84, 86, 89,
    90, 92–94
peace, *passim*
    p. encampments, 109
Peaceful Persuasion (Gorsevski), 33
Peacemakers in Action (Tanenbaum
    Center for Interreligious Under-
    standing), 35
peacemaking, 47
    p. virtues, 13–22
pedagogy, 63, 65, 133, 135, 137, 142–
    144, 146–148
Pedagogy of the Oppressed (Freire), 146
Perkins, Victor, 79
perpetrators, 52–54
Persia, 71
Picasso, Pablo, 134
    The Old Guitarist, 134
pity, 85, 91
placebo effect, 4
Plato, 103

Platoon (Stone), 93
plowshare witness, 123, 129, 131
Poe, Danielle, 119
poetry, 72, 101, 108, 110, 119
Poland, 6, 41, 44, 45
police, 112
politicians, 5, 67
pollution, 8
"The Popular Wobbly" (Slim), 115
Pork Chop Hill (Milestone), 76
"The Potential of Theory" (Jacobs), 126
power, 14, 19, 21, 33, 36, 40, 46, 93
    arts and music, p. of, 57, 68, 77
    collective p., 107, 108
    powerless, p. of the, 7
"There is Power in a Union" (Bragg), 112
"The Preacher and the Slave" (Hill), 112
Prelude (Wordsworth), 98
Prince, Camilo Salazar, 99
principles, 41, 102
    abstract p. 32
    metaphysical p., 71
privilege, 1, 7, 8, 110, 133, 137, 138,
    144, 146, 148
profiteers, 54
propaganda, 34, 50, 69, 76
psychoanalytic theory, 126
psychodrama, 50
psychology, 5, 14, 31, 92
    p. anguish/pain, 5, 146
    p. barrier, 56
    p. conditioning, 87
    p. damage, 139
    p. experience, 77
    p. factors, 57, 135
    p. functions, 14, 15, 146
    past and present, p. intersection of,
    135
    p. problems, 53
    socio-p. background to conflict, 50
    p. well-being, 147
Pumpkin (Abrams and Broder), 136–138
Puppetistas, 114, 116
pyramid, Mayan, 71

Quebecois of Canada, 40

Quilapayun of Chile, 117
Qur'an, 71

Rabbit Proof Fence (Noyce), 136–138, 141
race, 62, 139, 144–146, 149
Rank, Carol, 68
ratha, 71
rationalistic behavior, 63
Rayle, Joseph, 59
reachable, the, 26, 27
Read, Herbert, 72
    "Art and Society," 72
Reagan, Ronald, 5
Reagon, Bernice Johnson, 111
    If You Don't Go, Don't Hinder Me, 111
reality (*atman*), 25, 26, 57, 96, 97, 118,
    121, 135, 136, 140, 145
rebel, 1, 3, 7, 112, 143
The Rebel (Camus), 1
"The Rebel Girl" (Dickens), 112
rebirth, 99
redemption, 24, 98, 100
"To Reflect and Trust" (Bar On), 54
refugees, 16–18, 53
refusal, great, 1, 3, 7
regret, 83, 120
relationship(s), 10, 16, 19, 31, 32, 40, 60,
    61, 64, 67, 68, 71, 72, 96, 101,
    138, 142
    God, r. with, 123
    horizontal vs. vertical r., 121–132
    interracial r., 145, 146
    natural vs. civil r., 127
    oppressor-oppressed r., 146
    submissive r., 122
relativism, 2, 42
Renoir, Jean, 76–80, 88
    The Grand Illusion, 77–79, 88
repression, 115, 117, 118
republics, 7–10
resilience, 5
resources, 1, 8, 10, 35, 37, 39, 50, 52, 56, 70
respect(ful), 20, 34–36, 42, 44, 56, 63,
    67, 68, 125, 127, 141
responsibility, 8, 20, 34, 40, 63, 110,
    136, 137, 139, 147

the "Rest" countries, 56
revenge, 46, 50
rhetoric, 102
   nonviolent r., 31–37
rhythm, 78, 89, 102, 108, 109
Rice, Condoleezza, 9
Rickman, Jolie, 115
   "Romero," 115
   Sing it Down, 115
rights, 9, 43, 63
   Bill of R., 8, 42
   children's r., 42
   civil r., 6, 7, 35, 107, 109–114
   collective r., 47
   group r., 39, 41, 45
   human r., 34, 36, 41, 42, 45, 46, 114, 139
   individual r., 42, 45
   minority r., 41, 42
   Native Americans' r., 142
   political r., 46
   religious r., 69
   territorial r., 42
   veto r., 47
   Women's r., 42
   workers' r., 113
Rodgers, Carl, 31
Rodríguez, Silvio, 117, 118
role-play, 52
Roma (Gypsies), 41, 43
Rome, Imperial, 71
"Romero" (Rickman), 115
Romero, Óscar, 114, 115
Roosevelt, Franklin Delano, 5
Rorty, Amelie O., 21
Rose, Kenneth, 103
Rosenberg, Marshall, 31–33, 37
   Nonviolent Communication, 33
Rothermel, Dennis, 75
Rwanda, 40, 46

sabotage, 112
sacrifice, 75–78, 81, 82, 94, 95, 103, 129, 131
Said, Edward, 68
sales markets, 56
Satir, Virginia, 50

satire, 112, 113, 115
satyagraha (passive resistance), 23, 26, 28–30, 64
Saving Private Ryan (Spielberg), 98
Sayers-Walker, Katina, 133
   "Culturally Relevant Teaching," 136
scaffolding , 63
Schell, Jonathan, 60
Schicksalsgemeinschaften, 49, 50
School of the Americas (SOA), United States Army, 107, 114, 115
   SOA Watch, 107, 109, 113–116
Schur, Thomas, 95, 99
Seeger, Pete, 112, 114
self, 15, 21, 25, 57, 83, 96, 120–122, 125, 135
   s.-care, 21
   s.-centeredness, 62
   s.-consciousness, 86, 91
   s.-defense, 39, 50
   s.-determination, 41, 109
   s.-help groups, 19
   s.-interest, 14, 29, 62, 148
   s.lessness, 29, 30
   s.-preservation, 21, 64
   s.-serving attitude, 8, 63
   s.-sufficiency, 9, 10, 59
   s.-worth, 20
self-fulfilling prophesy, 2, 4–6
sensory experience, 108
"The Sentiment of Rationality" (James), 2
September 11th, 36, 44
Serb(ia)(s), 30, 41, 44
settler colonies, 42, 43
The Seville Statement on Violence, 34
sharing, 88
   power s., 46
   wealth s., 45
Sharp, Gene, 33
Siegel, Donm 81
   Hell is for Heroes (Siegel), 81
Silentio, Johannes, 5
Sing it Down (Rickman and Katteau), 115
Singin'est Movement, 113–116
Sinhalese, 40

sit-ins, 109
slave(ry)(s), 99, 109–112, 140
Slim, T-Bone, 115
    "The Popular Wobbly," 115
Slote, Michael, 13
Smaczny, Paul, 69
    Knowledge is the Beginning, 69
Smith, Adam, 10
SOA Watch vigil. See School of the
    Americas, United States Army
social action(s), 6, 7
social movements, 7, 34, 59, 107–110, 115
Social Security system, 43
social system(s), 49, 51, 52, 57, 61, 65
sociopolitical issues, 108, 116, 126, 127
Socrates, 3
soldier(s), 21,
    anti-war film, s. depicted in, 75–101
    Latin American s., 113
    Salvadoran s., 115
solidarity, 69, 76, 109, 117, 118
    racial s., 146
Solidarity, 6, 7
Solidarity, 112
"Solidarity Forever" (Chaplin), 112
song, 88–90, 92. *See also* lyrics; melody;
    music; *nueva canción*
    nonviolent transformative action, s.
        and, 107–118
Song Dynasty, 71
Songs to Fan the Flames of Discontent
    (IWW), 112
Sosa, Mercedes, 117, 118
South Africa, 6, 7, 35
    South African resisters, 29
South America, 107
South Ossettia, 44
Soviet Union (USSR), 44
Speth, James, 10
Spielberg, Steven, 98
    Saving Private Ryan, 98
spirit, 28, 89
Starhawk, 109
status quo, 7–9, 56, 59, 133, 137, 146–148
Stevens, George, 76
Stevens, Wallace, 134, 149

The Man with the Blue Guitar, 134, 149
Stone, Oliver, 76
Platoon, 93
Story of G. I. Joe (Wellman), 76
storytelling, 114
strategic allies, 56
stress, 3, 5
stupa, 71
subjectivity, 108, 120, 121, 122. See also
    intersubjectivity
    White s., 146
subtlety, 102
sufferers, 28, 29
surviv(al)(ors), 2, 3, 6, 15, 24, 27, 81, 84,
    86, 92, 98
    human species, s. of, 127
    individual vs. group s., 29, 30
    torture s., 114
susceptibility, 14, 16, 86
Swanton, Christine, 16
"In the Sweet By and By (Bennett)
Sweet Honey in the Rock, 111
sympathy, 77, 79, 88
system(s) (ecological) theory, 61–65
Systemic Constellations, 49–57

tactics
    action t., 112
    nonviolent t., 20
    military t., 77, 83
    scare t., 101
Tainos of Puerto Rico, 143, 144
Tamils in Sri Lanka, 40
Tanenbaum Center for Interreligious
    Understanding, 31, 35
Tanovic, Danis, 82
    No Man's Land, 82
Taoism, 71
Taylor, Yvonne, 69
Tchaikovsky, Pyotr Ilyich, 77
teach(ers)(ing), 14, 61–63, 124, 136, 139
    t. anti-war film, 104
    t. classroom management skills, 59
    t. conflict resolution, 59
    critical pedagogy, t. and, 133, 148, 149
    King's t., 20, 21

teach(ers)(ing), *con't.*
    t. peace, 7, 60, 64, 80, 104, 105
    t. power and privilege, 137, 144–146
    t. social justice, 134, 135, 140
    student-t. relationship, 122, 128, 137
    test, t. to the, 64
    t. without theory, 143
    t. tolerence, 67
Teaching Tolerance, 67
tension, 50, 79, 111, 126
territory of origin, 50
terror(ists), 78, 80, 82, 83, 93, 99
    t. activity, 36, 44, 63
    war on t., 8, 9
theater, 108, 114
Theater of the Oppressed, 114
"They Go Wild, Simply Wild over Me"
    (McCarthy and Fisher), 115
They Were Expendable (Ford), 76
Third World countries, 55, 56
threat, 4, 7–10, 14–16, 19–22, 29, 33, 40,
    43, 44, 62, 84, 124, 128, 129
Three Cups of Tea (Mortenson), 36
Tiffany, Ann, 115
tipping point phenomena, 5
Title IX, 59
tolerance, 67–73
torture, 114–117
transformati(on)(ve action), 20, 23, 27,
    30, 33, 34, 55, 57, 59, 67, 68, 70,
    83, 92, 107–121, 129, 137, 139,
    143, 144, 146
transgenerational legacies, 52
trauma(s), 49, 50, 54, 56, 121
Tree Model psychoanalytical approach,
    54
Trumbo, Dalton, 101
    Johnny Got His Gun, 101
truth (*satya*), 6, 21, 23, 24, 26, 29, 45,
    50, 67, 102, 110, 141
Tubman, Harriet, 110
Tutsis, 40

uncertainty, 1, 2, 50
unification, 9, 109, 148
United Nations

UN Charter, 39, 40
UN convention and declarations, 42
UN Educational, Scientific, and
    Cultural Organization
    (UNESCO), 69
UN International Covenant on Civil
    and Political Rights, 46
UN peacekeeping troops, 83
UN Security Council, 40
Un Universal Declaration of Human
    Rights (UDHR), 41
United States, 1, 7, 8, 10, 41, 42–46, 53,
    60, 62, 110, 114, 130–132, 141,
    142, 145, 147
U. S. civil rights movement, 6, 35,
    109
U. S. culture of death, 128
U. S. labor movement, 112
U. S. militarism, 124
U. S. nuclear buildup, 123
U. S. Senate, 72
United States Army School of the Amer-
    icas (SOA), 107, 109, 115, 116
SOA Watch, 113, 114
us/them opposition, 50, 62
USA PATRIOT Act, 9
USSR. *See* Soviet Union (USSR)
utopian thinking, 7, 9, 10, 18, 33, 126

values, 9, 16, 17, 32, 67, 108, 135
    capitalism, v. associated with, 147
    Christian v., 124, 128, 131
    competing v., 59
    dominent culture, v. of, 139
veterans, 76, 103, 104
victim(ization)(s), 9, 26–29, 53, 54, 82,
    90, 94, 101, 114, 116
video games, 79
"*Vientos del pueblo*" (Jara), 116
Vietnam War, 129, 130
violence, 19–21, 23, 24, 26–30–37, 47, 50,
    53, 60, 62–65, 69, 78, 88, 90, 92–
    94, 97, 99, 102–104, 109, 112,
    116–118, 124, 127, 130, 131
virtue(s)
    peacemaking v., 13–22

virtue(s), *con't.*
  warlike v., 75, 77, 82, 86
  willingness to die for a cause seen as a
    v., 29, 30
voice-over, 83, 91, 95, 97–99
Volkan, Vamik, 49, 54
"Volver a los diecisiete" (Parra), 118
vulnerability thesis, 13–22
Vygotsky, L. S., 63

A Walk in the Sun (Milestone), 79
War on Terror, 8, 9
War Requiem (Britten), 78, 93
war(fare)(ism), 8–10, 31, 32, 34, 40, 43,
  44, 62, 65, 67–69, 72, 73, 109,
  120, 123, 140
  anti-w. activists, 119
  anti-w. film, 75–105
  unethical w., 130
weapons of mass destruction, 1
Wellman, William, 76
  Story of G. I. Joe, 76
Werner, Richard, 1
"We Shall Overcome" (unknown), 111
West vs. Rest countries, 56
West-Eastern Divan, 68
Western Hemisphere Institute for Securi-
  ty Cooperation (WHINSEC),
  107, 114
Westphalian sovereignty, 40
White(ness)(s), 19, 20, 22, 62, 63, 137,
  140–143, 146, 149
  W. guilt, 142, 145, 146
  W. ideology, 147

W. man's burden, 139
W. oppressors, 146
W. privilege, 144–146, 148
W. subjectivity, 146
W. supremacy, 146, 148
"Whiteness and Critical Pedagogy" (Al-
  len), 146
"The Will to Believe" (James), 2
"Winds of the People" (Rossman and
  Vernier), 116, 117
Wobblies. See Industrial Workers of the
  World
Wolf language, 31, 32. *See also* Giraffe l.
wom(an)(en), 16, 20, 37, 43, 46, 120–
  122, 126, 144
  anti-war films, w. depicted in, 77, 88
  educated Muslim w., 36
  family, w. reduced to role in, 127
  w.-mother dyad, 120
  peace encampments, w.'s, 109
  w. rights, 42
Wordsworth, William, 98
  Prelude, 98
work stoppages, 109, 112
World Economic Forum International
  Meeting, 9
World War I, 40, 41, 43, 82,
World War II, 7, 8, 39, 42, 43, 87, 103

Yacoobi, Sakena, 36
Yupanqui, Atahualpa, 117

Zinnemann, Fred, 76
Zulu (Endfield), 93

VIBS

The **Value Inquiry Book Series** is co-sponsored by:

Titles Published

Volumes 1 - 181 see www.rodopi.nl

182.   David Boersema and Katy Gray Brown, Editors, *Spiritual and Political Dimensions of Nonviolence and Peace.* A volume in **Philosophy of Peace**

183.   Daniel P. Thero, *Understanding Moral Weakness.* A volume in **Studies in the History of Western Philosophy**

184.   Scott Gelfand and John R. Shook, Editors, *Ectogenesis: Artificial Womb Technology and the Future of Human Reproduction.* A volume in **Values in Bioethics**

185.   Piotr Jaroszyński, *Science in Culture.* A volume in **Gilson Studies**

186.   Matti Häyry, Tuija Takala, Peter Herissone-Kelly, Editors, *Ethics in Biomedical Research: International Perspectives.* A volume in **Values in Bioethics**

187.   Michael Krausz, *Interpretation and Transformation: Explorations in Art and the Self.* A volume in **Interpretation and Translation**

188.   Gail M. Presbey, Editor, *Philosophical Perspectives on the "War on Terrorism."* A volume in **Philosophy of Peace**

189.   María Luisa Femenías, Amy A. Oliver, Editors, *Feminist Philosophy in Latin America and Spain.* A volume in **Philosophy in Latin America**

190.   Oscar Vilarroya and Francesc Forn I Argimon, Editors, *Social Brain Matters: Stances on the Neurobiology of Social Cognition.* A volume in **Cognitive Science**

191.   Eugenio Garin, *History of Italian Philosophy.* Translated from Italian and Edited by Giorgio Pinton. A volume in **Values in Italian Philosophy**

192.   Michael Taylor, Helmut Schreier, and Paulo Ghiraldelli, Jr., Editors, *Pragmatism, Education, and Children: International Philosophical Perspectives.* A volume in **Pragmatism and Values**

193.   Brendan Sweetman, *The Vision of Gabriel Marcel: Epistemology, Human Person, the Transcendent.* A volume in **Philosophy and Religion**

194.	Danielle Poe and Eddy Souffrant, Editors, *Parceling the Globe: Philosophical Explorations in Globalization, Global Behavior, and Peace.* A volume in **Philosophy of Peace**

195.	Josef Šmajs, *Evolutionary Ontology: Reclaiming the Value of Nature by Transforming Culture.* A volume in **Central-European Value Studies**

196.	Giuseppe Vicari, *Beyond Conceptual Dualism: Ontology of Consciousness, Mental Causation, and Holism in John R. Searle's Philosophy of Mind.* A volume in **Cognitive Science**

197.	Avi Sagi, *Tradition vs. Traditionalism: Contemporary Perspectives in Jewish Thought.* Translated from Hebrew by Batya Stein. A volume in **Philosophy and Religion**

198.	Randall E. Osborne and Paul Kriese, Editors, *Global Community: Global Security.* A volume in **Studies in Jurisprudence**

199.	Craig Clifford, *Learned Ignorance in the Medicine Bow Mountains: A Reflection on Intellectual Prejudice.* A volume in **Lived Values: Valued Lives**

200.	Mark Letteri, *Heidegger and the Question of Psychology: Zollikon and Beyond.* A volume in **Philosophy and Psychology**

201.	Carmen R. Lugo-Lugo and Mary K. Bloodsworth-Lugo, Editors, *A New Kind of Containment: "The War on Terror," Race, and Sexuality.* A volume in **Philosophy of Peace**

202.	Amihud Gilead, *Necessity and Truthful Fictions: Panenmentalist Observations.* A volume in **Philosophy and Psychology**

203.	Fernand Vial, *The Unconscious in Philosophy, and French and European Literature: Nineteenth and Early Twentieth Century.* A volume in **Philosophy and Psychology**

204.	Adam C. Scarfe, Editor, *The Adventure of Education: Process Philosophers on Learning, Teaching, and Research.* A volume in **Philosophy of Education**

205.	King-Tak Ip, Editor, *Environmental Ethics: Intercultural Perspectives.* A volume in **Studies in Applied Ethics**

206.   Evgenia Cherkasova, *Dostoevsky and Kant: Dialogues on Ethics.* A volume in **Social Philosophy**

207.   Alexander Kremer and John Ryder, Editors, *Self and Society: Central European Pragmatist Forum*, Volume Four. A volume in **Central European Value Studies**

208.   Terence O'Connell, *Dialogue on Grief and Consolation.* A volume in **Lived Values, Valued Lives**

209.   Craig Hanson, *Thinking about Addiction: Hyperbolic Discounting and Responsible Agency.* A volume in **Social Philosophy**

210.   Gary G. Gallopin, *Beyond Perestroika: Axiology and the New Russian Entrepreneurs.* A volume in **Hartman Institute Axiology Studies**

211.   Tuija Takala, Peter Herissone-Kelly, and Søren Holm, Editors, *Cutting Through the Surface: Philosophical Approaches to Bioethics.* A volume in **Values in Bioethics**

212.   Neena Schwartz: *A Lab of My Own.* A volume in **Lived Values, Valued Lives**

213.   Krzysztof Piotr Skowroński, *Values and Powers: Re-reading the Philosophical Tradition of American Pragmatism.* A volume in **Central European Value Studies**

214.   Matti Häyry, Tuija Takala, Peter Herissone-Kelly and Gardar Árnason, Editors, *Arguments and Analysis in Bioethics.* A volume in **Values in Bioethics**

215.   Anders Nordgren, *For Our Children: The Ethics of Animal Experimentation in the Age of Genetic Engineering.* A volume in **Values in Bioethics**

216.   James R. Watson, Editor, *Metacide: In the Pursuit of Excellence.* A volume in **Holocaust and Genocide Studies**

217.   Andrew Fitz-Gibbon, Editor, *Positive Peace: Reflections on Peace Education, Nonviolence, and Social Change.* A volume in **Philosophy of Peace**

CPSIA information can be obtained at www.ICGtesting.com
Printed in the USA
LVOW06s0257130115

422598LV00001B/373/P